Antique Trader®

Pottery & Porcelain
CERAMICS

Price Guide

7TH EDITION

D0006626

INTRODUCTION BY DAVID RAGO

Published by

Krause Publications, a division of F+W Media, Inc.
700 East State Street • Iola, WI 54990-0001
715-445-2214 • 888-457-2873
www.krausebooks.com

To order books or other products call toll-free 1-800-258-0929
or visit us online at www.krausebooks.com

Cover photography courtesy
Rago Arts and Auction Center, Lambertville, New Jersey.

ISBN-13: 978-1-4402-3970-0
ISBN-10: 1-4402-3970-3

Designed by Jana Tappa
Edited by Paul Kennedy

Printed in China

Squat vessel with leaves and buds, Boston, ca. 1905, circular pottery stamp,
7" x 7-1/2"...**$6,875**

Contents

Roseville, Della Robbia vase, 15 ½" x 6", with wild roses and cut-out rim, Zanesville, Ohio, ca. 1910...............**$43,750**

Your best friend? Education

Whenever we are asked about what to collect we always stress that you should collect what you like and want to live with. Collecting is a personal matter and only you can determine what will give you the most satisfaction. With the incredible diversity of ceramics available, everyone should be able to find a topic they will enjoy studying and collecting.

No matter your passion, whether it is an entire line of Fiesta or prized piece from George Ohr, always remember that education is your best friend. It will serve you well when all else fails. To get the most from your pursuits read everything you can get your hands on, and purchase the best references available for your library. New research materials continue to become available for collectors and learning is an ongoing process.

It is also very helpful to join a collectors' club where others who share your enthusiasm will support and guide your learning. Fellow collectors often become friends and sources for special treasures to add to your collection. Dealers who specialize in a ceramics category are always eager to help educate and support collectors and many times they become a mentor.

With the very ancient and complex history of ceramic wares, it's easy to understand why becoming educated about your special interest is of paramount importance. There have been collectors of pottery and porcelain for centuries, and for nearly as long collectors have had to be wary of reproductions or reissues. In Chinese ceramics, for instance, it has always been considered perfectly acceptable to copy as closely as possible the style and finish of earlier ceramics and even mark them with period markings on the base. The only problem arises when a modern collector wants to determine whether their piece was produced over 200 years ago or barely a century ago.

With European and, to some extent, American wares, copying of earlier styles has also been going on for many decades. As far back as the mid-19th century, copies and adaptations of desirable early wares were finding their way onto the collector market. By the late 19th century, in particular, revivals of 18th century porcelains and even some early

19th century earthenware were available, often sold as decorative items and sometimes clearly marked. After 100 years, however, these early copies can pose a real challenge for the unwary.

Even more troublesome for collectors is the flood of reproductions produced during the past 30-40 years. Not only are high-end early wares copied even more modern, collectible wares have fallen victim to this problem. For instance, McCoy Pottery, never an expensive line, has seen a large number of "copies" hit the market. Cookie jars, in fact, have been one of the hardest hit areas of ceramics collectibles with not only McCoy cookie jars out there but also many of the Shawnee Pottery jars as well as some from other cookie jar makers of the past. In addition, the popular Little Red Riding Hood and other figural pieces made by Shawnee are being offered. With a little checking you can find many of these "copies" online. Many of the patterns made by the Roseville Pottery have also been widely reproduced in recent years. For at least 20 years porcelain pieces carrying "Hand-Painted Nippon" fake marks have been offered by reproduction wholesalers. When

Newcomb College, tall vase, 15 ¼" x 7 ½", carved by Sadie Irvine, pine trees with green needles on bright blue trunks against a blue-green and ivory ground, 1909 .... **$96,000**

first manufactured these pieces and the misleading marks were fairly easy to identify. That has changed as more sophisticated processes are used to create much better quality reproductions with "realistic" markings.

Again, education is the key. Read, seek out the advice of trusted experts, and ask questions. As with anything in life, do your homework and remember it's always a good idea to buy from a reliable source.

Another area that calls for special caution on the part of collectors, especially the inexperienced, is that of damaged or repaired pieces. A wise collector will always buy the best example they can find and it is a good policy to buy one extra fine piece rather than a handful of lesser examples. You never want to pass up a good buy. But, in the long run, a smaller collection of choice pieces will probably bring you more satisfaction (and financial reward) than a large collection of moderate quality.

Purchasing a damaged or clearly

Louis Comfort Tiffany, exceptional cabbage-shaped vase, 8 ½" x 8", in mottled polychrome matte glaze $50,020

repaired piece is a call only you can make. Generally, we don't recommend it unless the piece is so unique that another example is not likely to come your way in the near future. For certain classes of expensive and rare ceramics, especially early pottery that has seen heavy use, a certain amount of damage may be inevitable and even acceptable. The sale price, however, should reflect this fact.

Restoration of pottery and porcelain has been a fact of life for decades. Even in the early 19th century before good glues were available, "make-do" repairs were sometimes done to pieces using small metal staples. Today some collectors even seek out these quaint examples of early recycling. Since the early 20th century glue and repainting have been common methods used to mask damage to pottery and porcelain and these repairs can usually be detected today with a strong light and the naked eye.

The problem in recent decades has been the ability of restorers to completely

Rookwood, "Chief Hollow Horn Bear, Sioux," 16" x 15", 1900, standard glaze pillow vase by Matthew A. Daly, shows striking detail of a Native American Chief in full headdress and breast plate **$76,375**

mask any sign of previous damages using more sophisticated repair methods. There is nothing wrong with a quality restoration of a rare piece as long as the eventual purchaser is aware such work has been done.

It can take more than the naked eye and a strong light to detect some invisible repairs today and that's where the popular black light can help. Many spots of repair will fluoresce under the black light. Even a black light won't reveal everything which is why it is always recommended to do business with someone with a good reputation and who guarantees money-back satisfaction when making a major purchase.

Ceramics, in addition to their beauty and charm, also offer the collecting advantage of durability and low-maintenance. It's surprising how much pottery and porcelain from two centuries ago is still available to collect. There were literally train cars full of it produced and sold by the late 19th century, and such wares are abundantly available and often reasonably priced. Beautiful dinnerware and colorful vases abound in the marketplace and offer

Grueby, gourd-shaped vase with tooled and applied full-height ribbed leaves, 9 ¼" x 8 ½" covered in feathered matte green glaze, extremely rare **$84,000**

exciting collecting possibilities. They look wonderful used on today's dining tables or gracing display shelves.

A periodic dusting and once-a-year washing in mild, warm water is about all the care they will require. Of course, it's not recommended you put older pottery and porcelains in your dishwasher where rattling and extremely hot water could cause damage. And, of course, it's more satisfying to hold a piece in your hand in warm soapy water in a rubber dishpan (lined with towels for added protection) and caress it carefully with a dishrag. The tactile enjoyment of holding the object brings a new dimension to collecting.

Whatever sort of pottery or porcelain appeals to you most, whether it is 18th century Meissen or mid-20th century California-made pottery, you can take pride in the fact that you are carrying on a collecting tradition that goes back centuries. Back to the days when only the crowned heads of Europe could vie for the finest and rarest ceramics with which to accent their regal abodes.

George Ohr, rare corseted teapot, 6 ¾" x 8", with two different glazes, Biloxi, Miss., 1890s.. $46,875

The Evolution of the American Art Pottery Market

By David Rago

David Rago oversees Rago Arts and Auction Center (known as Rago's), the largest and leading auction house in New Jersey. He is an author who lectures nationally and is an expert appraiser for the hit PBS series, *Antiques Roadshow*, where he specializes in decorative ceramics and porcelain.

While the market for American decorative ceramics is relatively young, especially when compared to those of traditional antiques, it's been 40 years since the landmark exhibition The Arts and Crafts Movement in America first put the material on the map. During that span markets for some American companies came and went, while select others have seen almost a continuous upward spiral. This brief article will describe some of those disparities and explain why they exist.

Early on, before 1980, collectors and dealers both were mostly left to their own devices in determining what was good, rare, or even available. Who knew? There were very few books in print and most of them were incomplete if not outright misleading. Pricing was like throwing a dart at numbers. Imagine, if you can, the total absence of auction records, online pricing information, or eBay. If you had a push button phone you were on the cutting edge of existing technology.

So we stumbled, gathering at the few shows where art pottery might be for sale, laboring through books like Lucille Henzke's American Art Pottery or the Purviance spiral bounds, both of which mixed serious work with flower shop ware, reflecting more the confusion than dispelling it. It is for the reasons above that early collectors bought things like Japanese influenced Rookwood, Limoges-style faience, and other such art ware that had a foundation in cultures other than American. Never mind that it was derivative, inferior and little more than a rest stop on the way to discovering the best of what was made here.

To illustrate, in 1970 when James Carpenter brought the 10,000-piece cache of George Ohr pottery to New Jersey from Biloxi, Mississippi, it proved almost impossible to sell. There was no market to speak of for even better known names such as Rookwood or Roseville, much less the weird creations by the Mad Pottery of Biloxi. Red, twisted, scrunched, crimped 8-inch, two handled vases with black drips and the occasional applied snake didn't sell well in Biloxi 70 years earlier, and they found little more acceptance in sylvan New Jersey in 1970. What did initially sell of Ohr's work were his early, more traditional, folk pottery pieces bought by prominent folk art dealers and collectors in and around the New York area. They were something

Newcomb College, rare tall vase, 11 ½" x 5 ½", carved by Sadie Irvine, fenced-in cabin under moss-laden live oaks and a full moon, 1922 .... **$22,325**

George Ohr, vase with two ribbon handles, 8 ½" x 5 ¾", covered in a spectacular red and green mottled glaze. Stamped G.E. OHR, Biloxi, Miss **$84,000**

this nascent market could get their heads around. But like the Japanese and French influenced ware described above, it really had little to do with the heart of the matter. (Let's use that piece of Ohr above to show price progression. That 8-inch scrunched vase in 1975 would sell for $500)

The Jordan Volpe gallery opened in 1975 and, while the famous institution showcased a balance of great art and terrible ethics (one owner, Todd Volpe, spent 27 months in jail for fraud), it succeeded in defining the future of the art pottery market. They championed George Ohr as well as Robineau, Grueby, Newcomb College, and a host of other potteries heretofore known only to a few stalwart collectors and academics. By the mid 1980s American art pottery was no longer a secret. (Our red-scrunched Ohr vase is now a $10,000 piece)

The next big thing was the Boston Museum of Fine Art's sensational Arts

and Crafts exhibition, "The Art That is Life". Princeton came first, but Boston took things to a whole other level. Though the show included all aspects of Period material such as furniture, lighting and textiles, it also displayed the beauty, diversity and accessibility of decorative ceramics. Furniture was mostly angular and deep brown. Textiles were lovely but flat and, by nature, dull. Pottery stood out, the Cartier diamond pin on the basic black dress of the staid Arts and Crafts interior. And it was small, easy to transport and trade, and most of all fun.

It was during this time that the

Iowa College Pottery,
  Mary L. Yancey, vase,
  9 1/4" x 5", carved with
  blue daisies on yellow
  ground, 1920s..... **$45,000**

markets for important potteries such as Newcomb College, Marblehead, Ohr, Grueby and works by Frederick Rhead separated themselves from the pack. Certainly the average artist decorated piece of Rookwood or nicely glazed Fulper continued to find new homes, but the gap between the early collectors and the new wave of serious buyers was widening. Hollywood, and Hollywood money, entered the mix. Barbra Streisand featured a piece of Teco on the cover of one of her albums. Brad Pitt and Joel Silver were consistent players at auction. Suddenly many of the schoolteachers and academics that bulwarked the early collectors could no longer afford the insurance premiums for, much less the prices, art pottery was now costing. Many of them cashed in pieces they'd taken off the market 20 years earlier. The second generation of collecting art pottery began.

At this time the darlings of the market were mostly the high-end companies mentioned above, but new scholarship was finding print at a startling rate. When the Paul Evans, book on art was published in 1975 you might see only a two-page chapter on an important but obscure pottery such as Arequipa or North Dakota School of Mines. But by the mid 1990s you could find monographs on individual artists or these companies alone. This in turn encouraged even more collecting and prices rose (with the exception of the 1993 recession) inexorably. (Our red Ohr vase? $50,000)

Enter the millennium. Swept up along with the excesses of the dot-com boom, Arts and Crafts material was at an all-time high. Furniture, wrought copper and art pottery objects were finding new buyers including public and private museums as well as determined collectors. Even after the dot-com crash prices held steady for most Period material, though there was some softening by 2005 for commercial ware such as production Roseville and non-artist decorated Rookwood. (The Ohr? $100,000)

September 2008 was a different matter; with the cratering of Lehman Brothers and the credit default swap fiasco. In fairness, ALL markets, antiques and otherwise, suffered through much of 2009. But it remains clear that the forty-year run the Arts and Crafts market had enjoyed was at least slowing down and, in some places, coming to a standstill. Collecting is generational and perhaps younger collectors aren't interested in buying what their parents coveted. The demographic is aging and the under-40 crowd is buying Modern.

This is most apparent in prices for Mission furniture, where all but the very best, in pristine condition, is selling for a fraction of what they'd have brought a decade ago. This is less true for art pottery, however. You probably don't need another bookcase, and changing one out for an upgrade is a lot of work, between emptying, moving the old one out, moving the new one in, and refilling. Not so for your ceramics collection, where you can more easily add or subtract pieces. You can't mail a bookcase using UPS.

While work by some famous companies sell for below historic record prices, we're seeing staggering levels for the Period's best. Average pieces of Newcomb College have settled at about 80% of their high, but that elusive 1% of their production will easily sell for over $100,000. Grueby pottery also has faltered as of late, but the past few years have seen their best examples match or exceed past results. On the other end of the scale, production Roseville pieces are a full 35% lower than a decade ago, which suggests this is the best time in years to pursue such work.

We realized a record price for a piece of American art pottery six years ago when we sold a vase by Frederick Rhead, from his Santa Barbara Pottery (circa 1915), for $519,000. More recently, we sold another piece by Rhead, from his tenure at University City (circa 1911), for $637,000. And finally, that Ohr vase? It is valued at $150,000 on today's market.

All markets are always in a state of flux. What remains constant is the desire of American collectors, surfing the ebb and flow of value but continuing to collect, preserve and educate. While the current climate in some collecting areas has definitely cooled, the market for most art pottery is doing just fine.

Newcomb College, exceptional early vessel, 7 ½" x 9 ½", carved by Marie de Hoa LeBlanc, features five stylized blue and white rabbits, 1902 ....**$84,000**

Rago Arts Ceramics Gallery

The following images and those in the previous pages are from a collection of favorites and best-selling pieces as selected by Rago Arts and Auction Center.

Arequipa, exceptional and large vase, 10" x 5", 1912, decorated with irises and leaves on a purple ground. Marked 670 Arequipa/California............................ **$74,750**

George Ohr, bisque vase, 9" x 5", with folded rim, deep in-body twist, dimpled middle, and notched pattern on base and neck. Incised on body, "Made in the presence of owner John Power/By his friend/G E Ohr/Biloxi 1-24-1903," and on bottom, "Mary had a little Lamb & Ohr has a little Pottery." **$23,000**

Rookwood, vase, 13 ¼" x 10 ½" decorated by William Hentschell, 1929, perfectly fired. Flame mark/XXIX/WEH/6080.............................$14,400

Grueby, three-color squat vessel, 4 ¼" x 9 ½", rare, decorated with tooled and applied water lilies and lily pads in yellow and green against a leathery dark green ground, 1914.. **$54,625**

Roseville, Tourist 10" wall pocket. Stamped 1209.....................**$5,185**

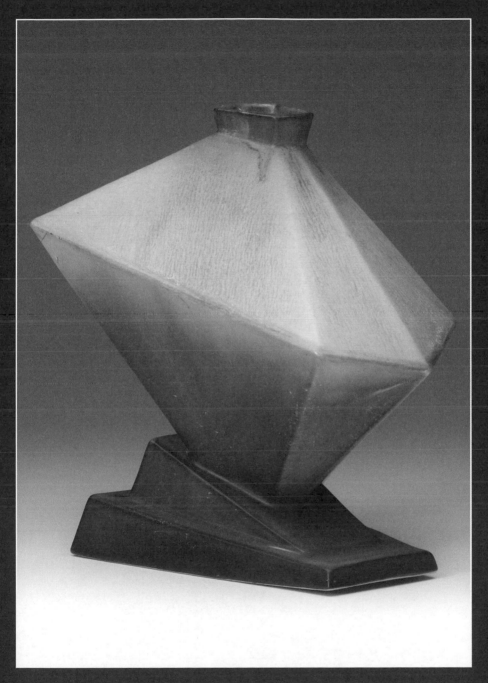

Roseville, rare Futura "Tank" vase, 10" x 9", in blue to ivory shaded glaze. Unmarked **$22,800**

George Ohr, oversized pitcher, 5 ½" x 8", with mottled raspberry, blue and green glaze, Biloxi, MS, ca. 1900. Stamped G.E. OHR, Biloxi, Miss **$50,000**

Fulper, rare corseted vase, 11 ¼" x 8 ¼", Copperdust Crystalline glaze, raised racetrack mark **$11,160**

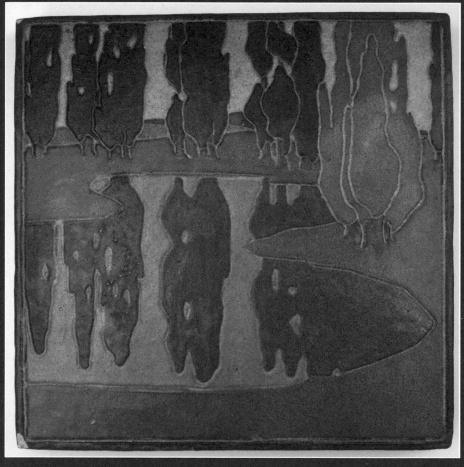

Marblehead, tile incised with a landscape of poplar trees reflected in a pond. Tile mounted in new Arts and Crafts frame. 6-inch square **$114,000**

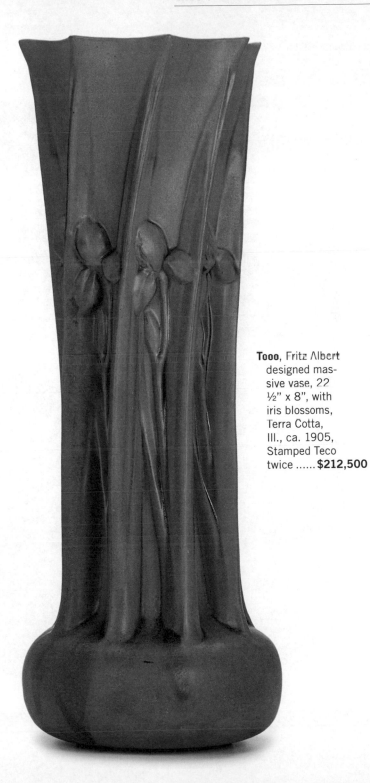

Tooo, Fritz Albert designed massive vase, 22 ½" x 8", with iris blossoms, Terra Cotta, Ill., ca. 1905, Stamped Teco twice **$212,500**

Teco, massive architectonic corseted vase, 18" x 10 ½" with four buttressed handles, covered in a smooth matte green glaze with charcoaling. Stamped Teco 416......**$60,000**

Marblehead, Arthur Hennessey exceptional carved vase, 7" x 4", with stylized blossoms.One of only four known.. **$134,200**

Frederick Hurten Rhead signed four-part tile panel with peacock, 20 ¾" square, University City, Mo., 1910 .... **$637,500**

George Kendrick Grueby, rare seven-handled vase, Boston, Mass., ca. 1900, 10 ¾" x 8 ½" **$37,500**

Rhead Pottery, Santa Barbara, Calif., iconic Arts and Crafts piece, tall vase etched with a stylized landscape, 11 ¼" x 6" **$516,000**

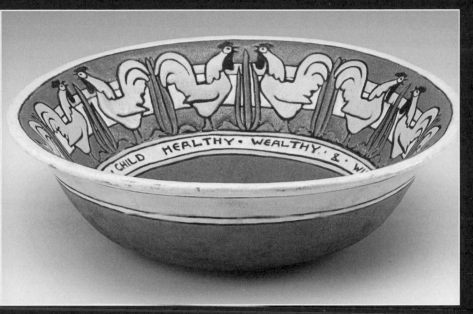

Frances Rocchi, Saturday Evening Girls, important, early and large center bowl, 3 ½" x 12 ¼", with roosters in cuerda seca on green ground, Boston, 1909, incised "Early to bed & early to rise makes a child healthy, wealthy & wise." Signed with bowl shop mark, SEG/FR 18-6-09 .... **$96,875**

Fulper, rare mushroom-shaped lamp, 17" x 17", covered in Leopard-Skin Crystalline glaze, shade inset with leaded glass, on a flaring, two-socket base.........**$36,000**

Shapes & Marks

The following line drawings illustrate typical shapes found in pottery and porcelain pitchers and vases. These forms are referred to often in our price listings.

PITCHER: Barrel-shaped

PITCHER: Jug-type

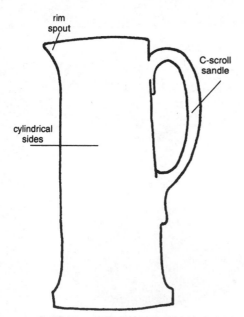

rim spout

C-scroll sandle

cylindrical sides

PITCHER: Tankard-type with cylindrical sides, C-scroll handle, and rim spout.

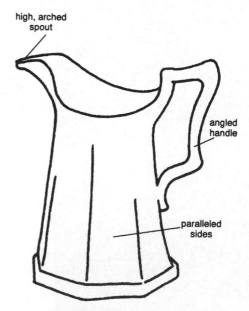

high, arched spout

angled handle

paralleled sides

PITCHER: Tankard-type with panelled (octagonal) sides, angled handle and high, arched spout.

VASES

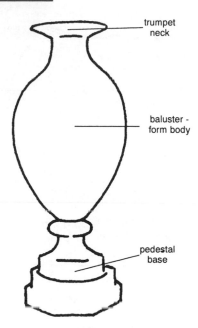

trumpet neck

baluster - form body

pedestal base

VASE: Baluster-form body with trumpet neck on a pedestal base

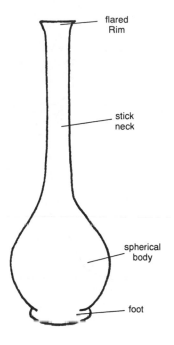

flared Rim

stick neck

spherical body

foot

VASE: Bottle-form Spherical footed body tapering to a tall stick neck with flared rim

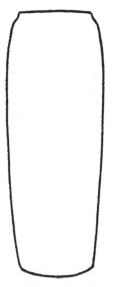

VASE: Cylindrical

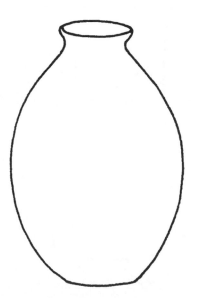

VASE: Ovoid body, tapering to a short, flared neck.

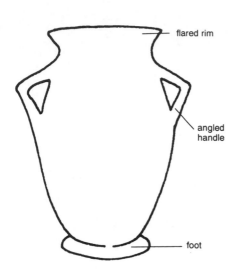

flared rim

angled
handle

foot

VASE: Ovoid, footed body with
flared rim & angled handles

molded
rim

flattened
sides

knob
feet

VASE: Pillow-shaped with
molded rim; on knob feet.

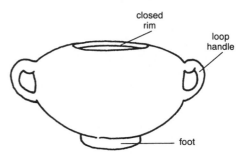

closed
rim

loop
handle

foot

VASE OR BOWL VASE: Spherical, footed
body with closed rim and loop handles.

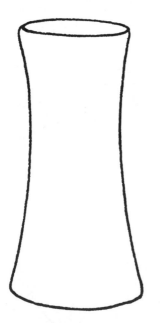

VASE: Waisted
cylindrical form.

VASE: Squatty bulbous body
with lobed sides.

MARKS

Abingdon

Various Amphora-Teplitz Factory
1880s-1930s

Austrian

Bauer

Beatrix Potter Backstamps

BEATRIX POTTER'S
"Mr Jackson"
F. Warne & Co.Ltd.
© Copyright 1974
BESWICK ENGLAND

© F. Warne & Co. 1988
Licensed by Copyrights
Studio of Royal Doulton
England

ROYAL ALBERT ®
ENGLAND

Blue Ridge
Hand Painted
Underglaze
Southern Potteries Inc.
MADE IN U.S.A.
Blue Ridge Dinnerwares

Boch Freres Mark

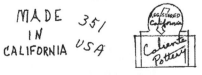
Brayton Laguna

Buffalo Pottery

Caliente

Cambridge

Catalina Island Pottery

CERAMIC ARTS STUDIO

Ceramic Arts Studio

Clarice Cliff

Cleminson

Clewell Wares

Clifton

Cowan

deLee Art

Derby & Royal Crown Derby

Fiesta

Franciscan

Frankoma

Fulper

Gallé Pottery

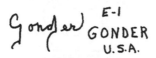

Gonder

GRUEBY

Grueby Pottery

Hall

Hampshire

Harker

Haviland

Hull

Jugtown Pottery

Lenox China

Longwy

McCoy

Meissen

Meissen

Minton

MOORCROFT

Moorcroft

Newcomb College Pottery

NILOAH

Niloak Pottery

Noritake

North Dakota School of Mines

GEO. E. OHR
BILOXI, MISS.

Ohr Pottery

Owens Pottery

 S.E.G.

Paul Revere

ZANEWARE
MADE IN U.S.A.

Peters & Reed

Pickard

HOWARD
PIERCE   Howard Pierce
Pierce   Claremont, Calif   Hp

Howard Pierce

 HENRIOT
QUIMPER

Quimper

R.S. Prussia & Related

Red Wing

Rookwood

Rosenthal

Royal Bayreuth

Royal Doulton

Royal Dux

Royal Vienna

Royal Worcester

Hedi Schoop
HOLLYWOOD CAL.
HEDI SCHOOP
HOLLYWOOD. CALIF.
Hedi Schoop

Schoop

Sèvres

Shelley

Stangl

Teco

Tiffany Pottery

Early Van Briggle Pottery

Vernon Kilns

Warwick

Watt Pottery

Early Wedgwood

Weller

Wheatley

Zsolnay

Amphora

THE AMPHORA CO. began in the country village of Turn, in the Teplitz region of Bohemia. The Teplitz region supported the highest concentration of ceramic production, not only in Bohemia, but throughout all of the Austro-Hungarian Empire.

Amphora's aim was always to produce richly ornamented porcelain luxury items. In addition to the American exports, there were sales to European dealers. Through world exhibitions and international trade shows, Amphora's collections received many significant awards and certificates.

By 1900 Amphora was at the pinnacle of its success. After World War I, in 1918, Czechoslovakia was established. The company continued production until the end of the 1930s.

—Phil & Arlene Larke

Daughter of the Rhine vase, applied jewels and enameled flowers, marked on underside, illustrated in House of Amphora, p. 188, mint condition, 18-1/2" h.............................. **$15,000**

Dragon vase, baluster form, applied dragon with spread wings in bronzed iridescent finish, head on lip with open mouth, jagged teeth and spiral horns, bottom impress marked Amphora with written 52, very good to excellent condition, 14" h...................... **$10,350**

Porcelain bust, "Sappho," early 20th century, marked
RSTK Amphora, 17" x 11-1/2" x 7"........**$344**

Vase, portraiture of "Maiden in the Woods," pink
and blue flowers enameled in her hair, burnished
gold highlights trees, rim and base, impressed
Amphora, maroon logo Turn Teplitz Bohemia,
RS+K for Reissner, Stellmacher & Kessel beneath,
perfect condition, 4-1/2" h. **$1,000**

Double vase, applied leaves and
flower clusters, marked on bottom with crown above Austria
Amphora, 10-3/4" h...**$475**

Art Nouveau, double-handle vase
with grapes in relief, signed,
13-1/2" h................. **$300**

Terra cotta bust of fancy woman,
20" h. **$550**

Vase, Reissner, Stellmacher & Kessler, female bust beside conch shell, raised on tree form base, 25-3/4" h........**$375**

Iridescent glazed vase, early 20th century, Secessionist, urn-form with horizontal ribbing and raised stylized flowers, impressed Amphora within oval and number 3773, 12-1/2" h.....**$1,100**

Stellmacher vase, two applied salamanders and fiddlehead ferns, Stellmacher mark, illustrated in House of Amphora, p. 228, mint condition, 16" h..... **$8,500**

Vase, two-tone blue and gold iridescent tones with pinched twist design, marked, 7" h..............**$275**

Grape vine vase, basket woven form with gilt handles at top, green grape vine pattern with clusters of blue grapes, signed Amphora on bottom, very good condition, 13" h. **$300**

Vase, maiden and swan by Ernst Wahliss, base stamped, 9" h. **$350**

Belleek

THE NAME BELLEEK refers to an industrious village in County Fermanagh, Northern Ireland, on the banks of the River Erne, and to the lustrous porcelain wares produced there.

In 1849, John Caldwell Bloomfield inherited a large estate near Belleek. Interested in ceramics and having discovered rich deposits of feldspar and kaolin (china clay) on his lands, he soon envisioned a pottery that would make use of these materials, local craftspeople and water power of the River Erne. He was also anxious to enhance Ireland's prestige with superior porcelain products.

Bloomfield had a chance meeting with Robert Williams Armstrong who had established a substantial architectural business building potteries. Keenly interested in the manufacturing process, he agreed to design, build, and manage the new factory for Bloomfield. The factory was to be located on Rose Isle on a bend in the River Erne.

Bloomfield and Armstrong then approached David McBirney, a highly successful merchant and director of railway companies, and enticed him to provide financing. Impressed by the plans, he agreed to raise funds for the enterprise. As agreed, the factory was named McBirney and Armstrong, then later D. McBirney and Co.

Although 1857 is given as the founding date of the pottery, it is recorded that the pottery's foundation stone was laid by Mrs. J.C. Bloomfield on Nov. 18, 1858. Although not completed until 1860, the pottery was producing earthenware from its inception.

With the arrival of ceramic experts from the (William Henry) Goss Pottery in England, principally William Bromley, Sr. and William Wood Gallimore, Parian ware was perfected and, by 1863, the wares we associate with Belleek today were in production.

With Belleek Pottery workers and others emigrating to the United States in the late 1800s

Marks:

American Art China Works - R&E, 1891-1895
AAC (superimposed), 1891-1895
American Belleek Co. - Company name, banner & globe
Ceramic Art Co. - CAC palette, 1889-1906
Colombian Art Pottery - CAP, 1893-1902
Cook Pottery - Three feathers with "CHC," 1894-1904
Coxon Belleek Pottery - "Coxon Belleek" in a shield, 1926-1930
Gordon Belleek - "Gordon Belleek," 1920-1928
Knowles, Taylor & Knowles - "Lotusware" in a circle w/a crown, 1891-1896
Lenox China - Palette mark, 1906-1924
Ott & Brewer - crown and shield, 1883-1893
Perlee - "P" in a wreath, 1925-1930
Willets Manufacturing Co. - Serpent mark, 1880-1909
Cook Pottery - Three feathers with "CHC"

Finely decorated, large Willets (American) bowl, circa 1900, hand-painted band of flowers including peonies around body with geometric border and low circular foot, marked Belleek Willets on base with serpent mark and hand-painted inscription MIDDLETON, 3-3/4" h., 9-3/4" dia. **$300**

and early 1900s, Belleek-style china manufacture, known as American Belleek, commenced at several American firms, including Ceramic Art Company, Colombian Art Pottery, Lenox Inc., Ott & Brewer, and Willets Manufacturing Co.

Throughout its Parian production, Belleek Pottery marked its items with an Irish harp and wolfhound and the Devenish Tower. The first period mark of 1863 through 1890 is shown below. Its second period began with the advent of the McKinley Tariff Act of 1891 and the (revised) British Merchandise Act as Belleek added the ribbon "Co. FERMANAGH IRELAND" beneath its mark in 1891. Both the first and second period marks were black, although they occasionally appeared in burnt orange, green, blue or brown, especially on earthenware items. Its third period begin in 1926, when it added a Celtic emblem under the second period mark as well as the government trademark "Reg No 0857," which was granted in 1884. The Celtic emblem was registered by the Irish Industrial Development Association in 1906 and reads "Deanta in Eirinn," and means "Made in Ireland." The pottery is now utilizing its 13th mark, following a succession of three black marks, three green marks, a gold mark, two blue marks and three green. The final green mark was used only a single year, in 2007, to commemorate its 150th anniversary. In 2008, Belleek changed its mark to brown. Early earthenware was often marked in the same color as the majority of its surface decoration. Early basketware has Parian strips applied to its base with the impressed verbiage "BELLEEK" and later on, additionally "Co FERMANAGH" with or without "IRELAND." Current basketware carries the same mark as its Parian counterpart.

The item identification scheme is that followed within the works by Richard K. Degenhardt: *Belleek The Complete Collector's Guide and Illustrated Reference* (both first and second editions). Additional information, as well as a thorough discussion of the early marks, is located in these works as well as on the Internet at Del E. Domke's website: http://home.comcast.net/~belleek_website.

Rare porcelain vase, triple fish motif, 15-1/2" h. x 7" x 7"..................... **$450**

Vase, 1891-1926, second period black mark, modeled as two entwined fish supporting coral-form stem beneath nautilus shell, rocky stepped base applied with shells and coral, 12-1/4" h. x 6" w. x 5" d.............. **$700**

Willets dragon vase, good condition, 7" h., 8" dia.. **$90**

Porcelain vase, painted all-around scene after "The Birth of Venus" by Casper-Philipp, good condition, 16-1/4" h. x 5-1/4" dia. **$1,100**

Ceramic pitcher, silver overlay, Willets Manufacturing Co., circa 1890, marks to ceramic: (W on plinth), BELLEEK, WILLETS; marks to silver: STERLING, minor rubbing to silver overlay, 9-1/4" h. **$1,000**

Porcelain figure, "Meditation," 1891-1926, standing, classically robed female in contemplative pose, second period black mark, 14-3/4" h................**$1,000**

Basket, 19th century, rim decorated with flowers and shamrocks, marked "Belleek Co. Ireland.".. **$50**

Three pieces, green mark dish, 7-1/4" dia.; green mark jug, 4-1/4" h., green mark bowl, 4-1/2" dia. **$60**

Sugar bowl and cream jug, 1863-1890, sugar bowl with first period black mark and impressed mark, inscribed in blue M0072203, modeled as conch shell supported on pierced coral-form base, ivory luster glaze; cream jug with partially rubbed mark (apparently first period black), impressed Belleek Fermanagh, impressed with symbol, modeled as nautilus shell with applied coral-form handle extending to base molded with shells, matte ivory glaze; sugar bowl 4" h. x 6-1/2" w, x 6-1/4" d.; cream jug 4-3/4" h. x 6-3/4" w. x 3-1/4" d. **$850**

Eight saucers, each with second period black mark, in two patterns, together with a Belleek Collectors Society plaque, issued 1979, diameter of largest 7"....... **$150**

Three-piece painted set, pot, sugar and creamer, third period black mark, 1926-1946, together with two marked steins, one Belleek piece cracked..................... **$100**

Partial tea service, most pieces dated 1863-1890, platter with first period black mark (17-3/4" w. x 14-1/4" d.), cream jug with first period black mark (3-1/2" h. x 4-1/2" w. x 3-1/2" d.), sugar bowl with first period black mark and impressed Belleek (3" h. x 3-3/4" dia.), three teacups with first period black mark and one teacup with first period red mark (2" h. x 3-1/2" dia.), three saucers with first period black mark and one saucer with first period red mark (5-1/4" dia.), kettle, unmarked (6" h. x 8" w. x 6" d.), various ivory-colored glazes, 12 pieces... **$700**

Bennington Pottery

BENNINGTON POTTERY WARES, which ranged from stoneware to parian and porcelain, were made in Bennington, Vermont, primarily in two potteries, one in which Captain John Norton and his descendants were principals, and the other in which Christopher Webber Fenton (also once associated with the Nortons) was a principal. Various marks are found on the wares made in the two major potteries, including J. & E. Norton, E. & L. P. Norton, L. Norton & Co., Norton & Fenton, Edward Norton, Lyman Fenton & Co., Fenton's Works, United States Pottery Co., U.S.P. and others.

The popular pottery with the mottled brown on yellowware glaze was also produced in Bennington, but such wares should be referred to as "Rockingham" or "Bennington-type" unless they can be specifically attributed to a Bennington, Vermont factory.

Bennington, Vermont flint enamel lion, circa 1850, impressed Lyman Fenton & Co., standing figure with coleslaw mane, front paw resting atop globe on stepped plinth, 9-1/2" h., 11" l. **$10,073**

Bennington spittoon, good condition, 4" h., 8" dia **$45**

Four Bennington marbles, 19th century, one with blue and brown glaze over white ground, two with brown glaze, one with yellowish glaze, all in excellent condition, diameter of largest 1-1/2". **$125**

Three Bennington Pottery and flint enamel book bottles, attributed to Lyman & Fenton, Bennington, Vermont, circa 1849, larger flask embossed "BENNINGTON COMPANION," smaller two embossed "DEPARTED SPIRITS," largest 8" h. x 6" w. x 3" d., smaller two 5-3/4" h. x 4" w. x 2" d.. **$800**

Bennington Pottery bottle, figure of man, by David Gil, circa 1970, 10" h. **$75**

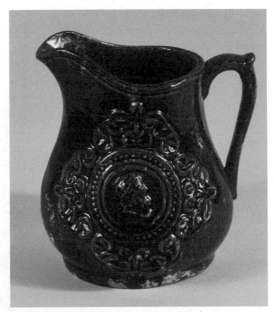

Bennington pottery pitcher, 19th century, Rockingham glaze with classical profiles in relief, 9" h. x 8" w. x 6-1/4" d................. **$50**

Clarice Cliff

CLARICE CLIFF WAS a designer for A.J. Wilinson, Ltd., Royal Staffordshire Pottery, Burslem, England, when it acquired the adjoining Newport Pottery Co., whose warehouses were filled with undecorated bowls and vases. In about 1925, Cliff's flair with the Art Deco style was incorporated into designs appropriately named "Bizarre" and "Fantasque," and the warehouse stockpile was decorated in vivid colors. These hand-painted earthenwares, all bearing the printed signature of designer Clarice Cliff, were produced until World War II and find enormous favor with collectors.

Note: Reproductions of the Clarice Cliff "Bizarre" marking appear on the market occasionally.

Fantasque ware vase, England, 20th century, Wilkinson Ltd., frieze-decorated in Broth pattern with green, red, and black banding, shape 194, backstamp, 11" high.......................**$1,304**

Bizarre ware charger, England, 20th century, Wilkinson Ltd., Rhodanthe pattern, backstamp, 18" diameter...................... **$652**

Moonlight vase, shape 370, printed factory marks, 6 1/2" high, 6 1/2" diameter... **$1,188**

Bowl and vase, England, 20th century, Newport and Wilkinson potteries, Bizarre ware bowl in Delecia pattern, shape 636, 8" diameter; flared vase, polychrome enameled with landscape, spreading foot, 9" high; each with backstamp.............. **$356**

Brangwyn Panels commemorative charger, England, 20th century, Wilkinson Ltd., depicting a scene with world peoples and animals in jungle setting, reverse with hand-painted inscription "The Brangwyn Panels Designed For the Royal Gallery of the House of Lords 1925 First Exhibited at Olympia 1933. Painted By Clarice Cliff From One of the Panels. A Wilkinson Ad. Royal Staffordshire. Pottery. Burslem Staffordshire," with Frank Brangwyn's monogram and signature, 17 1/4" diameter.. **$2,963**

Four Forest Glen pattern items, England, 20th century, Newport and Wilkinson potteries, three-piece tea service: teapot, 3-1/4" h., sugar and creamer, jam pot with red base and patterned lid, 4-1/8" dia.. **$516**

Wall pocket, England, 20th century, Newport Pottery Company, female nymph with flowers in her hair, with backstamp, 9" high... **$296**

Wall hanging, England, 20th century, female head adorned with flowers, designer's signature on reverse, 6 5/8"..... **$243**

Bizarre ware bowl, England, 20th century, Newport Pottery Company, Delecia pattern with pansies and ribbed sides, backstamp, 9 1/4" diameter. **$296**

Planter, England, 20th century, Wilkinson Ltd., Woodland pattern, three shaped feet, backstamp, 7 1/2" diameter.........**$365**

Bizarre ware bowl, England, 20th century, Wilkinson Ltd., ribbed body decorated with polychrome landscape dotted with cottages, shape 633, backstamp, 9 1/4" diameter. **$296**

Bowl, England, 20th century, Wilkinson Ltd., Rhodanthe pattern, backstamp, 8 1/2" diameter.................. **$296**

Fantasque ware vase, England, 20th century, Wilkinson Ltd., Brown Lily pattern with polychrome banding, shape 269, backstamp, 5 7/8".......................**$415**

Bizarre ware covered pot, England, 20th century, Newport Pottery Company, Delecia pattern with pansies, shape 335, wicker handle, backstamp, 6 1/4" diameter.................**$385**

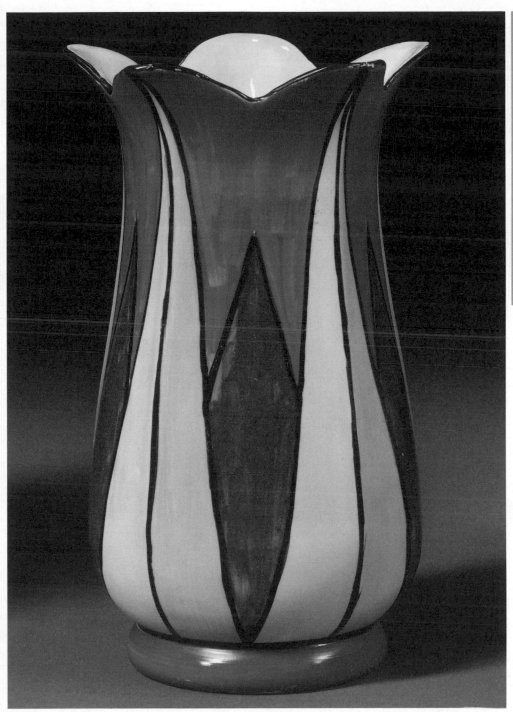

Bizarre ware vase, England, 20th century, Newport Pottery Company, tulip-form, polychrome geometric pattern, shape 361, backstamp, 8 1/4" high...**$652**

Bizarre ware vase, England, 20th century, Wilkinson Ltd., Rhodanthe pattern, baluster shape, backstamp, 10 5/8" high. **$593**

Bizarre ware vase, England, 20th century, Newport Pottery Company, baluster-form with molded decoration and matte glaze in pastel colors, shape 390, backstamp, 8 1/2" high. **$326**

Four Bizarre ware items, England, 20th century, Newport and Wilkinson potteries, Athens jug in Delecia pattern with backstamps for both firms and indistinct raised numbers, 7-1/4" h.; bowl with painted scene of tree and patch of flowers repeated on each side, 8" dia.; two tapered vases in My Garden pattern, one with orange ground, the other blue, 7-5/8" h.; each with backstamp. **$425**

Five tableware items, England, 20th century, Newport and Wilkinson potteries, Delecia Citrus pattern oblong dish, 11-5/8" l.; Rhodanthe pattern sugar sifter, 5" h.; My Garden cylindrical covered sugar with floriform finial, 3-1/8" h.; jam pot with yellow rose set against fuchsia spiral, 4" h.; toast rack with polychrome decoration of flowers and etched fields, 6" l. **$711**

House and Bridge tea set, Stamford teapot, sugar bowl (restored) and creamer, two teacups and a saucer, printed marks, teapot 4 1/2" high x 5" wide x 3" deep. **$2,250**

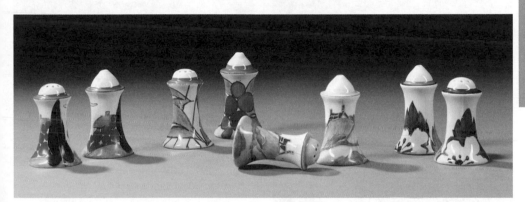

Fours pairs of Bizarre ware salt and pepper shakers, England, 20th century, Newport Pottery Co., two pairs Alpine and Berries patterns, one pair with brown flowers and green leaves and the other with thatched roof, 3-1/4". **$668**

Five items, England, 20th century, Newport and Wilkinson potteries, Bizarre ware vase with orange-leaf tree with black branches on yellow and white ground with cloud outlines and a band stylized green shrubbery, 8" h.; "Indian Summer" vase with flared black-lined rim, body with flared middle decorated with blue and black floral band, 7-5/8" h.; Bizarre ware Athens jug in Forest Glen pattern, 6" h; pair of Bizarre ware vases in Applique pattern, each incised "265," 6" h; each with backstamp. **$5,629**

Bizarre ware jug and coffeepot, England, 20th century, Wilkinson Ltd., each decorated with the Aurea pattern to a ribbed body, jug, 8 7/8" high, Lynton shape coffeepot 7 1/2" high, each with backstamp, jug with raised "563 GREEK" to base. ... **$459**

Two figural condiment servers, England, 20th century, Newport Pottery Company, shaker on spreading foot, painted as a sailor, 3 3/8" high; jam pot with handle modeled as a human head and further decorated with polychrome banding, 4 3/8" high; each with backstamp. **$563**

Bizarre ware Lotus Jug, England, 20th century, Wilkinson Ltd., ribbed body, Pine Grove pattern, backstamp and hand-painted blue "S," 11 3/8" high. **$1,126**

Two Bizarre ware jugs, England, 20th century, Wilkinson Ltd., each Aurea pattern to ribbed body, one Lotus form, 9 7/8" high, the other with spout, base with raised "563 GREEK," 9" high; each with backstamp. **$444**

Bizarre ware bowl, England, 20th century, Newport and Wilkinson potteries, green band to rim and interior with polychrome design of flowerheads and tree, three feet, backstamps for both firms, 7" diameter. **$326**

Three Bizarre ware items, England, 20th century, Newport Pottery Co., pitcher in Secrets pattern with additional "Fantasque" label to stamp, 7-1/2" h.; bowl in Cafe-au-Lait pattern, 10" dia.; miniature clog in Gayday pattern, 6"; each with backstamp. **$889**

Five-piece Bizarre ware partial tea set, England, 20th century, Newport Pottery Co., Sungay pattern, teapot, creamer, open sugar, teacup and saucer, dish, each with backstamp, teapot 5-3/4". **$1,067**

Bizarre ware vase, England, 20th century, Wilkinson Ltd., Aurea pattern, shape 362, backstamp, 8" high. ... **$474**

Eight-piece Fantasque Bizarre ware partial tea set, England, 20th century, Newport Pottery Co., Gibraltar pattern, teapot, creamer, open sugar, two coffee cups, two teacups and saucers, one dish, each with backstamp, teapot 5-3/4". **$2,963**

Bizarre ware vase, England, 20th century, Newport Pottery Company, slightly tapered and ribbed body, Goldstone pattern with gilt and black spheres and fine gilt banding, shape 630 L/S, backstamp, 8" high. **$237**

Five-piece Bizarre ware partial tea set, England, 20th century, Newport Pottery Co., Windbells pattern, teapot, creamer, open sugar, and two cups and saucers, each with backstamp, teapot 5" h. **$1,007**

Six Bizarre ware tableware items, England, 20th century, Newport and Wilkinson potteries, ovoid sugar sifter with design of thatched roof, 4-3/4" h.; two spice shakers with tapered ribbed bodies, one Aurea pattern, the other a geometric diamond design, 4-3/4" h.; Melon pattern jam pot with fruit finials, 3" h.; pair of cube-form Aurea pattern candlesticks, 2-1/4" h. **$830**

Seven Bizarre ware spice shakers, England, 20th century, Newport and Wilkinson potteries, two pairs of conical sugar sifters, one with partially etched design of flowers and fields, the other with thatched roof, height to 3-1/8"; small set of salt and pepper shakers and jam pot in bright hues, height to 1-7/8"... **$911**

Three Bizarre ware dishes, England, 20th century, Newport and Wilkinson potteries, octagonal Nasturtium pattern center bowl, 9"; octagonal Orange Roof Cottage plate also stamped "Fantasque," 9-3/8"; Rhodanthe pattern Biarritz-form plate, also stamped "The Biarritz Royal Staffordshire Great Britain Regd. No. 784849," 9"; each with backstamp. **$563**

CLARICE CLIFF

Five Bizarre ware conical sugar sifters, England, 20th century, Newport and Wilkinson potteries, one each Autumn Crocus, Rhodanthe, Aurea, and Gibraltar patterns, one with applied blue flowers to base on white ground, each with backstamp, 5-1/2" h. **$2,844**

Five-piece Bizarre ware partial tea set, England, 20th century, Wilkinson Ltd., each in Cabbage Flower pattern and Lynton-form, coffeepot, milk jug, creamer, open sugar, and cup and saucer, each with backstamp, coffeepot 7 1/8" high. **$521**

Cookie Jars

COOKIE JARS, COLORFUL and often whimsical, are popular with collectors. They were made by almost every manufacturer in all types of materials. Figural character cookie jars are the most popular with collectors.

Cookie jars often were redesigned to reflect newer tastes. Hence, the same jar may be found in several different variations, and these variations can affect the price.

Many cookie-jar shapes were manufactured by more than one company and, as a result, can be found with different marks. This often happened because of mergers. Molds also were traded and sold among companies.

For more information on cookie jars, see *Warman's Cookie Jars Identification and Price Guide* by Mark F. Moran.

Carousel by Red Wing, with distinct color and decorating styles, each 8" tall, 1950s, marked with two styles of ink stamp................ **$800 each**

Drum Major by Shawnee, 10" tall, late 1940s, impressed mark, "U.S.A.," also found marked "#10" and rarely in gold trim. This example ....
$700+; with gold trim, $1,200+

Pinocchio, two versions, by California Originals, both 12 1/4" tall, impressed marks on bottom, "Calif. Orig. G-131 USA." Also found unmarked or with only an impressed "USA." Unlike some other older jars, the color variations in these Pinocchios do not affect value. ....**$1,200+ each**

ABC Bear by Sierra-Vista, 11 3/4" tall, late 1950s, with original foil label, "Genuine hand Painted Starnes California U.S.A.," otherwise unmarked.............. **$400+**

Dog with Basket by Brush, 12" tall, unmarked (sometimes found with paper label)............ **$800+**

Water Lily blue cookie jar (1-8") by Roseville, raised mark, 9" by 10 1/4"................ **$400-$500**

Golfing Fred and Dino by American Bisque, 14 1/4" tall, 1960s, impressed mark on back, "U.S.A." (Beware of smaller reproductions.).................. **$1,500+**

Castle Turret, distributed by Cardinal, airbrush colors, 11 1/2" tall, 1950s, marked on reverse, "Cardinal Copyright (symbol) 310 USA." .... **$175-$200**

Balloon Lady by Pottery Guild of America, 11 3/4" tall, 1940s, unmarked................ **$175+**

Gleep by Haeger, 11" tall, 1960s, ink-stamped on bottom, "Haeger USA Copyright (symbol)," foil label, "Glaze Tested United States Pottery Association." **$300**

Queen by Hedi Schoop, 13 1/4" tall, 1950s, marked inside lid, "Hedi Schoop 2" and on bottom, "Hedi Schoop." .... **$700-$800**

Leprechaun (in red) by McCoy, 12" tall, 1950s, unmarked, never put into wide production, but no one is certain just how many were made. (Widely reproduced slightly smaller.) . ... **In red, $3,000+**

Clown by Regal China, 12" tall, 1950s, marked, "Translucent Vitrified China Copyright (symbol) C. Miller– 54-439A." ....**$700+**

Little Boy Blue marked "Hull-Ware Boy Blue U.S.A. 971-122" with cold paint. This jar was not produced, and there are only a few known to exist. **$5,000**

Watermelon by Metlox, 10 1/8" tall, 1960s, impressed mark on bottom, "Made in Poppytrail Calif." with gold and brown foil label, "Metlox Manufacturing Co."....................**$1,000+**

Little Old Lady by Abingdon, 9" tall, circa 1950, ink-stamped "Abingdon USA" and impressed "471." (Also found with other under-glaze decorations and in solid colors, similarly priced.) ...... **$600+**

COOKIE JARS

Fawn at Stump by Ungemach, 9 1/4" tall, 1950s, impressed mark, "U.S.A." on the back. .... **$300+**

Humpty Dumpty by Purinton, 10 1/2" tall, 1950s, unmarked. .... **$225-$250+**

Queen Bee by Starnes, 10 3/4" tall, 1950s, unmarked................**$375+**

Jocko by Robinson Rans-bottom, with unusual glaze decoration, 12" tall, 1950s, impressed mark, "RRPCo. USA Roseville O." ....
This example, $750+; in normal colors, $350-$400

Mammy by National Silver, with cold-paint highlights on mouth, 9 1/2" tall, 1940s, marked on bottom, "USA NSCO." (Some-times found with foil labels and the mark "NASCO.") .... **$500+**

Plaid Dog by Brayton Laguna, 9" tall, 1950s, marked inside the lid with a hand-written "H" and stamped on the bottom, "Brayton California USA." ..... **$500+**

Castle by Twin Winton, 10" tall, introduced in 1954, this example slightly later, soft impressed mark, "The Twin Wintons Copyright (symbol)." Found in other color combinations..... **$250-$300**

Rocking Horse by William Hirsch, 12" tall, raised mark on the bottom, "Copyright (symbol) 1950 Wm. Hirsch California." **$100**

Cowan

R. GUY COWAN opened his first pottery studio in 1912 in Lakewood, Ohio. The pottery operated almost continuously, with the exception of a break during World War I, at various locations in the Cleveland area until it was forced to close in 1931 due to financial difficulties.

Many of the 20th century's finest artists began with Cowan and its associate, the Cleveland School of Art. This fine art pottery, particularly the designer pieces, is highly sought after by collectors.

Many people are unaware that it was due to R. Guy Cowan's perseverance and tireless work that art pottery is today considered an art form and found in many art museums.

Chinese bird vase, marked (die impressed) Cowan seal, excellent condition, 11-1/4" h. **$110**

Two-handled vase, green glaze, impressed Cowan mark, 8" x 7". **$25**

Vase with volcanic-like glaze, black over April green flambé, marked with Cowan die impressed logo, excellent original condition, 7" x 11". **$190**

Swirl Dancer flower figure, original ivory, die impressed logo, 10-1/4" h. **$270**

Jazz Bowl, rare smaller form, melon green glaze, designed and signed by Viktor Schreckengost, 8-1/4" h. and 13-5/8" dia. Known as shape X-42, the small Jazz Bowl is thought to be much less common than its larger counterpart. **$22,000**

Delft

IN THE EARLY 17th century, Italian potters settled in Holland and began producing tin-glazed earthenwares, often decorated with pseudo-Oriental designs based on Chinese porcelain wares. The city of Delft became the center of this pottery production and several firms produced the wares throughout the 17th and early 18th century. A majority of the pieces featured blue on white designs, but polychrome wares were also made. The Dutch Delftwares were also shipped to England, where eventually the English copied them at potteries in such cities as Bristol, Lambeth, and Liverpool. Although still produced today, Delft peaked in popularity by the mid-18th century.

Two polychrome floral-decorated Delft plates and charger, 18th century, plates with similar floral central and rim decoration, imperfections, 7-7/8" dia., 8-7/8" dia., 13-3/4" dia. **$960**

Polychrome floral-decorated Delftware bowl, England, 18th century, round footed bowl, center with blue inscription "Success to Trade," exterior decorated with spray of blossoms and leaves, repaired, glaze wear, 4-3/8" h., 10-3/4" dia. **$1,020**

William & Mary figural-decorated Dutch Delft charger, 18th century, rim deco-rated with flowers and birds, table foot pierced for hanging, imperfections, 13-1/2" dia. **$1,920**

Large chinoiserie-decorated Delft bowl, England or Continental, 18th century, piecrust rim, waterway scene with fisher-men, chips, hairline, 4" h., 12-1/4" dia. ..**$840**

Dutch Delft floral-decorated barber bowl, 18th century, oval, center decorated with cobalt animal and bird figures and flowers, wide fluted floral-decorated rim, table foot pierced for hanging, hairline, minor rim chips, 3" h., 10-7/8" dia........ **$750**

Dutch Delft charger with lion and gate decoration, 18th century, circular form with dark cobalt designs of standing lion before curved gate with two col-umns, flanked by trees and foliage, rim decorated with three repeating panels of flowers, chinoiserie figure in a landscape, rim chips, 13-7/8" dia. **$720**

DELFT

Delft plate decorated with a woman holding a cornucopia and a flower stem, late 18th century, rim repair, glaze wear on rim, 8-7/8" dia. **$180**

Delft charger with cobalt flower basket decoration, 18th century, minor rim chips, 13-3/4" dia................................ **$360**

Large Delftware bowl, Britain, late 18th century, ornamented with polychrome bird in a garden in center, floral rim, rim chips, crazing, 2-1/2" h., 13-1/2" dia. ... **$360**

Dutch Delft tobacco jar, 19th century, ovoid form with blue decoration depicting Indian smoking pipe, seated on plinth set with large jar labeled "ST. DOMINGO," with a tobacco plant, barrels, and distant ships, domed brass cover, minor glaze loss and chips, 12" h. **$3,000**

Dutch Delft tobacco jar, 18th century, ovoid form with blue decoration, labeled "MARTE-NIEK" within rococo cartouche surrounded by scrolling foliage topped by flower-filled vase, domed brass cover, minor glaze loss, 15-1/4" h................ **$960**

Dutch Delft tobacco jar, 18th century, ovoid form with blue decoration, labeled "ST. OMER" within rococo cartouche surrounded by scrolling foliage topped by flower-filled vase, domed brass cover, minor glaze loss, 15-1/2" h................ **$960**

Delftware vase, Continental (Dutch), 17th century, tin-glazed earthenware two-handled vase with Baroque decoration, marine landscape on one side and man with tricornered hat in hand on the other, blue and white and marked in blue AKQ for Q. Kleynoven, (1680) and numbered, 337/14, 6-1/4" h. **$300**

Dutch Delft tobacco jar, 19th century, ovoid form with blue decoration depicting Indian smoking pipe, seated on plinth set with large jar labeled "STRASSBUR[G]" and other tobacco-related material with distant ships, domed brass cover, minor chips, 14" h. **$3,120**

Large Dutch Delft tobacco jar, 18th century, ovoid form with blue decoration, labeled "STRAATS/ BURGER" within rococo cartouche surrounded by scrolling foliage topped by flower-filled vase, brass cover, minor glaze loss, 16" h............. **$1,140**

Doulton and Royal Doulton

DOULTON & COMPANY, Ltd., was founded in Lambeth, London, in about 1858. It operated there until 1956 and often incorporated the words "Doulton" and "Lambeth" in its marks. Pinder, Bourne & Company Burslem was purchased by the Doultons in 1878 and in 1882 became Doulton & Company Ltd. It added porcelain to its earthenware production in 1884. The "Royal Doulton" mark has been used since 1902 by this factory, which is still in operation. Character jugs and figurines are commanding great attention from collectors at the present time.

John Doulton, the founder, was born in 1793. He became an apprentice at the age of 12 to a potter in south London. Five years later, he was employed in another small pottery near Lambeth. His two sons, John and Henry, subsequently joined their father in 1830 in a partnership he had formed with the name of Doulton & Watts. Watts retired in 1864 and the partnership was dissolved. Henry formed a new company that traded as Doulton and Co.

In the early 1870s, the proprietor of the Pinder Bourne Co., located in Burslem, Staffordshire, offered Henry a partnership. The Pinder Bourne Co. was purchased by Henry in 1878 and became part of Doulton & Co. in 1882.

With the passage of time, the demand for the Lambeth industrial and decorative stoneware declined, whereas demand for the Burslem manufactured and decorated bone china wares increased.

Doulton & Co. was incorporated as a limited liability company in 1899. In 1901, the company was allowed to use the word "Royal" on its trademarks by Royal Charter. The well-known "lion on crown" logo came into use in 1902. In 2000, the logo was changed on the company's advertising literature to one showing a more stylized lion's head in profile.

Today Royal Doulton is one of the world's leading manufacturers and distributors of premium grade ceramic tabletop wares and collectibles. The Doulton Group comprises Minton, Royal Albert, Caithness Glass, Holland Studio Craft and Royal Doulton. Royal Crown Derby was part of the group from 1971 until 2000 when it became an independent company. These companies market collectibles using their own brand names.

Character Jugs

Anne Boleyn, large, D 6644, 7-1/4" h........... **$85**

Aramis, large, D 6441, 7-1/4" h..................... **$90**

'Arriet, large, D 6208, 6-1/2" h................... **$65**

Beefeater, large, D 6206, 6-1/2" h. **$125**

Catherine Howard, large, D 6645, 7" h. **$115**

Blacksmith, D 6571, large, 7" h. **$100**

Capt. Henry Morgan, large, 6-3/4" h. **$100**

Catherine Parr, large, D 6664, 6-3/4" h. **$220**

Capt Hook, large, D 6597, 7-1/4" h. **$500**

'Ard of 'Earing, large, D 6588, 7-1/2" h. **$1,250**

Bacchus, large, D 6499, 7" h. $100

The Fortune Teller, large, D 6497, 6-3/4" h. $200

Anne of Cleves, large, D 6653, 7-1/4" h.... **$240**

Catherine of Aragon, large, D 6643, 7" h.. **$100**

Left: Cliff Cornell, large, variation No. 1, light brown suit, brown and cream striped tie, 9" h. **$450**

Right: Cliff Cornell, large, variation No. 3, dark brown suit, green, black and blue designed tie, 9" h. **$750**

The Clown with white hair, large, D 6322, 7-1/2" h. **$1,000**

Don Quixote, large, D 6455, 7-1/4" h. **$60**

Falstaff, large, D 6287, 6" h. **$100**

The Gardener, large, D 6630, 7-3/4" h...........**$150**

The Guardsman, large, D 6568, 6-3/4" h. **$95**

George Washington and George III, large, D 6749, 7-1/4" h. **$125**

Groucho Marx, large, D 6710, 7" h.................**$155**

Gulliver, large, D 6560, 7-1/2" h....................**$675**

Gladiator, large, D 6650, 7-3/4" h.................... **$600**

Henry VIII, large, D 6642, 6-1/2" h. **$125**

Izaac Walton, large, D 6404, 7" h. **$85**

Hamlet, large, D 6672, 7-1/4" h. **$150**

John Peel, large, D 5612, 6-1/2" h. **$100**

Johnny Appleseed, large, D 6372, 6" h. **$350**

Jane Seymour, large, D 6646, 7-1/4" h. **$100**

Louis Armstrong, large, D 6707, 7-1/2" h. **$185**

The Lawyer, large, D6498, 7" h. **$90**

Lord Nelson, large, D 6336, 7" h. **$325**

Lumberjack, large, D 6610, 7-1/4" h. **$100**

Parson Brown "A," large, D 5486, 6-1/2" h. **$125**

Mr. Pickwick, large, D 6060, 5-1/2" h. **$150**

Robin Hood, 2nd version, large, D 6527, 7-1/2" h....... **$65**

Robin Hood, 2nd version, small, D 6234, 3-1/4" h. **$20**

Merlin, large, D 6529, 7-1/4" h. **$100**

Paddy, large, D 5753, 6" h. **$120**

Old King Cole, large, D 6036, 5-3/4" h. **$230**

Mad Hatter, large, D 6598, 7-1/4" h. **$185**

The Ringmaster, large, D 6863, 7-1/2" h..........**$150**

Santa Claus, doll and drum handle, large, D 6668, 7-1/2" h..........**$185**

St. George, large, D 6618, 7-1/2" h. **$175**

The Walrus & Carpenter, large, D 6600, 7-1/4" h. **$130**

Tony Weller, large, D 5531, 6-1/2" h.........**$230**

Robinson Crusoe, large, D 6532, 7-1/2" h. **$175**

The Sleuth, large, D 6631, 7" h.................**$100**

William Shakespeare, large, D 6689, 7-3/4" h. **$125**

Simple Simon, large, D 6374, 7" h............... **$500**

Ugly Duchess, large, D 6599, 6-3/4" h. **$675**

Yachtsman, large, D 6626, 8" h. **$150**

Sairey Gamp, large, No. 5451, 6-1/4" h. **$65**

Scaramouche, large, first version, D 6558, 7" h. .**$775**

Veteran Motorist, large, D 6633, 7-1/2" h..........**$125**

Sir Thomas More, large, D 6792, 6-3/4" h..........**$210**

Dickensware items: "The Artful Dodger" candlestick, "Old Peggoty" pitcher, "Little Nell" pitcher, "Bill Sykes" cream jug, each with deep green line rims, ombre burnt orange grounds to rims and black outlines over-enameled in colors, 20th century, excellent condition, 4" to 5-3/4" h. overall. **$127**

Four Series Ware items: "Coaching" pitcher with rope-twist handle, No. D2416, and three others with house in rustic scenery, all with dark green line rims, printed marks, 1920s and later, smallest pitcher undamaged, remaining with light to moderate glaze crazing, 4-1/2" to 6-1/8" h overall. **$92**

Four Series Ware pitchers: "Katherine" small-sized jug, "Woolsey" mid-sized jug, small "Bluebell Gatherers" jug, small "Queens and Ladies" creamer, No. D3159. "Woolsey" and "Queens" pitchers with dark green line rims, remaining two with brown line rims, each with printed marks, 1930s and later, 3-7/8" to 6-7/8" h. overall. $92

Four Series Ware items, clockwise from top left: "Queen Elizabeth at Old Moreton" double-handled dish with black line rims, "Henry VIII at Hampton Court" quatrefoil-form dish with brown line rim, "Romeo" with brown-line rim, and "Bluebell Gatherers" cereal bowl with light green line rim, each with printed marks, 1920s and later, very good overall condition, various sizes. ..$69

Three Series Ware items: hatpin holder, possibly "Henry VIII at Hampton Court," No. D3858, "Pottery in the Past" loving cup, No. D6696, and "Thomas Touchy" tankard from "Sir Roger de Coverly" series, No. D3618; 1920s and later, loving cup undamaged, hatpin with minor crazing and kiln-splitting to base, tankard cracked at rim, glaze crazing, loving cup 6-1/8" h, hatpin 5" h, tankard 5-1/2" h. **$92**

Four Series Ware items: "Bird Feeder & Flowers" child's mug, creamer No. D1404, "Juliet" double-handled covered sugar bowl, No. D3696, and "Night Watchman" candlestick, No. D2002; 1920s and later, glaze crazing, various sizes.. **$115**

Flambé landscape vase with scene of thatch-roofed house along road with flowers in foreground, "woodcut" style, bearing Royal Doulton inkstamp insignia, paper label attached to bottom, excellent original condition with short minor scratch, 9" h. **$160**

Flambé scenic vase of landscape showing thatch-roofed houses along road with flowers in foreground, "woodcut" style, marked with Royal Doulton insignia, excellent original condition with a few short scratches, 11-3/8" h. ... **$130**

Pair of Lambeth whiskey jugs, salt glaze stoneware, registry #4818, marked Doulton Lambeth, late 19th century, 8". **$30**

Early Lambeth vase decorated in 1878 with white daisies on blue ground, wrapped with dragon, impressed Doulton logo, date and incised monogram of artist (appears to be JWT), chip at base in area with prior restoration, two short minor firing separations to bottom, slight lean to vase, 14" h. **$1,500**

Fiesta

THE HOMER LAUGHLIN China Co. originated with a two-kiln pottery on the banks of the Ohio River in East Liverpool, Ohio. Built in 1873-'74 by Homer Laughlin and his brother, Shakespeare, the firm was first known as the Ohio Valley Pottery, and later Laughlin Bros. Pottery. It was one of the first white-ware plants in the country.

After a tentative beginning, the company was awarded a prize for having the best white-ware at the 1876 Centennial Exposition in Philadelphia.

Three years later, Shakespeare sold his interest in the business to Homer, who continued on until 1897. At that time, Homer Laughlin sold his interest in the newly incorporated firm to a group of investors, including Charles, Louis, and Marcus Aaron and the company bookkeeper, William E. Wells.

Under new ownership in 1907, the headquarters and a new 30-kiln plant were built across the Ohio River in Newell, West Virginia, the present manufacturing and headquarters location.

In the 1920s, two additions to the Homer Laughlin staff set the stage for the company's greatest success: the Fiesta line.

Dr. Albert V. Bleininger was hired in 1920. A scientist, author, and educator, he oversaw the conversion from bottle kilns to the more efficient tunnel kilns.

In 1927, the company hired designer Frederick Hurten Rhead, a member of a distinguished family of English ceramists. Having previously worked at Weller Pottery and Roseville Pottery, Rhead began to develop the artistic quality of the company's wares, and to experiment with shapes and glazes. In 1935, this work culminated in his designs for the Fiesta line.

For more information on Fiesta, see *Warman's Fiesta Identification and Price Guide* by Glen Victorey.

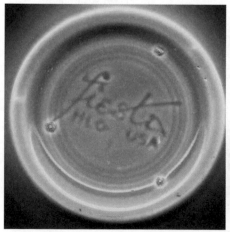 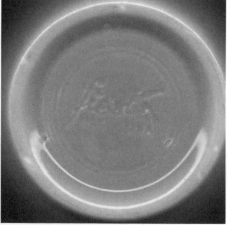

Bottom of No. 1 mixing bowl in green, showing sagger pin marks, the "Fiesta/HLCo. USA" impressed mark, and the faint "1" size indicator. The impressed size mark on the bottom of the No. 2 mixing bowl in yellow is too faint to be seen in this image.

Fiesta Colors

From 1936 to 1972, Fiesta was produced in 14 colors (other than special promotions). These colors are usually divided into the "original colors" of cobalt blue, light green, ivory, red, turquoise, and yellow (cobalt blue, light green, red, and yellow only on the Kitchen Kraft line, introduced in 1939); the "1950s colors" of chartreuse, forest green, gray, and rose (introduced in 1951); medium green (introduced in 1959); plus the later additions of Casuals, Amberstone, Fiesta Ironstone, and Casualstone ("Coventry") in antique gold, mango red, and turf green; and the striped, decal, and Lustre pieces. No Fiesta was produced from 1973 to 1985. The colors that make up the "original" and "1950s" groups are sometimes referred to as "the standard 11."

In many pieces, medium green is the hardest to find and the most expensive Fiesta color.

Bottom of a teacup saucer in turquoise, showing sagger pin marks and the "Genuine Fiesta" stamp.

Bottom of 6" bread plate in turquoise, showing "Genuine Fiesta" stamp.

Examples of impressed Fiesta bottom marks.

FIESTA

Fiesta Colors and Years of Production to 1972

Antique Gold—dark butterscotch 1969-1972
Chartreuse—yellowish green 1951-1959
Cobalt Blue—dark or royal blue.. 1936-1951
Forest Green—dark hunter green.. 1951-1959
Gray—light or ash gray 1951-1959
Green—often called light green when comparing it
to other green glazes; also called "Original" green................................ 1936-1951
Ivory—creamy, slightly yellowed 1936-1951
Mango Red—same as original red 1970-1972
Medium Green—bright rich green... 1959-1969
Red—reddish orange .... 1936-1944 and 1959-1972
Rose—dusty, dark rose 1951-1959
Turf Green—olive.. 1969-1972
Turquoise—sky blue, like the stone.. 1937-1969
Yellow—golden yellow 1936-1969

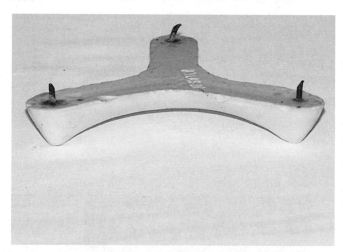

Fiesta pieces were glazed on the underside, so before being fired, each piece was placed on a stilt to keep it off the floor of the kiln. The stilt was made up of three sagger pins positioned an equal distance from each other to form three points of a triangle. If you inspect the underside of any piece of Fiesta, which has a completely glazed bottom, you will notice three small blemishes in a triangular pattern. Later in Fiesta's production run, the undersides of pieces were glazed and then wiped, creating a dry foot, before going into the kiln to be fired.

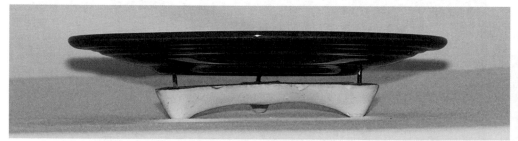

A 9" cobalt blue plate rests on a stilt with sagger pins to show the basic idea of how it worked. Please note that this stilt is not the exact one that would have been used by Homer Laughlin China Co., but rather an updated style in use today by many ceramic studios.

Two different impressed marks on the bottoms of relish tray inserts.

Notice the different bottoms of two ashtrays. The left one has a set of rings with no room for a logo. The right aswhtray has rings along the outer edge, opposite of the ring pattern on the ashtray above. The red example is an older example. The yellow ashtray with the logo can be dated to a time period after 1940.

An ink stamp on the bottom of a piece of Fiesta.

FIESTA

Dessert bowl, yellow. **$60**

Stack of four ashtrays in red, cobalt blue, ivory and yellow. ....
$95, $95, $95, and $85, respectively

Footed salad bowl, ivory. **$550**

Covered onion soup bowl, ivory. **$775**

4-3/4" fruit bowl, cobalt blue. **$35**

Cream soup cup, gray. **$75**

#1 mixing bowl, red with an ivory lid.
.... **$300 bowl, $1,250-$2,000 lid**

11-3/4" fruit bowl, light green. **$395**

#2 mixing bowl, in turquoise with a cobalt
blue lid. ....**$150 bowl, $1,250-$2,000 lid**

Individual salad bowl, yellow. **$145**

#3 mixing bowl, with a yellow lid. ....
$150 bowl, $1,250-$2,000 lid

5-1/2" fruit bowl, red. **$45**

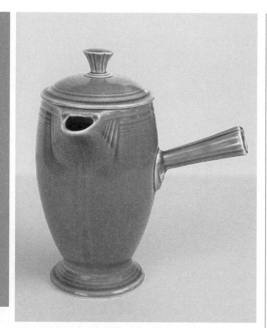

Demitasse coffeepot, light green. **$600**

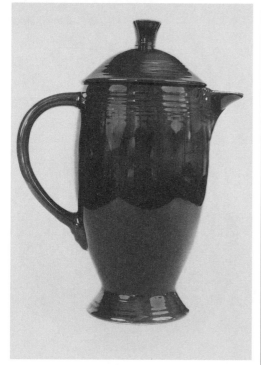

Coffeepot, cobalt blue. **$325**

#4 mixing bowl, ivory. **$175**

#6 mixing bowl, cobalt blue. **$400**

#7 mixing bowl, ivory. **$650**

Sweets comport, cobalt blue. $150

8-1/2" nappy, red. $70

Ring-handle creamer, turquoise. $35

Stick-handle creamer, yellow. $65

Demitasse cup and saucer,
   cobalt blue. $115/set

Eggcup, red.. $80

Covered sugar bowl and stick-handle creamer, red............................... $95 and $75, respectively

Three Tom & Jerry mugs in yellow, light green, and red............... $75, $75, and $95, respectively

Marmalades, red and ivory, including glass spoons with colored tips. .... **$425 and $400, respectively**

Two mustards, red and ivory...................
$350 and $450, respectively

Promotional French casserole, yellow with yellow cover .... **$275-$325**

Rare promotional salad bowl, cobalt blue, with Kitchen Kraft red spoon and yellow fork.
This was the Promotional Salad Set that sold between 1940 and 1943.
Bowls were usually yellow .... **$2,000 for bowl**

Teacup and saucer, yellow..................... **$39/set**

Disk water pitcher, turquoise................... **$185**

Ice pitcher, light green. **$185**

DripCut syrup pitcher, ivory...................... **$525**

Two-pint jug, red. **$175**

FIESTA

6" and 7" plates, medium green... **$35 each**

10-1/2" compartment plate, red. **$85**

9" plate, yellow.. **$25**

12" compartment plate, light green. **$125**

Deep plate, rose. **$65**

FIESTA

13" chop plate, yellow. $65

10" plate, cobalt blue. $50

Shakers, turquoise (note color variation).... **$35/pair**

Oval platter, cobalt blue. $65

Sauceboat, yellow. $75

Medium teapot, ivory. $295

10" vase, ivory...$1,150

8" vase, yellow. **$785**

Utility tray, red. $65

Carafe, red. $395

Water tumbler, light green.......................... $90

Tripod candleholders,
yellow, light green, and
ivory. .... **$725 each pair**

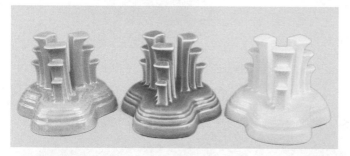

**Two covered onion soup
bowls and lids**, ivory. Lid
on left is typical production
style with flared knob and
shorter flange ring; lid on
right is early production
style with more tapered
knob and deeper flange
ring. More common one on
left is approximately **$775**.
No established value for
one on right.

#3 mixing bowl, red $175

Bowl lids, light green, red, and yellow ....**$1,250-$2,000 each**

4 3/4" fruit bowl, red $40

4 3/4" fruit bowl, turquoise, cobalt blue, ivory,
  yellow and light green... **$35 each**

Bud vase, red. **$155**

Dessert bowls, cobalt blue and turquoise..$65
Dessert bowls, red $75

FIESTA

Covered casserole, red...$300
Covered casserole, yellow $250

Demitasse coffeepot, green. $600
Demitasse cups, red...$100
Demitasse cups, cobalt blue, ivory, and turquoise ....$95 each
Demitasse cups, yellow and green ....$85 each

Comport, cobalt blue...$150
Sauceboat, light green $80

Oval platter, medium green $250

FIESTA

Disk water pitcher, red $225

Teacup and saucer, cobalt blue $39/set

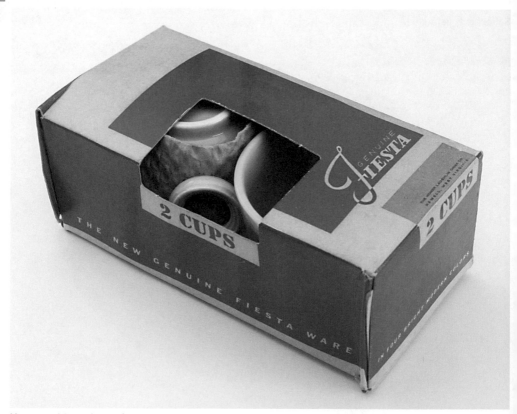

Unopened boxed set of two teacups, yellow.
Boxes can double or triple overall value of piece... $78-$117

Eggcup, yellow $70
Ashtray, light green $85

Demitasse cup and saucer, ivory $115/set
Demitasse cup and saucer, red..$125/set

Tom & Jerry mugs, forest green and chartreuse....................................$95
Tom & Jerry mugs, gray $85

Promotional juice tumbler, red **$75**

12" compartment plate, red **$145**

8", 10", and 12" vases in turquoise, yellow, and cobalt blue......................................
$800, $1,150, and $1,950, respectively

Deep plate, chartreuse **$75**

Medium teapot, turquoise........................ **$295**

Special order promotional disk juice pitcher, red $650
Juice tumbler, chartreuse $950
Juice tumbler, yellow $65
Juice tumbler, rose $95
Juice tumbler, turquoise $70

7" plates, light green, cobalt blue,
   turquoise, and yellow .... $15 each
7" plates, red $20

Two-pint jug, turquoise $135
Two-pint jug, red $175

Relish tray, ivory with cobalt blue, light
   green, red, turquoise, and yellow inserts. $425

Frankoma

JOHN FRANK STARTED his pottery company in 1933 in Norman, Oklahoma. However, when he moved the business to Sapulpa, Oklahoma, in 1938, he felt he was home. Still, Frank could not know the horrendous storms and trials that would follow him. Just after his move, on Nov. 11, 1938, a fire destroyed the entire operation, which included the pot and leopard mark he had created in 1935. Then, in 1942, the war effort needed men and materials, so Frankoma could not survive. In 1943, John and Grace Lee Frank bought the plant as junk salvage and began again.

The time in Norman had produced some of the finest art ware that John would ever create and most of the items were marked either "Frank Potteries," "Frank Pottery," or to a lesser degree, the "pot and leopard" mark. Today these marks are avidly and enthusiastically sought by collectors. Another elusive mark wanted by collectors shows "Firsts Kiln Sapulpa 6-7-38." The mark was used for one day only and denotes the first firing in Sapulpa. It has been estimated that perhaps 50 to 75 pieces were fired on that day.

The clay Frankoma used is helpful to collectors in determining when an item was made. Creamy beige clay known as "Ada" clay was in use until 1953. Then a red brick shale was found in Sapulpa and used until about 1985 when, with the addition of an additive, the clay became a reddish pink.

Rutile glazes were used early in Frankoma's history. Glazes with rutile have caused more confusion among collectors than any other glazes. For example, a Prairie Green piece shows a lot of green but it also has some brown. The same is true for the Desert Gold glaze; the piece shows a sandy-beige glaze with some brown. Generally speaking, Prairie Green, Desert Gold, White Sand, and Woodland Moss are the most puzzling to collectors.

In 1970, the government closed the rutile mines in America, and Frankoma had to buy it from Australia. It was not the same, so the results were different. Values are higher for the glazes with rutile. Also, the pre-Australian Woodland Moss glaze is more desirable than that created after 1970.

After John Frank died in 1973, his daughter, Joniece Frank, a ceramic designer at the pottery, became president of the company. In 1983, another fire destroyed everything Frankoma had worked so hard to create. They rebuilt, but in 1990, after the IRS shut the doors for nonpayment, Joniece, true to the Frank legacy, filed for Chapter 11 (instead of bankruptcy), so she could reopen and continue the work she loved.

In 1991, Richard Bernstein purchased the pottery, and the name was changed to Frankoma Industries. The company was sold again in 2005 to Det and Crystal Merryman. Yet another owner, Joe Ragosta, purchased the pottery in 2008.

Frankoma Pottery was closed for good in 2010, with a factory closeout auction in Oklahoma in 2011.

Bucking Bronco bookends, Model No. 423, Prairie Green glaze, 5 1/2" h. .... **$560 pr.**

Carafe and cover, footed bulbous body tapering to short cylindrical neck, domed cover with rounded tab handle, made from No. 93 pitcher mold created in 1940 and discontinued in 1964, made for an organization, below five-point colored star is the name "Ted Witt," reverse incised with sailboat on water and dates 1946-47, turquoise glaze, marked "Frankoma," 6 1/2" h .. **$90**

Bowl, deep round shape with three full-figure Tiki gods around sides, incised "Club Trade Winds, Tulsa, Okla. 6," Prairie Green, Sapulpa clay, early 1960s, 6 1/4" dia., 3 1/2" h. **$195**

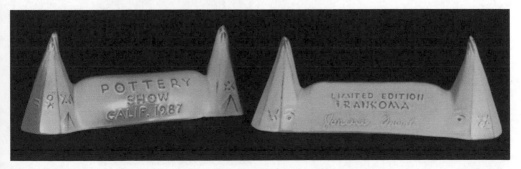

Sign advertising "Pottery Show – Calif. 1987," Prairie Green glaze, 9" l. **$115**

Christmas card in form of figural fish tray,
marked "1960 the Franks, Frankoma
Christmas Frankoma," Woodland Moss
glaze, 4" l. **$95**

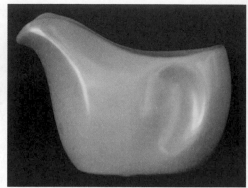

Christmas card in form of creamer, Model
No. 560, "Xmas – The Franks – 1948"
incised into Ada clay, Prairie Green glaze,
rare, 2 1/4" h. **$125**

Flower holder, model of miniature hobby
horse, marked "Frankoma," 1942, Ada
clay, Prairie Green glaze, rare, 3 1/2" h.. **$340**

Stein, footed,
advertising-
type, for John
Frank Memo-
rial Charity
Golf Tourna-
ment, blue,
150 created,
1973. .... **$30**

Vase, miniature spherical ringed shape,
marked "Frankoma 500," Desert Gold
glaze, Ada clay, 2 3/4" h **$190**

Wall pocket, fig-
ural, Billiken,
marked "Tulsa
Court, No.
47, R.O.J.,"
Prairie Green
glaze, Ada
clay, 7" h. ....
$178

Salt and pepper shakers in form of bull heads, Ada clay, matte yellow glaze, 1 3/4" h.....................................**$165 pr.**

Model of Pekinese dog standing on hind legs, designed by Joseph Taylor, 1934-38, marked "Frankoma," glossy black glaze, 7 1/2" h. **$590**

Trivet, eagle sitting on branch, large wings fill up most of space, Peach Glow glaze, Model No. 2tr, 6" sq. **$76**

Figure of Indian chief, No. 142, Desert Gold glaze, Ada clay, 7" h. .**$190**

Wall plaque, figural, modeled as head of Peter Pan, designed by Joseph Taylor, made 1936-38 and 1972-75, Ada clay, Prairie Green glaze, 6" h. **$148**

Vase, stovepipe, marked "Frankoma," Prairie Green glaze with silver overlay, 1940s, 8 3/4" h. **$645**

Fulper Pottery

FROM THE "GERM-PROOF FILTER" to enduring Arts & Crafts acclaim – that's the unlikely journey of Fulper Pottery, maker of the early 20th-century uniquely glazed artware that's become a favorite with today's collectors.

Fulper began life in 1814 as the Samuel Hill Pottery, named after its founder, a New Jersey potter. In its early years, the pottery specialized in useful items such as storage crocks and drain pipes fashioned from the area's red clay. Abraham Fulper, a worker at the pottery, eventually became Hill's partner, purchasing the company in 1860. Renamed after its new owner, Fulper Pottery continued to produce a variety of utilitarian tile and crockery. By the turn of the 20th century, the firm, now led by Abraham's sons, introduced a line of fire-proof cookware and the hugely successful "Germ-Proof Filter." An ancestor of today's water cooler, the filter provided sanitary drinking water in less-than-sanitary public places, such as offices and railway stations.

In the early 1900s, Fulper's master potter, John Kunsman, began creating various solid-glaze vessels, such as jugs and vases, which were offered for sale outside the pottery. On a whim, William H. Fulper II (Abraham's grandson, who'd become the company's secretary/treasurer) took an assortment of these items for exhibit at the 1904 Louisiana Purchase Exposition—along with, of course, the Germ-Proof Filter. Kunsman's artware took home an honorable mention.

Since Chinese art pottery was then attracting national attention, Fulper saw an opening to produce similarly styled modern ware. Dr. Cullen Parmelee, who headed up the ceramics department at Rutgers, was recruited to create a contemporary series of glazes patterned after those of ancient China. The Fulper Vasekraft line of art pottery incorporating these glazes made its debut in 1909. Unfortunately, Parmelee's glazes did not lend themselves well to mass production; they did not result in reliable coloration. Even more to their detriment, they were expensive to produce.

In 1910, most of Parmelee's glazes disappeared from the line. A new ceramic engineer, Martin Stangl, was given the assignment of revitalizing Vasekraft. His most notable innovation: steering designs and glazes away from reinterpretations of ornate Chinese classics and toward the simplicity of the burgeoning Arts & Crafts movement. Among his many Vasekraft successes: candleholders, bookends, perfume lamps, desk accessories, tobacco jars, and even Vasekraft lamps. Here, both the lamp base and shade were of pottery; stained glass inserts in the shades allowed light to shine through.

Always attuned to the mood of the times, William Fulper realized that by World War I the heavy Vasekraft stylings were fading in popularity. A new and lighter line of Fulper Pottery Artware, featuring Spanish Revival and English themes, was introduced. Among the most admired Fulper releases following the war were Fulper Porcelaines: dresser boxes, powder jars, ashtrays, lamps, and other accessories designed to complement the fashionable boudoir.

Fulper Fayence, the popular line of solid-color, open-stock dinnerware eventually known as Stangl Pottery, was introduced in the 1920s. In 1928, following William Fulper's death, Martin Stangl was named company president. The artware that continued into the 1930s embraced Art Deco as well as Classical and Primitive stylistic themes. From 1935 onward, Stangl Pottery became the sole Fulper output. In 1978, the Stangl assets came under the ownership of Pfaltzgraff.

Unlike wheel-thrown pottery, Fulper was made in molds; the true artistry came in the use of exceptionally rich, color-blended glazes. Each Fulper piece is one-of-a-kind. Because of glaze divergence, two Fulper objects from the same mold can show a great variance. While once a drawback for retailers seeking consistency, that uniqueness is now a boon to collectors: each Fulper piece possesses its own singular visual appeal.

Rare VaseKraft lamp, Flemington Green flambé glaze, circa 1908, glazed ceramic, leaded glass, two sockets, base with rectangular ink stamp, patent pending, no. 22, shade numbered 22/33/28, 22" x 16" **$13,750**

Flower jug, Copperdust Crystalline glaze, 1916-1922, incised racetrack mark, 12" x 8"... **$1,500**

Tall rare urn, blue and ivory flambé glaze, 1916-1922, raised racetrack mark, 14 1/2" x 9".. **$3,250**

Jar with pedestal, Cucumber Green crystalline glaze, 1916-1922, raised racetrack mark, 11 1/4" x 10 1/2"..................... **$4,063**

Jardiniere, Mirror Black glaze, 1910-1916, vertical black ink stamp, 8 1/4" x 10" **$3,000**

Rare VaseKraft lamp, Cat's Eye flambé glaze, circa 1908, glazed ceramic, leaded glass, two sockets, VaseKraft stamp, vertical rectangular ink stamp, patent pending, 17 1/2" x 14" **$9,375**

Art pottery candle sconce, 20th century, 10 3/4" high......................... **$395**

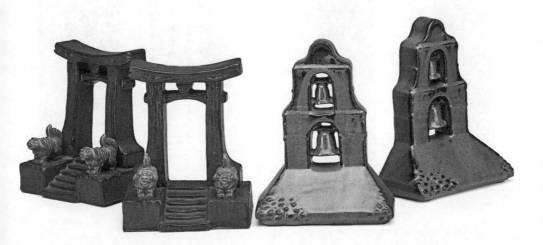

Two pairs of book blocks, Mission Bells and Chinese Gates, 1910-1916, Chinese Gates with vertical ink stamp, Mission Bells with paper label, 8" x 6 1/4", 7 1/4" x 5 1/2" **$1,250**

FULPER POTTERY

Handled vase with blue snowflake crystals over lilac gray, ink stamp racetrack mark, excellent original condition, 6" high **$200**

Urn, Green Crystalline glaze, 1910-1916, vertical rectangular ink stamp, 12" x 8 1/2" **$1,000**

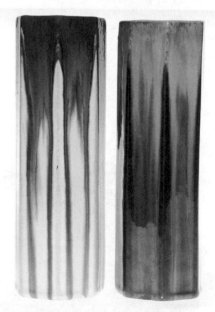

Pair of pillar candlestick vases, with glossy and mat glazes in several shades of green with touches of brown at rim, ink stamp racetrack logo, excellent original condition, 8 1/2" high.................................. **$425**

Two seven-sided vases, shape 445, each covered with drip glazes; 8-3/4" version with green and black flambé glaze and marked with Fulper paper sticker; 8-7/8" version in brown and blue glazes dripped over yellow, marked with early rectangular ink stamp, excellent original condition.... **$550**

4" cream pitcher and 4-5/8" lidded bowl, mat brown glaze, marked with early rectangular mark, mark on sugar cannot be read because glaze has covered it, each in excellent original condition. **$140**

"Bum" glazed ceramic doorstop, 1910s, unmarked, 8" x 9 1/2" x 6" **$1,375**

FULPER POTTERY

Vase with blue snowflake crystals, impressed oval Fulper logo, glazed over kiln kiss on fat part of vase, two uneven areas at rim, also glazed over, 9 1/2" high **$190**

Vase with cream flambé over Mirror Black glaze, raised vertical Fulper mark, several burst glaze bubbles and some tiny scratches, 16 1/2" high......................... **$850**

"Bell pepper" vase in bluish-green mat glaze with yellow on top, incised racetrack mark, excellent condition, 4 1/4" high.. **$350**

Vaz bowl in Mirror Black over cream flambé, marked with vertical Fulper ink stamp logo and Panama-Pacific Expo paper label, also bears remnants of another Fulper paper label, excellent original condition with slight crazing in bowl, 6 3/8" high................................. **$180**

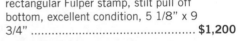

**Handled vase in Mirror Black over butter-
scotch glaze**, vertical racetrack ink stamp
logo, small open glaze bubble on inside
of rim, some kiln pulls on base, 11 3/4"
high... **$425**

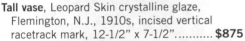

Tall vase, Leopard Skin crystalline glaze,
Flemington, N.J., 1910s, incised vertical
racetrack mark, 12-1/2" x 7-1/2"........... **$875**

**Flambé Chinese sleeping cat doorstop in
flambé Mirror Black with ivory glaze**,
rectangular Fulper stamp, stilt pull off
bottom, excellent condition, 5 1/8" x 9
3/4" **$1,200**

Compote with blue crystalline glaze, marked with early rectangular ink stamp, small grinding nicks at base, 6" x 10-3/4".. **$140**

Handled compote on raised base coated with mustard mat glaze, paler yellow interior encircled with streaks of brown-gray, center has splash of red-brown, unmarked, crazed interior, excellent original condition, 5" high x 12 1/2" wide **$200**

Squatty gourd vase with green glaze over blue with small patches of cobalt, Prang mark on bottom, 3 3/4" high x 6 3/8" diameter **$400**

Tapered gourd vase in green mat glaze with tan at rim, incised racetrack mark, excellent condition, 5 5/8" high x 9" wide **$275**

Vase with two squared handles, dark blue glaze dripped over Wisteria glaze, marked with larger rectangular ink mark, excellent original condition, 11" h. **$250**

Tall vase, Cucumber mat glaze, Flemington, N.J., 1910s, vertical racetrack stamp, 12-1/2" x
7-1/2"... **$1,250**

FULPER POTTERY

Vase with Chinese Blue glaze over Wisteria, marked with vertical "racetrack" logo, some glaze pulls to bottom of vase, some small glaze bubbles, 8" h. **$130**

Vase with flambé glazes of green, brown and blue covering exterior of vessel and running into interior, rectangular "Prang" ink stamp, excellent original condition, 7-5/8" h. **$325**

Two-handled vase, green glaze with large snowflake crystals, die-stamped with "incised" logo, excellent original condition, 8-3/4" h. ... **$225**

Vase, shape TP57 with three color glazes, beige, fawn and brown, marked with company's earlier squatty ink logo, excellent condition, 7-3/4" h................... **$250**

Vase with four buttresses, shape 47, blue, gold and red high glaze, die-stamped with "incised" logo, excellent original condition, 8" h. **$200**

Six-sided vase covered with mahogany flambé glaze in yellow, blue and brown, impressed with "incised" mark, excellent original condition, 10-3/4" h................. **$250**

Two vases with Wisteria glaze, 8-1/8" vase with green applied at rim, 7-3/4" vase impressed with pottery logo, other has oval inkstamp, some roughness at rim of smaller vase, both in original condition... **$150**

Leopard Skin three-handled vase with black and white crystals, marked with vertical ink stamp logo, 6-3/8" h. **$1,600**

Large early vase, 1909-1916 era, green dripped over Wisteria glazes, marked with rectangular Fulper ink stamp, excellent factory condition, 10-3/8" h. **$200**

Large vase with Ivory over Mahogany to Mirrored Black glazes with some blue accents, impressed with Fulper "incised" mark, excellent original condition with some grinding nicks at base, 12-1/4" h. . **$450**

Early corseted vase, gray and mahogany glazes, marked with rectangular ink stamp, excellent original condition, 7-1/8"......... **$325**

Vase, shape 523, mat maroon glaze over blue, marked with vertical ink stamp logo, excellent original condition, 10" h.. **$300**

Bud vase with stovetop neck, variegated blue mat glaze, large rectangular ink mark dating vase to 1909-1916 era, excellent original condition, 5 1/2" h. **$80**

Vase, shape 567, blue, green and purple glazes in both mat and glossy, raised Fulper logo, excellent original condition with some minor glaze bubbles, 6-5/8" h. **$375**

Vase, shape 17, textured brown glaze over blue high glaze, marked with Fulper rectangular ink stamp, small chip at base, 3-5/8".............. **$110**

Large urn-shape vase with two handles, blue green glaze with blue crystals, marked with large rectangular ink mark, professional restoration at base, 12" h. **$200**

Vase, shape 581, Cucumber Crystalline glaze or variant, snowflake crystals, vertical ink stamp symbol and incised D 581, excellent original condition with flat chip or pull to interior edge of foot ring, 9-1/2" h. **$200**

Vase, shape 537, blue, green and tan crystalline glaze, die-stamped "incised" logo, excellent original condition, 7-1/2" h................... **$200**

FULPER POTTERY

Vase, shape 537, black and yellow flambé glaze with blue highlights, marked with die-stamped "incised" logo, excellent original condition, 7-3/8". **$120**

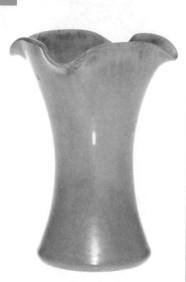

Vase with spouted rim and gloss green glaze, marked with early Fulper rectangular logo, few minor glaze bubbles, excellent condition, 7-1/4" h. **$100**

Cylinder vase, shape 57, dark blue glaze applied over Famille Rose, marked with "h," trial mark, and Fulper's earliest mark, excellent original condition, 8" h. **$180**

Three-handled "Bullet" vase with glossy green glazes applied over Wisteria mat glaze, vertical "racetrack" ink stamp, excellent factory condition, 6-1/4" h.... **$250**

Necked vase with mat Aqua Green Crystalline glaze, racetrack logo, excellent condition, 7 3/4" high **$150**

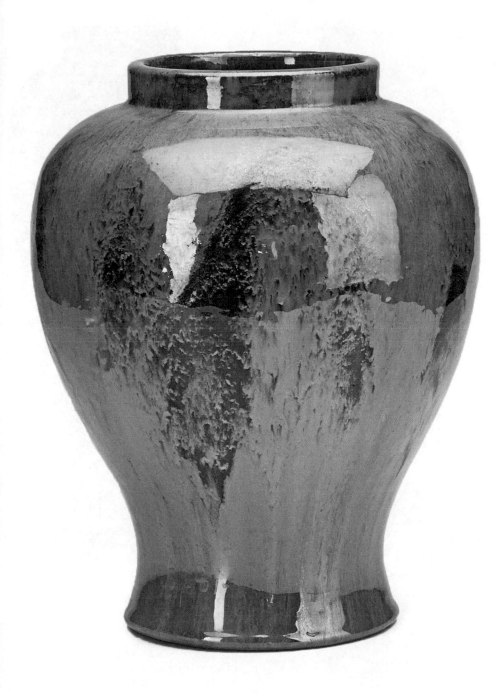

Baluster vase, Chinese Blue flambé glaze, 1916-1922, vertical incised racetrack mark, 11 1/2"
x 8 1/2".. **$1,750**

FULPER POTTERY

Vase with oatmeal glaze over Mirrored Black, impressed with die-stamped "incised" mark, shape 536, small grinding chips at base, 13-1/2" h....................... **$700**

Vase, 1916-1922 era, textured mat green glaze, die-stamped "incised" mark, excellent original condition, 7" h. **$250**

Lamp vase in Mirrored Black glaze over Copper Dust glaze, vase has 14 ribs, Mirrored Black has many small silver crystals, Copper Dust is totally crystallized; marked with vertical ink stamp logo offset to accommodate cast wiring hole, excellent original condition, 13" h. **$600**

Handled pitcher, Oriental form hybridized with addition of handle, 1916-1922, Copper Dust
   crystalline glaze, marked with die-stamped "incised" mark, three flat chips to foot ring, 11-
   3/8" h. **$1,800**

Gouda

GOUDA IS ONE of the decorative art world's strong and silent types, not withstanding its beautifully bright colors and rich floral and abstract designs – considered by many to be its calling card. While its place in today's market is less robust than some of its contemporaries, such as Weller and Rookwood, its pairing of subtle strength of identity and eye-catching design is what attracts people to it and makes it a collecting category to watch.

One of the indicators that Dutch pottery shouldn't be counted out is that higher-end pieces continue to attract attention, not unlike many other categories of antiques today.

"There appears to be a line in the sand with Gouda right now," said Stuart Slavid, vice president and director of Fine Ceramics, Fine Silver, European Furniture & Decorative Arts at Skinner, Inc. "Spectacular pieces are still doing very well, but there is very little or no movement at all for lower-end pieces."

The reasons for that vary, but some contributing factors appear to be advanced collectors looking for advanced pieces rather than more basic items; and the way in which people collect overall has changed some, Slavid explained.

"It used to be more people would start with good pieces, move to better pieces and then to great. Now more people with available discretionary income are starting with the very best pieces," he said.

Riley Humler, auction director and art pottery expert at Humler & Nolan, echoed Slavid's sentiments, adding that high-end pieces in every collecting arena are doing far better than the rest.

"I think the reason is serious collectors are looking for better pieces and avoiding lesser items," Humler said. "Quality has finally taken over for quantity. Part of that may be that serious collectors are generally older and have money. There are not enough young collectors to buy the more reasonable pieces, so one end of the market is

High glaze vase, Rozenburg den Haag, coiling design of butterflies and sunflowers, factory mark with data code and incised V.W 189, early 20th century, 19 1/2" h. **$4,444**

Two high glaze Zuid-Holland Gouda vases, tallest measuring 12" h., painted with florals, Netherlands, circa 1905. ....**$3,375**

doing fairly well and the other, not so well."

As with many situations, there are exceptions to the status quo, and that's also true in today's Gouda pottery market. While the most common Gouda pieces are seen in matte finishes, which are more modern and also more plentiful, early pieces, especially those with birds or butterflies under their gloss finishes, may be somewhat hard to find and tend to be more interesting, according to Humler.

Another example of an exception to the overall slowdown of interest in Gouda is white ground ware, which remains popular, according to experts at Rago Arts. At an unreserved auction on Jan. 12-13, 2013, at Rago Arts, the highlight of the 33 available lots of Gouda pottery was a pair of high-glaze white Zuid-Holland vases, circa 1905, featuring a floral motif, which sold for $3,375 – more than three times the lot's high estimate. Of the Gouda pieces featured at this sale, 22 commanded more than their low estimate, and of those 22 lots, eight fetched more than their high estimate.

Looking at the history of Gouda pottery, it's possible the founders of the earliest factories would be surprised to see what has become of their pottery — especially since many of the first companies to produce Gouda pottery did so to diversify their primary operation of clay pipe production. With an abundance of clay in the Gouda region of the Netherlands, it made good sense for the companies to expand into pottery; and the public demand confirmed it, according to information on the Museum Gouda website, www.museumgouda.nl.

It was 1898 when Plateelbakkerij Zuid-Holland, often referred to as PZH or Zuid-Holland, produced their first piece of Gouda pottery. Named for the region in the Netherlands, Gouda

High-glazed rectangular form vase, circa 1930, elongated stork designed in blue with Art Deco-influenced geometric floral accents, cream ground, marked 217, 12" h., hairline crack near base. **$338**

encompasses the pottery produced by several factories located there. While the earliest examples of Gouda were not the same as the brightly colored, matte glaze pieces collected today, they were often sought after for the same reason as today: décor for the home.

However, like many types of pottery, it didn't necessarily start out that way, said Joe Altare, founder of the Regina Pottery Collectors site (www.reginapottery.com). "One of the key points to remember about these wares is that some were designed as giftware and others for day-to-day use," Altare said. "Both were marketed to the middle class, who finally had discretionary income to purchase decorative, rather than utilitarian wares."

People, then and now, are drawn in by the remarkable colors and designs.

"I stumbled across my first piece, a Regina compote, on eBay about 10 years ago. I knew nothing about Gouda pottery or the Regina factory, but the design captivated me and I had to have it," said Altare. "The design, variety and quality of execution captured my attention, and the many untold secrets of the [Regina] factory have fueled my passion these many years."

Although many of the companies that produced Gouda pottery remained in operation through the mid-1960s and 1970s, many consider the heyday of Gouda to have lasted through the first three decades of the 20th century. In fact, in the 1920s, a quarter of the workforce in the Gouda region was employed in the pottery industry, according to Museum Gouda.

While Gouda pieces may not be setting high-profile auction records today, it remains a strong and serious representative of the ingenuity of decorative pottery. Plus, as more people are shopping at places like IKEA and Crate & Barrel for modern décor and furnishings, decorative pottery like Gouda lends itself nicely to that scene.

"I think Gouda fits very well in that space. It just hasn't caught on yet," said Slavid.

In addition to fitting into society's modern décor and design interests, another advantage for Gouda is that it is more affordable, according to Humler. "Even the best pieces are in most people's price range," he said.

With a history steeped in innovation primed by practicality and fans across the globe, a renewal and widespread rediscovery of Gouda pottery isn't out of the question.

— *Antoinette Rahn*

Experimental floor vase, Zuid-Holland Gouda pottery, 20th century, matte glaze, baluster-form with spreading foot and intricate decoration of three owls interspersed with Rorschachesque designs, cream-colored ground, painted Gouda Zuid Holland and incised 226 A, 25 3/4" h., short hairline crack on lip of rim. **$4,444**

Four pieces: Arnhem Gouda, Purdah bowl, lidded box, Olivia tray, Creta bowl, Netherlands..**$406**

Four pieces: Zuid-Holland Gouda, 20th century Goes tray, Goedewaagen Orchidee charger, Sabany, lidded dresser boxes, Netherlands, all marked.............**$344**

Nine pieces: two Unique Metalique vases, Muvlee bowl and pitcher, Deco bulbous vase, Unicum vase, pitcher in raspberry glaze, and two plates by Leendert Muller, all marked, 1930-1950s, Netherlands....**$313**

Three-piece clock garniture, Zuid-Holland Gouda pottery, Netherlands, circa 1910, clock 20 1/2"......................................**$1,750**

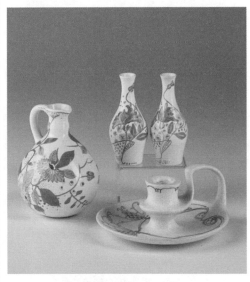

Four pieces: jug, pair of mini vases and chamberstick, Netherlands, circa 1910. . **$125**

Five piece grouping: Zenith Clematis jar-dinière (center back and measuring 10" x 15 1/2" x 13" dia.) and fire bottle (far right), three Ed Antheunis vases (starting at far left): Rola, Bagdhad and Rolf, all pieces circa 1920. .... **$219**

Five pieces of Gouda pottery, early 20th century, Netherlands, all marked, Violette jug with stopper (far left and tallest at 9 1/4"), Maas creamer (front left), double-handled bud vase (center), Rozenburg gourd-shape vase (back right), and bowl (far right). **$438**

Eight-piece grouping of marked pottery from Gouda and Arnhem, Netherlands, early 20th century, Francis and Feo tazzas (far left and far right front), footed Yannis bowl, 1926 (second from left front), Abo flaring low bowl, 1931 (front center), a tray and three vases (back row, left to right). **$500**

Six pieces, early 20th century, Nether-lands, all marked, Ponseav bud vase (back left), squat bowl (middle back), bottle-shaped vase with portrait (right middle and tallest piece measuring 11"), cup with tulips (back far right), double-handled bowl with irises (front left), bowl with tulips (front right). **$563**

Numbered Zuid-Holland Gouda matte glaze charger, circa 1925, Rosalie pattern, bird on branch centering blossoming branches, PZH factory mark, 14 1/4" dia... **$830**

Mat jug and vase painted with florals and birds, Netherlands, circa 1910. .... **$563**

Pairing, early 20th century PZH modern Gouda vase with Rembrandt inkwell. **$219**

Rozenburg den Haag Gouda high glaze charger from the Netherlands, early 20th century, decorated with a bouquet of flowers on pale yellow, deep green, and deep blue ground, painted factory mark, 17 1/2" dia. **$1,007**

Seven pieces: 20th century Zuid-Holland Gouda vases, bowl, gourd-form vase, framed watercolor. $438

Seven pieces, 20th century Zuid-Holland Gouda: charger, footed bowl, bottle-shaped vase, lantern, Crocus chambersticks, Blaren bowl. $563

Nine pieces: 20th century Goedewaagen/ Distel bowl, Ivora plaque, Schoonhoven lidded Isis box, PZH Helene bud vase, salt and four pieces featuring windmill and sailboat paintings...........................$156

Fourteen pieces: Chambersticks, candlesticks, basket, inkwell, vases, tray, bowl, lidded jar, all from the 1920s, Netherlands. $813

16-piece Ispahan tea set: teapot, creamer, sugar, tall pitcher, and set of six cups and saucers, Netherlands..............................$88

Four pieces: footed Gouda bowl and jug in Clareth pattern, Clara vase and Barbara low bowl, all signed with pattern name...$344

Grueby

THE GRUEBY FAIENCE and Tile Co., established in Boston in 1891, produced impressive fine art pottery. Choice pieces were created with molded designs on a semi-porcelain body. The ware is marked and often bears the initials of the decorators. The pottery closed in 1907.

GRUEBY

Vase, tall swelled cylindrical body tapering to short flaring neck, fine slightly streaked matte green glaze, some pinhead-sized burst bubbles, area of think glaze on side, impressed round mark, 12 1/2" h. **$2,760**

George Kendrick designed rare seven-handled vase, Boston, ca.1900, circular Grueby pottery stamp/5, 10-3/4" x 8-1/2"..**$37,500**

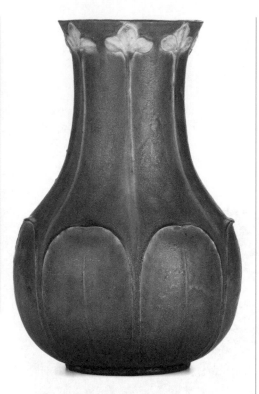

Large bulbous vase with yellow trefoils
and rounded leaves, Boston, ca. 1905,
circular stamp WP, 13" x 8"................ **$6,875**

Early large vase with light green irises,
Boston, ca. 1900, circular faience stamp
EWR 161, 13" x 8-1/4". **$28,750**

Squat vessel with leaves and buds, Boston,
ca. 1905, circular pottery stamp, 7" x
7-1/2"... **$6,875**

Vessel with leaves, matte-green glaze,
Boston, ca. 1905, circular stamp, 4-1/2"
x 5-1/2". **$2,875**

Three water lily tiles, Boston, 1910s, all stamped BOSTON, 6" sq. ea...................................**$938**

Large rare tile with forest decoration, Boston, 1910s,
unmarked, 12" sq. x 2"... **$9,375**

Vase, tall slender gently tapering cylindrical body molded with full-length pointed leaves alternating with flower buds around slightly flaring and scalloped rim, thick suspended green matte glaze, by Annie Lingley, impressed mark, minor grinding to foot chip, minor chip repair at rim, 9" h......**$2,880**

Two architectural tiles with geometric pattern, Boson, ca.
1915, green tile stamped BOSTON 5635?, 1" x 8" sq.. **$1,000**

GRUEBY

Vase, wide squatty bulbous body molded with repeating design of wide rounded overlapping leaves, wide shoulder to wide, short rolled neck, dark green matte glaze, signed "W.P.," restored rim chips, 5 1/2" dia. **$960**

Scarab paperweight in mat blue glaze, impressed with Grueby faience logo, original Grueby sticker, small glaze chips and some glaze skips at base, 1-3/8" x 3-7/8"......... **$350**

Early tall vase with yellow buds, Boston, ca. 1900, circular faience stamp, 23, 11-1/2" x 5-1/4".**$6,875**

Vase, wide ovoid body with short rolled neck, thick medium brown matte glaze, impressed mark, glaze pucker near base, 6 1/8" h........ **$1,150**

Vase, lower portion with ribbed design, signature mat green glaze, impressed pottery logo, incised with a conjoined RE possibly for Ruth Erikson, excellent, original condition, 8-3/4" h. x 9-1/4" w. **$2,500**

Vase, wide ovoid body tapering to a short molded neck, sides incised with wide, tall pointed leaves, thick green matte glaze, Grueby sticker on bottom and impressed initials, 5" h. **$1,495**

Bowl-vase, wide flat mouth above swelled tapering sides, overall blue matte glaze, impressed mark, 6" dia., 5" h. **$575**

Early squat vessel with two rows of leaves, Boston, ca. 1900, circular faience mark, M.S., 5" x 7". **$5,938**

Vase, footed bulbous ovoid body tapering to a molded mouth, sides molded with full-length tapering pointed leaves, fine matte green glaze, modeled by Wilhelmina Post, few minor high point nicks, impressed company mark and artist logo, 6 5/8" h.**$3,565**

Vase, wide ovoid lower body molded with arched overlapping leaves issuing slender stems and flowers to wide angled shoulder tapering to short cylindrical neck, fine green matte glaze, designed by Lillian Newman, paper company label with "1623" and paper "tulip" label and symbol, 9 3/4" h.....**$3,450**

"Kendrick" design, tall ovoid body below wide squatting incurved neck, sides and neck carved with wide pointed veined leaves, green glaze, dark brown interior glaze, unmarked but remnant of original paper label, drilled hole in bottom, small filled-in base chip, original quality oil font, 12 5/8" h. **$10,449**

Cuenca tile, oak, unusual size, Boston, ca. 1905, initialed G.A., 6" x 6-3/4". **$2,125**

Haeger

SLEEK. SINUOUS. COLORFUL and cutting edge. Timeless, trim of line, and, above all, thoroughly modern. That's the hallmark of Haeger Potteries. Since its 1871 founding in Dundee, Illinois, the firm has successfully moved from the utilitarian to the decorative. Whether freshly minted or vintage, Haeger creations continue to provide what ads called "a galaxy of exquisite designs ... visual achievements symbolizing expert craftsmanship and pottery-making knowledge."

Today's collectors are particularly captivated by the modernistic Haeger output of the 1940s and '50s – from "panther" TV lamps and figurines of exotic Oriental maidens to chomping-at-the-bit statuary of rearing wild horses and snorting bulls. But the Haeger story began long before then, with the Great Chicago Fire of 1871.

Founder David Haeger had recently purchased a budding brickyard on the banks of Dundee's Fox River. Following the fire, his firm produced bricks to replace decimated Chicagoland structures. For the next 30 years, industrial production remained the primary emphasis of the Haeger Brick and Tile Co. It wasn't until 1914 that the company, now under the guidance of Edmund Haeger, noted the growing popularity of the Arts & Crafts movement and turned its attention to artware.

From the very beginning, Haeger was distinguished by its starry roster of designers. The first: J. Martin Stangl, former glaze wizard for Fulper. The design emphasis of Stangl and his early Haeger successors was on classically simple, uncluttered Arts & Crafts

Royal Haeger pottery vase, stamped at underside, 12" h. x 8" w........**$15**

Deer figure with original label, 14" h...........**$60**

stylings. Haeger's roster of pots, jugs, vases, bowls, and candleholders all proved big hits with buyers.

An early zenith was reached with a pavilion at the 1934 Chicago World's Fair. In addition to home environment settings accented with Haeger, there was an actual working factory. Once fair-goers had viewed the step-by-step pottery production process, they could purchase a piece of Haeger on the way out. The World's Fair brought Haeger to America's attention – but its grandest days of glory were still ahead.

The year 1938 saw the promotion of Edmund Haeger's forward-thinking son-in-law, Joseph Estes, to general manager, the arrival of equally forward thinking designer Royal Arden Hickman, and the introduction of the popular "Royal Haeger" line.

Royal Haeger pottery "Haeger Award 1947" head form sculpture designed by R. Rush, very good condition with kiln imperfection marks on base, 12-1/4" h. **$30**

The multi-talented Hickman, snapped up by Haeger after stays at J.H Vernon, Kosta Crystal, and his own Ra Art, quickly made his mark. Earlier Haeger figurals were generally of animals and humans at rest. Under the guidance of Hickman, and the soon-to-follow Eric Olsen, motion was key: leaping fish, birds taking wing, and a ubiquitous snarling black panther. The energetic air of underlying excitement in these designs was ideally suited to the action-packed atmosphere of World War II, and the postwar new day that followed.

In 1944, Hickman left Haeger following a dispute over lamp production, returning only for occasional free-lance assignments. The 1947 arrival of his successor, Eric Olsen, coincided with the official celebration of Haeger's "Diamond Jubilee"; that's when much of the Olsen line made its debut. From towering abstract figural lamps to long-legged colts, self-absorbed stalking lions, and mystic pre-Columbian priests, his designs were ideal for the soon-to-be-ultra-current "1950s modern" décor.

"A work of art," Olsen stated, "is not only based on the 'beautiful,' but also on such ingredients as interest, character, craftsmanship, and imagination."

Royal Haeger large blue frothy bottle vase on stand, partial foil label at neck, vase affixed to stand, 16" h. x 8" dia. **$20**

Today, "The Haeger Potteries" continues as a family affair under the leadership of Joseph Estes' daughter, Alexandra Haeger Estes. And whether collectors favor the early Arts & Crafts pieces, the modernistic designs of the 1940s and '50s, or examples of today's output, one constant remains: This is artware collectors are eager to own. Retailer Marshall Field & Co. said it best in 1929: "Haeger Pottery will become an indispensible charm in your home!"

Royal Haeger Earthwrap vase, marked on base Royal Haeger USA, 11" h. x 5-1/2" dia............ **$30**

Pair of Royal Haeger leopard bookends with mat black and burnt orange glaze, both marked Royal Haeger, one marked R617 USA 1903-30D, the other marked R618 USA 1904-30D, mint condition, 11" and 8" h... **$325**

Two vases, each in handled baluster form with modeled textured glaze, larger vase 10" h. x 14" dia. **$30**

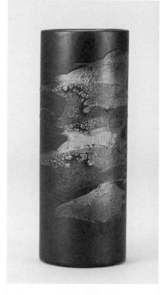

Royal Haeger Earthwrap vase, marked Royal Haeger USA on base, 10-3/4" h. x 4" dia. **$30**

Hall China

FROM TEAPOTS TO toilet seats, Hall China has, quite literally, produced it all. One of the most recognizable names in American pottery manufacture, Hall owes it longevity to a unique combination of product reliability and an uncanny ability to adapt to the particular needs of the times.

Founded in 1903 by Robert Hall, the firm was a restructuring of the defunct East Liverpool (Ohio) Pottery Co., a conglomeration of five smaller Ohio potteries. Hall's plans for his new company ended abruptly with his death in 1904; it fell to his son, Robert Taggart Hall, to carry out his father's ambitious agenda.

First up: cutting production costs by finding a white china compound requiring only single-firing that would not craze. During 10 years of experimentation, the company sustained itself by producing such utilitarian whiteware as jugs, mugs, and, yes, even toilet seats. In 1911, new production manager Jackson Moore successfully developed a leadless glaze that met the single-fire, non-crazing, cost-effective requirements Hall had been seeking. That new formula proved to be the formula for Hall China's enduring success.

The company's earliest sales boom was due, in large part, to the onset of World War I. Since European imports were curtailed, it fell to domestic manufacturers, such as Hall, to produce the sort of heavy-duty china cookware required by large-scale entities, ranging from restaurants and hospitals, to the United States government.

Cooks exposed to Hall china were impressed by its durability, and, at war's end, the company made a seamless expansion into production of retail consumer ware. Promoting

Basket shape Chinese red teapot, covered. **$250**

McCormick Teahouse design teapot, covered, upright rectangular cottage-form with color transfer-printed design of an earlier English teahouse, 1985. .... **$75**

itself as the "World's Largest Manufacturer of Fireproof Cooking China," Hall became particularly known for its extensive line of brightly colored and gilded, imaginatively shaped teapots.

Hall's association with teapot production proved particularly fortunate. In an effort to boost sales (particularly during the Depression years of the 1930s), Hall produced specific lines of china that other manufacturers offered as premiums to their customers. Among the tie-in clients: Standard Coffee, General Electric, Hotpoint, and Jewel Tea. Hall's exclusive Autumn Leaf pattern for Jewel Tea was both affordable and attractive, attracting consumers then and collectors now. Autumn Leaf quickly expanded its borders beyond teapots, covering a full range of dinnerware and decorative accessories, from cookie jars and canister sets to salt-and-peppers and serving dishes.

The seemingly endless array of Autumn Leaf pieces keeps collectors hopping. Its ubiquitous presence is rivaled only by that of another Hall pattern, Red Poppy, a premium for Grand Union. Like Autumn Leaf, Red Poppy was produced in a dizzying array of shapes and for a multitude of uses. The simple, homespun designs of both patterns, the general usefulness of the ware, as well as remarkable durability, have kept them favorites throughout the decades.

Hall kept abreast of changing tastes in the mid-20th century by releasing patterns by such "name" designers as Eva Zeisel. Among her most notable lines for Hall are 1949's Tomorrow's Classic and the 1956 release, Century. In later years, Donald Schreckengost contributed a line of whimsical Hall pieces, ranging from owl-shaped cookie jars to figural teapots, immortalizing in china such notables as Ronal Reagan.

Other sought-after Hall patterns include Wildfire, Meadow Flower, Blue Blossom, and Rose Parade. Some collections consist solely of Hall teapots; best-selling shapes were available in a rainbow of colors. Among the most instantly recognizable Hall teapots is the Arabian Nights-influenced Aladdin shape.

A 2010 merger with Homer Laughlin China Co. (the original manufacturer of the equally well-known Fiesta line) brought two of America's best-loved and longest-lived potteries under one roof. As the ongoing proliferation of Hall China collectors and clubs attests, good style never goes out of style.

Automobile shape Chinese red teapot, covered. $650

Kadota shape Crocus pattern coffeepot, covered, drip-type, all-china.... **$350**

Centennial shape teapot, covered, forest green with gold decoration...**$125**

Zephyr shape Fantasy pattern leftover container, covered.....................**$225**

Bellevue shape Orange Poppy pattern teapot, covered..................**$1,800**

Special Birdcage shape Jewel Tea Autumn Leaf pattern teapot, covered, specially produced for the Autumn Leaf Club in 1995.........................**$150**

Zephyr shape Blue Garden pattern water bottle, covered, refrigerator ware line. **$650**

Bowling ball shape turquoise teapot, covered.**$500**

Teapot, covered, Globe No-Drip pattern, dark pink with standard gold decoration...................**$90**

Zephyr shape Chinese red water bottle, covered, refrigerator ware line. **$650**

Cube shape teapot, covered, in green, marked "The Cube" with listing of design and patent numbers, licensed by Cube Teapots, Ltd., Leicester, England, circa 1930s, East Liverpool, Ohio. ... **$50**

Ansel shape Tricolator coffeepot, covered, yellow art glaze. **$75**

Miniature Aladdin shape teapot, covered, light blue glaze, unmarked, overall 7" l., 5" h. $15

Donut shape jug-type pitcher, large, Chinese red. $135

Moderne shape marine blue teapot, covered. $85

Los Angeles shape teapot, covered, cobalt blue with standard gold trim..................... $75

Donut shape Autumn Leaf pattern teapot, covered, 1993 reissue. $150

Commemorative Donut shape teapot, covered, part of a limited edition produced for the East Liverpool High School Alumni Association, No. 2 of 16, 1997... $100

Ball shape pitcher, No. 3, orchid. **$85**

Coffeepot, covered, Tricolator, Coffee Queen, yellow. **$35**

Irish coffee mug, footed, pale yellow, 6". **$15**

Birch shape Victorian line teapot, covered, blue with gold decoration. **$175**

Radiance shape drip jar, covered. **$60**

Cameo Rose pattern teapot, covered, on E-shape dinnerware body. **$75**

Haviland

SINCE ITS FOUNDING in 1840, the Haviland China Co. has produced over 60,000 chinaware patterns. The company's story is a unique one. Although based in the United States, Haviland China produced its wares in the French porcelain capital of Limoges, exporting those products for sale domestically. Over the years, Haviland has become so closely identified with Limoges that many have used the terms interchangeably, or assumed Haviland was yet another of the numerous French firms that made Limoges their manufacturing base.

The Haviland company was actually the result of its founder's quest for the "ideal" china. New York importer David Haviland was dissatisfied with the china then available for his clientele. Its varying coloration (never consistently white) and grainy, porous texture made it not only visually unappealing, but also unsuitable for long-term use.

Haviland's search led him to Limoges, already a busy hub of porcelain production, and home to over 40 manufacturing firms. The reason? The 1765 discovery of rare kaolin deposits in the Limoges vicinity. Kaolin was a necessary component of fine, hard paste porcelain. Blessed with abundant supplies of other necessities for porcelain manufacture (wood, water, and a willing work force), Limoges quickly gained renown for its superb product.

Impressed by the area's output—the porcelain had a pristine whiteness, as well as a smooth, non-porous finish—Haviland set up shop. The firm's dinnerware exports found immediate success, thanks to the delicate translucence of the ware and its exquisitely detailed decoration.

In the mid-19th century, at Haviland's peak of popularity, "fine dining" was a term taken seriously. Specific foods required specific serving dishes, and each course of a meal mandated its own type of tableware. Substituting a luncheon plate for a bread-and-butter plate was not only unthinkable, but in the worst possible taste. China cabinets in affluent homes were filled to overflowing, and much of that overflow was thanks to Haviland. Just a sampling from its vast dinnerware inventory includes: fish plates, bone plates, salad plates, chop plates, bon bon plates, and underplates; chocolate pots and coffee pots; bouillon cups, eggcups, and teacups; lemonade pitchers and milk pitchers; honey dishes and vegetable dishes; toast trays and celery trays; pudding sets and dessert sets; sauceboats and sauce tureens; broth bowls, soup bowls, and punch bowls. Imagine any conceivable fine dining need, and Haviland dinnerware was there to meet it.

Although dinnerware was its mainstay, Haviland also produced a multitude of other decorative yet useful porcelain housewares. Among them were dresser trays, hair receivers, ashtrays, and decorative baskets. A limited line of art pottery was also released from 1885 into the 1890s, utilizing the underglaze slip decoration technique known as "Barbotine." Developer Ernest Chaplet supervised this series for Haviland, in which pigments were combined with heavy white clay slip. The mixture, applied to the clay body of a piece, had the consistency of oil paint; the resulting finish had the texture of an oil painting.

Because various Haviland family members eventually branched out on their own, the porcelain markings are many. "H & Co." was the earliest, succeeded by such variations as "Haviland, France" and "Decorated by Haviland & Co." Theodore Haviland achieved much acclaim after forming his own firm in 1892, and those pieces are often marked "Theodore Haviland" or other variants of his name. (In 1941, the Theodore Haviland facility relocated to the United States.)

Twelve French Haviland porcelain gilt violet plates, circa 1900, signed A McM on reverse, designs are similar, not identical, one with edge chip, 8-1/2" dia. **$100**

"Old Paris" porcelain, early Limoges pair of large two-handled, pink-ground mantel garniture vases, circa 1855-1865, attributed to atelier of Haviland & Co., flattened ovate baluster form, handles formed as gilt large grape leaves, clusters and vines in high relief down sides, knotted vines under everted gilt rims, bodies enameled with gilt vermiculi, brocade, rocaille and other patterns to shoulders, faces painted in polychrome enamels with a queen seated in throne, gilt scrolls down vase backs, both incised 39, various other incised marks, possibly 4561, very good to good condition, 28" h. **$950**

Haviland set of four five-well porcelain oyster plates, pinwheel type mold, each with different background color and heavy gold decoration, 9". **$375**

Thirteen-piece porcelain game set, each with different decoration, 12 7-1/2" plates, 18" x 11" platter, marked CFH / GDM... **$130**

Six French Haviland Limoges hand-painted game decorated plates with floral and gilt borders, marked Haviland & Co. Limoges on base, 8-3/4" sq.............................. **$150**

Hull Pottery

THE A.E. HULL Pottery Co. grew from the clay soil of Perry County, Ohio, in 1905. By the 1930s, its unpretentious line of ware could be found in shops and, more importantly, homes from coast to coast, making it one of the nation's largest potteries. Leveled by flood and ensuing fire in 1950, like a phoenix, Hull rose from the ashes and reestablished its position in the marketplace. Less than four decades later, however, the firm succumbed after eight bitter strikes by workers, leaving behind empty buildings, memories and the pottery shown in this volume.

Addis Emmet Hull founded A.E. Hull Pottery in July 1905. By the time the company was formed, the Crooksville/Roseville/Zanesville area was already well established as a pottery center. Hull constructed an all-new pottery, featuring six kilns, four of them large natural gas-fired beehive kilns.

The early years were good to Hull. In fact, after only two years of operation, Hull augmented the new plant by taking over the former facilities of the Acme pottery. By 1910, Hull was claiming to be the largest manufacturer of blue-banded kitchenware in the United States. By 1925, production reached three million pieces annually.

No. 310, Orchid jardinière, 6". **$45-$100**

This early ware included spice and cereal jars and salt boxes. Some of these items were lavishly decorated with decals, high-gloss glazes or bands. This evolved into some early art ware pieces including vases and flowerpots. However, Hull could not keep up with the demand, especially the growing demand for artwares, which could be sold in five and dime stores. Hence, Addis Hull visited Europe and made arrangements to import decorative items from Czechoslovakia, England, France, Germany and Italy. To accommodate the influx of these items, Hull opened a facility in Jersey City, N.J. This arrangement continued until 1929, when import operations were discontinued.

In 1926, Plant 1 was converted to manufacture decorative floor and wall tiles, which were popular at the time. But by the time of Addis Hull's death in 1930, the company bearing his name was exiting the tile business. Plant 1, Hull's original, which had been converted to the now-discontinued line of tile production as well as being elderly, was closed in 1933.

When Addis Hull Sr. died in 1930, management of the works was passed to his son, Addis Hull Jr., who was involved in the formation of the Shawnee Pottery Co. By the late 1930s, Addis Junior left the family business and assumed the presidency of Shawnee.

World War II affected the entire nation, and Hull was no exception. This time period saw the production of some of Hull's most famous lines, including Orchid, Iris, Tulip and Poppy. Their airbrushed matte hues of pink, blue, green and yellow became synonymous with the Hull name. Sales of such wares through chain and dime stores soared.

The close of the decade saw the emergence of high-gloss glazed art pottery as the growing trend in decorative ceramics. Hull responded initially by merely changing the glaze applied to some of its earlier lines. Another significant development of the time was the growing

B-1, Crescent bowls, 5-1/2".. **$10-$15 each**

influence of designer Louise Bauer on Hull's lines. First and most notable was her 1943 Red Riding Hood design, but also significant were her Bow-Knot and Woodland lines.

While the late 1940s and early 1950s saw the demise of long-time rivals Weller and Roseville, business at Hull flourished. This is particularly surprising given that on June 16, 1950, the pottery was completely destroyed by a flood, which in turn caused the kiln to explode, and the ensuing fire finished off the venerable plant.

A new plant officially opened on Jan. 1, 1952. With the new plant came a new company name – Hull Pottery Co.

Hull entered into dinnerware manufacture in the early 1960s at the behest of one of its largest customers, the J.C. Penney Co. Penney, whose offers to purchase Pfaltzgraff dinnerware were declined by the manufacturer, turned to Hull to create a competitive line. Hull's response to this was the new House 'n Garden line, which would remain in production until 1967 and would grow to 100 items.

No. 53 Thistle vase, 6-1/2". .... **$40-$70**

During the 1970s and 1980s, the pottery was closed by no fewer than eight strikes, one of which lasted for seven weeks. The eighth and final strike by workers sounded the death knell for the pottery. In 1986, the Hull Pottery Co. ceased business operations. For more information on Hull pottery, see *Warman's Hull Pottery Identification and Price Guide* by David Doyle.

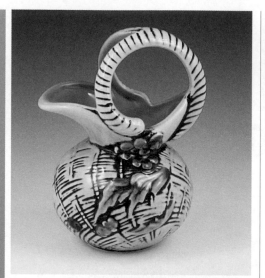

T1, Blossom Flite honey jug, 6"........... $20-$70

B5, Butterfly jardinière, 5".................. $20-$30

B-26, Bow-Knot pitcher-shaped wall pocket, 6". .... $60-$200

No. 132, Camellia/Open Rose hanging basket, 7". .... $40-$120

C314, Capri flying duck planter. .... $15-$30

O-6, Debonair pitcher, 5" tall x 6-1/2". $30-$40

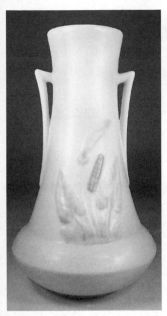

Calla Lily 560/33, mold vase, 10". ....$50-$150

No. 218 Granada vase, 9". ....$10-$20

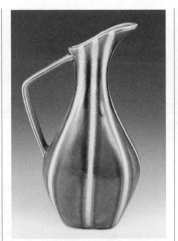

C56, Continental ewer, 12-1/2". ....$40-$80

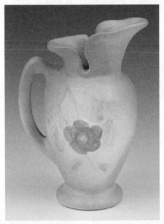

No. 520, Dogwood ewer, 4 3/4". ....$20-$45

No. 32, Early Artware vase, 8". ....$20-$40

No. 79 Fantasy bowl, 6 1//2" x 5-1/2".......$10-$15

No. 527, House 'n Garden French casserole with cover. .....$6-$7

HULL POTTERY

No. 91, novelty pigeon planter, 6-1/2" x
5-1/2". .... $45-$70

E-13, Ebb Tide candleholder, 2 3/4". ....
$40-$80 each

S15, Serenade fruit bowl, 7". .... $45-$80

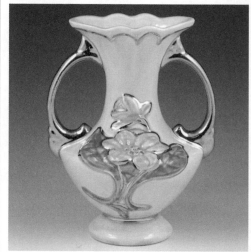

H-2, New Magnolia vase, 5-1/2". .... $25-$40

S23, Serenade ashtray, 13". .... $35-$45

No. 72 novelty flowered vase, 8-1/4" x 5
7/8". .... $35-$45

F433, Imperial pedestal ivy vase, 10". ...... **$20-$25**

No. 410, Iris bud vase was produced in two color schemes, with different decorations front and rear, 7-1/2". .... **$40-$70**

No. 425, Jubilee embossed jardinière, 5-1/2". .... **$5-$15**

No. 85, Mayfair bass viol planter or wall pocket, 7-1/4". .... **$25-$40**

S-4 Parchment and Pine vase, 10-1/2"....... **$35-$50**

No. 20, Magnolia vase, 15"................... **$175-$250**

No. 612 Poppy vase, 6-1/2". .... **$35-$100**

No. 1,Tokay cornucopia, 6-1/2". .... **$20-$30**

No. 113, Tulip flowerpot. .... **$60-$80**

L-4, Water Lily vase, 6-1/2". .... **$25-$35**

W24, Woodland Hi-Gloss ewer, 13-1/2". ....**$70-$180**

W-17, Wildflower vase, 12-1/2"..............**$70-$150**

W9, Royal basket, 8 3/4"................ **$45-$60**

W-4, Wildflower handled vase in dusty rose marked "Hull Art USA W-4-6-1/2"," 6-1/2". ..... **$35-$45**

W15, Woodland double bud vase, 8-1/2". **$30-$120**

Ironstone

DURABILITY: WHEN INTRODUCED in the early 1800s, that was ironstone china's major selling point. Durability also accounts for the still-ready availability of vintage ironstone china, literally centuries after it first captivated consumers. Unlike its fragile porcelain contemporaries, this utilitarian earthenware was intended to withstand the ravages of time—and it did.

Ironstone owes its innate sturdiness to a formula incorporating iron slag with the clay. Cobalt, added to the mix, eliminated the yellowish tinge that plagued earlier attempts at white china. The earliest form of this opaque dinnerware made its debut in 1800 England, patented by potters William and John Turner. However, by 1806 the Turner firm was bankrupt. Ironstone achieved its first real popularity in 1813, when Charles Mason first offered for sale his "Patent Ironstone China." Mason's white ironstone was an immediate hit, offering vessels for a wide variety of household uses, from teapots and tureens to washbowls and pitchers.

Although the inexpensive simplicity of white ironstone proved popular with frugal householders, by the 1830s in-mold and transfer patterns were providing a dose of visual variety. Among the decorative favorites: Oriental motifs and homey images such as grains, fruits, and flowers.

Mason's patented formula for white ironstone lasted for 14 years. Upon its expiration, numerous other potteries jumped into the fray. By the 1840s, white ironstone found its way across the ocean, enjoying the same success in the United States and Canada as it had in England. By the 1880s, however, the appeal of white ware began to fade. Its successor, soon overtaking the original, was ironstone's most enduring incarnation, Tea Leaf.

First marketed as Lustre Band and Sprig, the Tea Leaf Lustreware motif is attributed to Anthony Shaw of Burslem; his ironstone pieces of the 1880s featured hand-painted copper

Eagle shape white ironstone gravy boat, Davenport, circa 1859s **$110**

Rare Ceres shape ironstone eggcup, Elsmore & Forster, all white. **$225**

Figural hen-on-nest covered dish, all white. **$225**

lustre bands and leaves. Tea Leaf was, however, a decorative style rather than a specific product line. Since the design was not patented, potteries throughout England and the United States soon introduced their own versions. Design modifications were minor; today, collectors can assemble entire sets of ironstone in the Tea Leaf pattern from the output of different manufacturers. Although independently produced, the pieces easily complement each other.

During the late 1800s, ironstone tea sets were so ubiquitous that ornamenting them with a tea leaf was a logical choice. Buyers were intrigued with this simple, nature-themed visual on a field of white. Their interest quickly translated into a bumper crop of tea leaf-themed ironstone pieces. Soon, the tea leaf adorned objects with absolutely no relation whatsoever to tea. Among them: gravy boats, salt and peppers shakers, ladles, and even toothbrush holders and soap dishes.

There were, of course, more romantic rationales given for the introduction of the tea leaf motif. One holds that this decoration was the modern manifestation of an ancient legend. Finding an open tea leaf at the bottom of a teacup would bring good luck to the fortunate tea drinker. In this scenario, the tea leaf motif becomes a harbinger of happy times ahead, whether emblazoned on a cake plate, a candlestick, or a chamber pot.

For makers of Tea Leaf, the good fortune continued into the early 1900s. Eventually, however, Tea Leaf pieces became so prevalent that the novelty wore off. By mid-century, the pattern had drifted into obscurity; its appeal was briefly resuscitated with lesser-quality reproductions, in vogue from 1950 to 1980. Marked "Red Cliff" (the name of the Chicago-based distributor), these reproductions generally used blanks supplied by Hall China.

For today's collectors, the most desirable Tea Leaf pieces are those created during the pattern's late-Victorian heyday. Like ironstone itself, the Tea Leaf pattern remains remarkably durable.

New York shape teapot, luster band trim, Clementson. **$60**

Ceres shape dinner plate, dessert plate and handle less cup and saucer, green and copper luster trim. .... **$30-$50 set**

Corn & Oats shape white ironstone mug,
Davenport. .... **$90-$110**

Chinese shape white ironstone mug,
Anthony Shaw, circa 1858. .... **$90**

Alternate Panels ironstone compote, all
white. **$225**

**Classic Gothic Octagon shape white ironstone
soup tureen,** cover, undertray and ladle,
Samuel Alcock & Co., circa 1847... **$1,200 set**

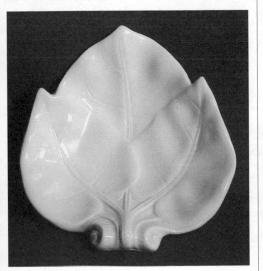

**Pond Lily Pad shape white ironstone relish
dish,** James Edwards. ....**$115-$130**

**Berlin Swirl shape white ironstone covered
vegetable tureen,** T.J. & J. Mayer. **$190**

Olympic shape white ironstone sugar bowl, covered, Elsmore & Forster, 1864. .... **$90**

Scalloped Decagon/ Cambridge shape white ironstone sugar bowl, Wedgwood & Co.........**$100**

Alternate Panels shape white ironstone teapot, unknown pottery, England, mid-19th century. ....**$125-$150**

Inverted Diamond shape white ironstone teapot, covered, T.J. & J. Mayer, England, circa 1840s........ **$250-300**

Sydenham shape white ironstone teapot, covered, copy of Victorian ironstone original design produced by Hall China for Red Cliff, circa 1960s. **$95**

Divided Gothic shape white ironstone washbowl and pitcher set, John Alcock, circa 1848......... **$400-$450 set**

Classic Gothic Octagon shape master waste jar, all white, Jacob Jurnival. ....**$950-$1,050**

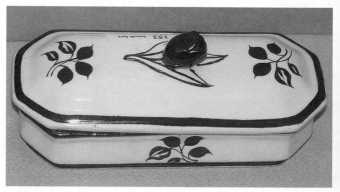

Tobacco Leaf pattern, Fanfare shape covered toothbrush box, Elsmore & Forster, rare. **$675**

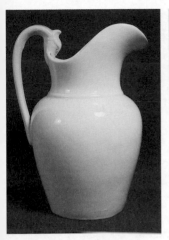

Dolphin-handled shape white ironstone wine pitcher, unmarked, circa 1850s. .... **$110-$130**

Ginger Jar shape Tea Leaf ironstone master waste jar, covered, Elsmore & Forster, rare............**$1,300**

Grape Octagon shape washbowl and pitcher set, luster band trim, unmarked................. **$225**

Imari-style soup bowls, English, 19th century, unmarked, 10 in. dia. **$150**

Empress shape Tea Leaf ironstone two-handled cream soup bowl, Micratex by Adams, circa 1960s. **$35**

Cable shape Tea Leaf ironstone butter dish, cover and insert, Anthony Shaw. **$60**

Lily of the Valley shape Tea Leaf ironstone chamber pot, Anthony Shaw. **$175**

Favorite shape Tea Leaf ironstone coffeepot, covered, Grindley. **$170**

Rare Paneled Grape shape jam server, covered, by J.F. .... **$110-$140**

Tulip shape white ironstone teapot, covered, trimmed in blue, Elsmore & Forster, England, circa 1855. .... **$290-$320**

KPM

KPM

KPM PLAQUES ARE highly glazed, enamel paintings on porcelain bases that were produced by Konigliche Porzellan Manufaktur (KPM), the King's Porcelain Factory, in Berlin, Germany, between 1880 and 1901.

Their secret, according to Afshine Emrani, dealer and appraiser at www.some-of-my-favorite-things.com, is KPM's highly superior, smooth, hard paste porcelain, which could be fired at very high temperatures.

"The magic of a KPM plaque is that it will look as crisp and beautiful 100 years from now as it does today," he said. Even when they were introduced, these plaques proved highly collectible, with art lovers, collectors, tourists, and the wealthy acquiring them for extravagant sums.

KPM rarely marketed painted porcelain plaques itself, however. Instead, it usually supplied white, undecorated ones to independent artists who specialized in this genre. Not all artists signed their KPM paintings, however.

While most KPM plaques were copies of famous paintings, some, commissioned by wealthy Americans and Europeans in the 1920s, bear images of actual people in contemporary clothing. These least collectible of KPM plaques command between $500 and $1,500 each, depending on the attractiveness of their subjects.

Gilded, hand-painted plaques featuring Middle Eastern or female Gypsy subjects and bearing round red "Made in Germany" stamps were produced just before and after World War I for export. They command between $500 and $2,000 each. Plaques portraying religious subjects, such

Plaque depicting a bearded man; impressed KPM and scepter mark, also incised "12. 9 3/4," signed "Horn" lower right; late 19th/early 20th century, carved painted wooden frame, 12 1/2" high x 10 1/2" wide. **$1,600**

as the Virgin Mary or the Flight into Egypt, command higher prices but are less popular.

Popular scenes of hunters, merrymakers, musicians, etc., generally fetch less than $10,000 apiece because they have been reproduced time and again. Rarer, more elaborate scenes, however, like "The Dance Lesson" and "Turkish Card Players" may be worth many times more.

Highly stylized portraits copied from famous paintings–especially those of attractive children or décolleté women–allowed art lovers to own their own "masterpieces." These are currently worth between $2,000 and $20,000 each. Romanticized portrayals of cupids and women in the nude, the most desirable KPM subjects of all, currently sell for up to $40,000 each. Portraits of men, it must be noted, are not only less popular, but also less expensive.

Porcelain plaque "Clementine" depicting an auburn-haired beauty adorned with sprigs of clementine leaves, after Conrad Kiesel (1846-1921, German); impressed KPM and scepter mark and incised "315-255" with a symbol, signed lower right "L. Schinzel"; late 19th century, 12 1/2" high x 10" wide, Italian Rococo-style carved gilt wood frame, overall 20 3/4" high x 15 3/4" wide x 3 3/4" deep. **$16,000**

Size also matters. A 4" x 6" inch plaque, whose subject has been repeatedly reproduced, may sell for a few thousand dollars. Larger ones that portray the same subject will fetch proportionately more. A "Sistine Madonna" plaque, fashioned after the original work by Rafael and measuring 10" x 7 1/2", might cost $4,200. One featuring the identical subject, but measuring 15" x 11", might cost $7,800. A larger plaque, measuring 22" x 16", might command twice that price.

The largest KPM plaques, measuring 22" x 26", for example, often burst during production. Although no formula exists for determining prices of those that have survived, Afshine Emrani said that each may sell for as much as $250,000. Rare plaques like these are often found in museums.

The condition of a KPM plaque also affects its price. Most, since they were highly glazed and customarily hung instead of handled, have survived in perfect condition. Thus those that have sustained even minor damage, like scratches, cracks, or chips, fetch considerably lower prices. Those suffering major damage are worthless.

KPMs painted plaques arouse so much interest and command such high prices that, over the last couple of years, unscrupulous dealers have entered the market. According to dealer Balazs Benedek, KPM plaques are "the mother of all fakes. About 90 percent of KPM plaques are mid- to late-20th century reproductions. And about 70 percent are not hand painted."

Collectors should be aware that genuine KPM paintings always boast rich, shiny, glazes that preserve their colors, and though subject matter may vary, they typically feature nude scenes, indoor portraits of women, or group gatherings in lush settings. Anything wildly different should raise suspicion.

Genuine KPMs, on their backs or edges, feature small icons of scepters deeply set in the porcelain, over the letters KPM. These marks are sometimes accompanied by an "H" or some other letter, which may indicate their production date or size. Some are imprinted with the size of the plaque as well, which facilitated sorting or shipping. Shallow or crooked imprints may reveal a fake.

– By Melody Amsel-Arieli

Two plaques, each titled verso, the first "Medea" after N. Sichel (Nathaniel Sichel, 1843-1907, German), the second "L'esclave" (The Slave) after de Chatillon (Joseph de Chatillon, 1808-1881, American); unsigned, each with impressed "KPM" and scepter mark; late 19th/early 20th century, each 9 1/4" high x 6 1/2" wide, wooden frame with old trade label verso, each overall 14 1/2" high x 11 1/2" wide. **$4,250**

Framed plaque, "The Young Jesus"; late 19th century, 8 1/2" x 6 1/4", frame 15" high. **$2,987**

Oval porcelain plaque, impressed scepter and KPM marks; late 19th century, 16 3/4" high. **$2,750**

Framed porcelain plaque of a man smoking a pipe; marks: (scepter) **KPM**, paper label reading 911 Rauchez; circa 1880-1900, 7 5/8" x 5 3/8", carved gilt frame 13" high x 10 3/4" wide.................................. **$2,510**

Rectangular porcelain plaque with hand-painted decoration of a self-portrait of artist Louise-Elisabeth Vigee Le Brun after the original painting; marks: **KPM scepter**; circa **1900**, 7" by 5 1/8", gilt frame 11 1/2" by 9 1/2"................... **$3,500**

Framed rectangular porcelain plaque with hand-painted decoration of a young classically dressed woman feeding pigeons; marks: (scepter) **KPM**; circa **1890**, 7 1/4" x 5", metal and enamel frame 11" x 8 1/5"........... **$4,481**

Framed rectangular plaque with hand-painted decoration of the Three Muses crossing a river into the forest; marks: (scepter) **KPM**, h, L, 275 223; circa 1890, 10 3/8" x 8 1/2", gilt wood frame 16 1/2" x 14 5/8"............................**$13,145**

Framed rectangular porcelain plaque by Franz Till, hand-painted decoration of a young girl holding a "catch the ball" toy; marks: (scepter) KPM, S, Fr. Till, Dresden; circa 1900, 6 1/2" high x 3 3/4" wide, frame 13" x 10 1/2".....................$813

Porcelain plaque of Lorelei, painted after Willhelm Kray (1828-1889), the winged beauty in diaphanous drapery and seated on a ledge in a misty landscape; unsigned, impressed monogram and scepter mark; late 19th/early 20th century, framed, sight size 15 1/4" x 9 7/8". **$13,000**

KPM Porcelain Plaque of the Virgin Mother and Christ Child, Germany, 19th century, oval, depicting mother and child on a blue enamel and gilt-star background, with impressed factory mark to back, in velvet lining and gilt frame, 7" high (sight), wd. 5" wide. Losses to gilt frame, plaque not examined outside of frame or velvet lining. **$365**

KPM Porcelain Portrait Plaque of a Woman, 19th century, the woman in a purple dress seated in a Victorian-style interior, impressed mark to base, 10 3/4" high, 8 7/8" wide. Good condition. No chips, cracks, or repairs. **$1,185**

KPM

Framed rectangular porcelain plaque by Ludwig Sturm, hand-painted decoration of nude female nymph with fish skin chased by a raven; signed L. Sturm, marks: (scepter) KPM, high, F; circa 1890, 14" x 8 7/8", frame 15 3/8" x 10 1/8". **$8,125**

Porcelain plaque depicting a female nude hovering over a moonlit lake holding a torch; unmarked, signed lower right "J. Sch./XR" with handwritten inscription verso, "Painted in the studio by J. Schumacher"; late 19th century, 11 3/4" high x 8 3/4" wide. Provenance: Collection of the estate of a resident of Artist Alley, Champion Place, Alhambra, California, prior to the 1960s............................. **$4,250**

A KPM Berlin porcelain mantel clock, underglaze blue scepter mark, red factory mark and black iron cross stamp, 21 1/2" high, 31" wide, 9 1/2" deep. **$27,500**

Framed rectangular porcelain plaque with hand-painted decoration of young woman in Renaissance dress kneeling in prayer; marks: (scepter) **KPM**, C; circa 1890, 8 1/2" x 6", gilt wood and velvet frame 18 1/8" x 16 1/8".................................. **$3,585**

Oval porcelain plaque with hand-painted decoration of a young shrouded woman looking upward; marks: (scepter) **KPM**, K; circa 1890, 8 7/8" x 6 1/2"............... **$2,330**

Framed porcelain plaque by Franz Till, hand-painted decoration of a boy in a white gown; marks: (scepter) KPM, S, Fr. Till, Dresden; circa 1900, 6 1/2" high x 3 3/4" wide, frame 13" x 10 1/2".......... **$594**

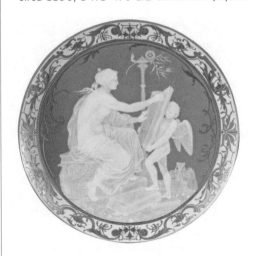

Porcelain pate-sur-pate charger of a seated Venus scribing in a book supported by Cupid, on rose ground with cream border and gilt accents; signed "E. Dietrich" with blue scepter and red globus cruciger marks; third quarter 19th century, approximately 13 1/2" diameter, framed................ **$10,000**

Framed porcelain plaque depicting Ruth after
Charles Landelle (French, 1821-1908);
marks: impressed (scepter over KPM), S,
33, 20, original paper labels to reverse inscribed Kunst Institut Fur Porzellan-Malerai,
Merkel-Heine, Wiesbaden, and 1119, Ruth
by Landelle; circa 1900, 13" x 7 7/8",
frame 22 1/4" x 20 1/4" wide.............. **$2,750**

Framed porcelain plaque, Ruth After Landelle;
marks: (scepter) KPM, high, signed Kronller;
circa 1900, 12 1/2" x 7 3/8", gilt wood
frame 19 1/4" x 14 1/2". **$2,390**

Framed porcelain plaque depicting
Bussende Magdalen after the painting
by Correggio (Italian, 1489-1534);
marks: lower right front: AH (conjoined),
impressed marks to reverse: (scepter)
KPM, high; circa 1890, 8 3/4" high x 10
7/8" wide, frame 11 1/8" x 13 1/4".... **$2,625**

Framed porcelain plaque, "Grape and Melon
Eaters" after Bartome Murillo; marks:
(scepter) KPM, high; circa 1900, 11 1/2" x
9 1/2", frame 19 3/4" x 17 1/2" ....**$1,912.**

KPM

Framed plaque, "Othello Pleading Before the Doge," depicts Othello pleading before the chief magistrate of Venice or Genoa and Brabantio, Desdemona at his side, member of the Senate looking on; signed "C. Hen" in lower right, which is unusual since most KPM art was not signed; circa 1900. ....$11,950

Porcelain vase with circular rim above scrolled handles entwined with serpents, elongated tapering body decorated with a frieze of mythological figures over a socle entwined with a serpent on a circular base raised on paw feet; underglaze blue scepter mark and overglaze blue beehive mark to underside; late 19th/early 20th century, 20 1/2" high x 5 3/4" diameter............... **$3,000**

Porcelain plaque depicting three nymphs, one seated on a chariot pulled by winged cherubs, and another about to be shot by Cupid; marks: (scepter) K.P.M., J, J, 315, 255; late 19th century, 10 1/8" x 12 3/4"....................................$7,768

Rectangular porcelain plaque based on Bartolom Esteban Murillo's "The Little Fruit Sellers," depicting a young girl and boy with a basket of grapes and apples; marks: (scepter), impressed KPM, high; late 19th century, 12 1/2" high..**$3,000**

Limoges

"LIMOGES" HAS BECOME the generic identifier for porcelain produced in Limoges, France, and the surrounding vicinity. More than 40 manufacturers in the area have, at some point, used the term as a descriptor of their work, and there are at least 400 different Limoges identification marks. The common denominator is the product itself: fine hard paste porcelain created from the necessary components found in abundance in the Limoges region: kaolin and feldspar.

Until the 1700s, porcelain was exclusively a product of China, introduced to the Western world by Marco Polo and imported at great expense. In 1765, the discovery of kaolin in St. Yrieixin, a small town near Limoges, made French production of porcelain possible. (The chemist's wife credited with the kaolin discovery thought at first that it would prove useful in making soap.)

Limoges entrepreneurs quickly capitalized on the find. Adding to the area's allure were expansive forests providing fuel for wood-burning kilns; the nearby Vienne River, with water for working clay; and a workforce eager to trade farming for a (hopefully) more lucrative pursuit. Additionally, as the companies would be operating outside metropolitan Paris, labor and production costs would be significantly less.

By the early 1770s, numerous porcelain manufacturers were at work in Limoges and its environs. Demand for the porcelain was high because it was both useful and decorative. To meet that demand, firms employed trained, as well as untrained, artisans for the detailed hand painting required. (Although nearly every type of Limoges has its fans, the most sought-after—and valuable—are those pieces decorated by a company's professional artists.) At its industrial peak in 1900, Limoges factories employed over 8,000 workers in some aspect of porcelain production.

A myriad of products classified as Limoges flooded the marketplace from the late 1700s onward. Among them were tableware pieces, such as tea and punch sets, trays, pitchers, compotes, bowls and plates. Also popular were vases and flower baskets, dresser sets, trinket boxes, ash receivers, figural busts, and decorative plaques.

Although produced in France, Limoges porcelain was soon destined for export overseas; eventually over 80 percent of Limoges porcelain was exported. The United States proved a particularly reliable customer. Notable among the importers was the Haviland China Co.; until the 1940s, its superior, exquisitely decorated china was produced in Limoges and then distributed in the United States.

By the early 20th century, many exporters in the United States were purchasing porcelain blanks from the Limoges factories for decoration stateside. The base product was authentically made in France, but production costs were significantly lower: Thousands of untrained porcelain painters put their skills to work for a minimal wage. Domestic decoration of the blanks also meant that importers could select designs suited to the specific tastes of target audiences.

Because Limoges was a regional designation, rather than the identifier of a specific manufacturer, imported pieces were often marked with the name of the exporting firm,

Eight porcelain Mary Bacon Jones-designed plates, circa 1905, each polychrome enamel-decorated design based on Rudyard Kipling's The Jungle Book, printed Wm. Guerin & Co. Limoges mark, 10 7/8" diameter. **$2,400**

followed by the word "Limoges." Beginning in 1891, "France" was added. Some confusion has arisen from products marked "Limoges China Co." (aka "American Limoges"). This Ohio-based firm, in business from 1902-1955, has absolutely no connection to the porcelain produced in France.

The heyday of quality French Limoges lasted roughly into the 1930s. Production continues today, but after World War II, designs and painting techniques became much more standardized.

Vintage Limoges is highly sought-after by today's collectors. They're drawn to the delicacy of the porcelain as well as the colors and skill of decoration; viewing a well-conceived Limoges piece is like seeing a painting in a new form. Valuation is based on age, decorative execution and, as with any collectible, individual visual appeal.

Porcelain game service, early 20th century, each piece decorated with different game bird in copse, signed de Solis, comprising one two-handled oval platter, 18 1/2" long, and 12 plates, 9 1/2" diameter. $875

Porcelain sugar and creamer with Great Seal of United States, Tressemanes & Vogt, France, 1892-1897, boat-shaped vessels with gilt foliate border, handles, and feet, one side decorated with polychrome and gilt seal, green "T & V LIMOGES FRANCE DEPOSE" backstamp, 2 7/8", 3" high. $480

Enamel on copper plaque depicting procession of the Magi, France, 19th century, after Benozzo Gozzoli (circa 1421-1497), in polychrome and gilt with raised "jewel" accents, back incised "France," metal frame, plaque 11" x 7". **$2,760**

Three Limoges porcelain ichthyological plates, retailed by Mansard, Paris, early 20th century, each decorated with fish swimming among waterweeds and shells with insects above, gilt heightened borders, green printed J.P./L factory mark and blue printed retailer's mark, 9 5/8" diameter, together with seven Wedgwood square form creamware dessert plates in the Wellesley pattern. $250

Haviland porcelain dinner service in nautical design made for English market, fourth quarter 19th century, each in pattern number 4651, some pieces with English registration diamond for 1871, handles in form of tied ropes and anchors, comprising two covered two-handled circular tureens, 10" long between handles; two oval two-handled oval tureens and one cover, 12" long between handles; one oval open vegetable dish, 9" long; oval platter, 11 1/4" long; circular cover; two pedestal baskets, 7 1/4" high; eight cups; five saucers, 4 1/2"-5" diameters; two breakfast cups; eight eggcups; 11 butter pats; one soup bowl, 9 1/2" diameter; six plates, 8 1/2" diameter; two plates, 8" diameter; two plates, diameter 5 1/4" diameter; similar Haviland Limoges oblong dish, 8 1/2" long. $750

Eleven hand-painted porcelain plates depicting orchids, early 20th century, retailed by Ovington Bros., New York, each with gilded border decorated with floral garlands, polychrome enameled orchids in center, signed "L. Meage," Latin names for specimens on reverse, 9 3/8" diameter.....................**$1,140**

Basket, round with flattened and scalloped gold rim and arched center gold handle, interior hand painted with pink and red roses and green leaves on pink to blue ground, artist-signed "Pierre," underglaze Limoges, France Mark 2 and overglaze Blakeman & Henderson decorating mark, 6" diameter, 2 1/2" high. **$350**

French bronze gilt enameled box, 2 1/4" high x 7" wide x 4 1/4" deep. **$850**

Pair of metal-mounted enamel vases, late 19th/early 20th century, each poly-chrome decorated with seated figure in landscape setting, 7 1/2" high. **$780**

Bonbon dish, long oval shape with scalloped and scrolled sides, hand painted with flow-ers and leaves on shaded green and yellow ground, artist-signed "Duval," underglaze green factory mark of Jean Pouyat, Mark 5, 5" x 9". **$550**

Vases, Louis XVI taste, round pedestal foot on four paw feet supporting baluster-form body with flaring neck, figural Grecian helmet handles at shoulder, deep gold ground with one side decorated with square reserve enclosing dockside scene with figures and sailing vessel, each reverse decorated with military trophies, circa 1900, 15 1/2" high.............. **$1,610 pr.**

Six hand-painted chargers, late 19th/early 20th century, Orientalist scene by Morley, four avian scenes by Boumy, Puisoye, Valantin, and Dubois, and unsigned pastoral scene, largest 13 1/2" diameter. **$531**

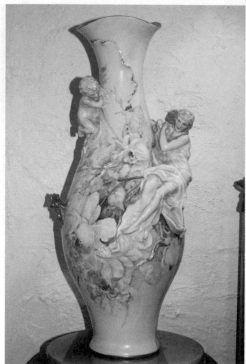

Vase, tall slender baluster shape with "blown out" figures of cherub and lady on sides with hand painted roses, underglaze green marked "CFH/GDM – France" (Charles F. Haviland), rare blank, circa 1891-1900, 23 1/2" high................. **$7,000**

Teapot, bulbous tapering ribbed body with wide domed cover with fancy loop finial, gold serpentine spout and C-scroll handle, star mark of the Coiffe factory and Flambeau China mark of decorating firm, also a Haviland & Co. mark, France, early 20th century................................ **$100**

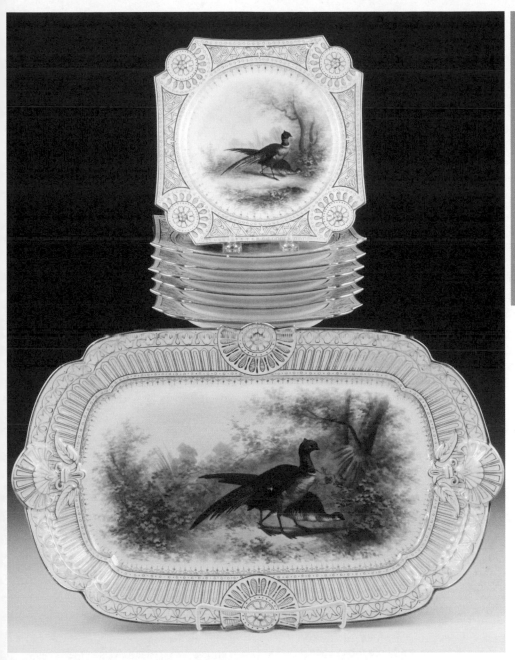

Eight-piece game set consisting of one platter and seven plates with hand-painted scenes of birds and forestry in center and gold decoration on borders, all stamped CFH/GDM on back, platter 18 1/4" long, plates 8 1/2" wide...**$600**

Ashtray-matchbox holder, squared dish base with cigarette indentation at each corner, vertical holder for matchbox in center, hand painted with violets on cream ground, underglaze Tresseman & Vogt Mark 7, rare. **$350**

Basket, long rectangular form with deeply scalloped sides, gold border band and arched flower-molded gold handle across center, interior hand painted at one end with large red roses and green leaves on dark green shaded to pale yellow ground, artist-signed "Segur," underglaze green factory mark of Jean Pouyat, 5" x 9"...... **$550**

◄ **Bawo & Dotter hand-painted covered handled tureen with matching floral serving platter**, each with floral designs with crimson ground and gild accenting, bottoms have green Limoges mark with gold Bawo & Dotter mark, serving platter signed Ribes, 19th/20th century; tureen 10 1/2" high x 15" long, platter 19" long x 12 3/4" wide.................................... **$610**

Ormolu mirror with Limoges enameled scene of maiden in distress being attacked by two bandits, maiden holding hand mirror high above her head and looking into distance as if signaling someone; enameled panel is artist signed, reverse side houses what appears to be original beveled glass mirror, mirror and enameled panel are housed in ormolu frame that swivels in matching stand decorated with lion's paw feet and gargoyles; very good to excellent condition with some minor pitting to silvering on mirror; mirror 10 1/4" high overall; Limoges panel approximately 4" x 5 3/4".. **$5,036**

Hand-painted punch bowl, late 19th/early 20th century, raised gold foliage with polychrome enameled fruiting grapevines, printed factory mark, 14" diameter. **$215**

Twelve dinner plates, French, early 20th century, white ground with bands of blue and gold in scrolling floral design, all marked..**$570**

LIMOGES

Hand-painted china four-piece dresser set, tray, hatpin holder, candleholder and pin box, three blanks with various Limoges, France markings, late 19th/early 20th century, candleholder with chip to rim, remainder undamaged, tray 9 1/4" x 13". $115

Late Victorian dessert set marked AL/ Limoges France, 11 3/4" x 15 5/8" oval platter with shell-molded scalloped rim with hand-painted colored daisies and heavy gold in center, and four matching plates, 8" diameter. $70

Set of 12 French shellfish plates, 9" diameter. $225

French enamel on copper vase, 19th century, 4" high. $300

Fruit bowl, oblong boat-shaped with high inward-scrolled gold end handles, raised on four gold feet, exterior hand painted with purple grapes and green leaves, heavy gold border band, amateur artist-signed, underglaze factory mark for Elite – L – France, circa 1900, 8" x 12 1/2" **$550**

Planter, round, upright waisted sides and slightly scalloped rim, raised on four gold scroll feet, decorated with large red and pink roses and green leaves on dark ground, underglaze green Tresseman & Vogt Mark 7, 8" diameter, 5 1/2" high. .. **$850**

Teapot, covered, bulbous tapering ovoid body with long serpentine spout, high C-form handle and low domed cover with loop finial, white with simple trim, mark of Tressemann & Vogt, Limoges, circa 1900. .... **$200**

Painting on porcelain, rectangular, scene of a couple in 18th century attire in garden, by unknown artist, underglaze factory green mark for Tresseman & Vogt, early 20th century, one of a pair, 11" x 14"....... **$1,500 ea.**

Sauceboat and undertray, footed boat-shaped vessel with scroll-molded rim and wide arched spout, ornate looped gold handle, hand painted with white roses on shaded pink, blue and green ground, matching décor on undertray, underglaze Elite factory Mark 5, 5" long, 6" high..................... **$275 set**

Hand-painted punch bowl, 6-3/4" x 16" diameter. $250

Bust of young boy, all white, mounted on gray socle base, after model by C. Houdon, green mark for Porcelain de Paris, France, circa 1920s, 15" high. **$1,500**

Bust of young girl, all white, mounted on gray socle base, after model by C. Houdon, green mark for Porcelain de Paris, France, circa 1920s, 15" high. **$1,500**

Majolica

IN 1851, AN English potter was hoping that his new interpretation of a centuries-old style of ceramics would be well received at the "Great Exhibition of the Industries of All Nations" set to open May 1 in London's Hyde Park.

Potter Herbert Minton had high hopes for his display. His father, Thomas Minton, founded a pottery works in the mid-1790s in Stoke-on-Trent, Staffordshire. Herbert Minton had designed a "new" line of pottery, and his chemist, Leon Arnoux, had developed a process that resulted in vibrant, colorful glazes that came to be called "majolica."

Trained as an engineer, Arnoux also studied the making of encaustic tiles, and had been appointed art director at Minton's works in 1848. His job was to introduce and promote new products. Victorian fascination with the natural world prompted Arnoux to reintroduce the work of Bernard Palissy, whose naturalistic, bright-colored "maiolica" wares had been created in the 16th century.

Wedgwood pitcher with Oriental motif, 7" high. **$157**

But Arnoux used a thicker body to make pieces sturdier. This body was given a coating of opaque white glaze, which provided a surface for decoration.

Pieces were modeled in high relief, featuring butterflies and other insects, flowers and leaves, fruit, shells, animals and fish. Queen Victoria's endorsement of the new pottery prompted its acceptance by the general public.

When Minton introduced his wares at Philadelphia's 1876 Centennial Exhibition, American potters also began to produce majolica.

For more information on majolica, see *Warman's Majolica Identification and Price Guide* by Mark F. Moran.

Delphin Massier grasshopper figural planter, early 20th century, signed, 6-1/2" x 12-3/4" x 3-1/2". **$3,125**

Other Majolica Makers

John Adams & Co., Hanley, Stoke-on-Trent, Staffordshire, England, operated the Victoria Works, producing earthenware, jasperware, Parian, majolica, 1864-1873. (Jasperware is a fine white stoneware originally produced by Josiah Wedgwood, often colored by metallic oxides with raised classical designs remaining white.)

Another Staffordshire pottery, **Samuel Alcock & Co.,** Cobridge, 1828-1853; Burslem, 1830-1859, produced earthenware, china and Parian.

The **W. & J.A. Bailey Alloa Pottery** was founded in Alloa, the principal town in Clackmannanshire, located near Edinburgh, Scotland.

The **Bevington** family of potters worked in Hanley, Staffordshire, England in the late 19th century.

W. Brownfield & Son operated in Burslem and Cobridge, Staffordshire, England from 1850-1891.

T.C. Brown-Westhead, Moore & Co. produced earthenware and porcelain at Hanley, Stoke-on-Trent, Staffordshire, from about 1862 to 1904.

The **Choisy-le-Roi** faience factory of Choisy-le-Roi, France, produced majolica from 1860 until 1910. The firm's wares are not always marked. The common mark is usually a black ink stamp "Choisy-le-Roi" pictured to the right with a large "HBm," which stands for Hippolyte Boulenger, a director at the pottery.

William T. Copeland & Sons pottery of Stoke-on-Trent, Staffordshire, England, began producing porcelain and earthenware in 1847. (Josiah Spode established a pottery at Stoke-on-Trent in 1770. In 1833, the firm was purchased by William Copeland and Thomas Garrett. In 1847, Copeland became the sole owner. W.T. Copeland & Sons continued until a 1976 merger when it became Royal Worcester Spode. Copeland majolica pieces are sometimes marked with an impressed "COPELAND," but many are unmarked.)

Jose A. Cunha, Caldas da Rainha, southern Portugal, also worked in the style of Bernard Palissy, the great French Renaissance potter.

Julius Dressler, Bela Czech Republic, was founded 1888, producing faience, majolica and porcelain. In 1920, the name was changed to EPIAG. The firm closed about 1945.

Eureka Pottery was located in Trenton, New Jersey, circa 1883-1887.

Railway Pottery was established by S. Fielding & Co., Stoke, Stoke-on-Trent, Staffordshire, England, 1879.

There were two **Thomas Forester** potteries active in the late 19th century in Staffordshire, England. Some sources list the more famous of the two as Thomas Forester & Sons Ltd. at the Phoenix Works, Longton.

Established in the early 19th century, the **Gien** pottery works is located on the banks of France's Loire River near Orleans.

Joseph Holdcroft majolica ware was produced at Daisy Bank in Longton, Staffordshire, England, from 1870 to 1885. Items can be found marked with "J HOLDCROFT," but many pieces can only be attributed by the patterns and colors that are documented to have come from the Holdcroft potteries.

George Jones & Sons Ltd., Stoke, Staffordshire, started operation in about 1864 as George Jones and in 1873 became George Jones & Sons Ltd. The firm operated the Trent Potteries in Stoke-on-Trent (renamed "Crescent Potteries" in about 1907).

In about 1877, **Samuel Lear** erected a small china works in Hanley, Staffordshire. Lear produced domestic china and, in addition, decorated all kinds of earthenware made by other manufacturers, including "spirit kegs." In 1882, the firm expanded to include production of majolica, ivory-body earthenware, and Wedgwood-type jasperware. The business closed in 1886.

Robert Charbonnier founded the **Longchamp** tile works in 1847 to make red clay tiles, but the factory soon started to produce majolica. Longchamp is known for its "barbotine" pieces (a paste of clay used in decorating coarse pottery in relief) made with vivid colors, especially oyster plates.

Hugo Lonitz operated in Haldensleben, Germany, from 1868-1886, and later Hugo Lonitz & Co., 1886-1904, producing household and decorative porcelain, earthenware, and metalwares. Look for a mark of two entwined fish.

The **Lunéville** pottery was founded about 1728 by Jacques Chambrette in the city that bears its name, in the Alsace-Lorraine region of northeastern France. The firm became famous for its blue monochromatic and floral patterns. Around 1750, ceramist Paul-Louis Cyfflé introduced a pattern with animals and historical figures. Lunéville products range from hand-painted faience and majolica to pieces influenced by the Art Deco movement.

The **Massier** family began producing ceramics in Vallauris, France, in the mid-18th century.

François Maurice, School of Paris, was active from 1875-1885 and also worked in the style of Bernard Palissy.

George Morley & Co. was located in East Liverpool, Ohio, 1884-1891.

Morley & Co. Pottery was founded in 1879, Wellsville, Ohio, making graniteware and majolica.

Orchies, a majolica manufacturer in northern France near Lille, is also known under the mark "Moulin des Loups & Hamage," 1920s.

Faïencerie de Pornic is located near Quimper, France.

Quimper pottery has a long history. Tin-glazed, hand-painted pottery has been made in Quimper, France, since the late 17th century. The earliest firm, founded in 1685 by Jean Baptiste Bousquet, was known as HB Quimper. Another firm, founded in 1772 by Francois Eloury, was known as Porquier. A third firm, founded by Guillaume Dumaine in 1778, was known as HR or Henriot Quimper. All three companies made similar pottery decorated with designs of Breton peasants, and sea and flower motifs.

The **Rörstrand** factory made the first faience (tin-glazed earthenware) produced in Sweden. It was established in 1725 by Johann Wolff, near Stockholm.

The earthenware factory of **Salins** was established in 1857 in Salins-les-Bains, near the French border with Switzerland. Salins was awarded with the gold medal at the International Exhibition of Decorative Arts in Paris in 1912.

Sarreguemines wares are named for the city in the Lorraine region of northeastern France. The pottery was founded in 1790 by Nicholas-Henri Jacobi. For more than 100 years, it flourished under the direction of the Utzschneider family.

Wilhelm Schiller and Sons, Bodenbach, Bohemia, was established 1885.

Thomas-Victor Sergent was one of the School of Paris ceramists of the late 19th century who was influenced by the works of Bernard Palissy.

St. Clement was founded by Jacques Chambrette in Saint-Clément, France, in 1758. Chambrette also established works in Lunéville.

The **St. Jean de Bretagne** pottery works are located near Quimper, France.

Vallauris is a pottery center in southeastern France, near Cannes. Companies in production there include Massier and Foucard-Jourdan.

Victoria Pottery Co. was located in Hanley, Staffordshire, England from 1895-1927.

Wardle & Co. was established 1871 at Hanley, Staffordshire, England.

Josiah Wedgwood was born in Burslem, Staffordshire, England, on July 12, 1730, into a family with a long pottery tradition. At the age of nine, after the death of his father, he joined the family business. In 1759, he set up his own pottery works in Burslem. There he produced cream-colored earthenware that found favor with Queen Charlotte. In 1762, she appointed him royal supplier of dinnerware. From the public sale of "Queen's Ware," as it came to be known, Wedgwood was able to build a production community in 1768, which he named Etruria, near Stoke-on-Trent, and a second factory equipped with tools and ovens of his own design. (Etruria is the ancient land of the Etruscans, in what is now northern Italy.)

Tile and iron planter, possibly Italy, 19th century, rectangular form with paneled sides, two polychrome enamel decorated portrait tiles to either side, floral decorated tile to either end, 16 3/4" long overall. **$660**

Minton chestnut bowl, England, circa 1870, polychrome decorated and modeled with chestnuts and leaves to scallop-edge shell-shaped bowl with robin's-egg blue interior, impressed mark, 10 1/2" long..**$180**

Hugo Lonitz fish-form covered tureen, Germany, late 19th century, polychrome enameled and inset with glass eyes, impressed factory mark and numbered 1347, incised lowercase "b," blue underglaze "KY," 17 1/2" long. **$861**

Minton pomegranate vase, England, date cipher for 1879, elongated neck, handle modeled as pomegranate tree branch with leaves and fruit radiating outward onto neck and body of vase, impressed mark, professional restoration to pomegranate and leaves, 21" high.................$510

George Jones fox tray, England, circa 1870, oval, leaf-molded dish adorned with fox head to one side, tail under rim, impressed and pad marks, repair to tip of one ear, 10" long..........$300

George Jones jardiniere, England, late 19th century, decorated with low relief scene of birds and cherry blossoms between basketweave pattern register to rim and base, pad mark, lower side of body with hairline and restoration, 10 1/2" high. $840

Minton bowl, England, date cipher for 1867, circular shape with pale pink exterior and orange interior, three frogs on faux cobblestone base, impressed factory mark and cipher marks, 4 1/8" high. **$984**

Hugo Lonitz model of swan, Germany, late 19th century, white glazed figure naturalistically modeled and seated atop stepped oval base, impressed mark, 4 3/4" high. **$600**

Pair of Joseph Holdcroft vases, England, circa 1875, each with register of white flowers to foot and rim, central high relief scene of bird and butterfly among vine and flower motif on cobalt ground, impressed mark, professional restoration to body of each, 10 3/8" high. .... **$480 pr.**

Rare Wardle three-piece tea set with matching tray, minor spout nick to teapot and creamer, staining to sugar bowl, tray 10 3/4" diameter.....................**$726**

English jardiniere in Egyptian taste, circa 1875, likely George Jones, square shape with canted corners and decorated with pharaoh busts and sphinxes on outset feet, unmarked, professionally restored hairline crack to one side, 2" hairline crack to base, two jardiniere feet professionally repaired, 8" high. **$584**

St. Clement rooster and duck figural pitchers, 11" and 13" high...... **$206**

Three-piece Royal Worcester candle set, England, late 19th century, each modeled as stylized Corinthian columns, one slightly larger with two sconces, impressed mark, two single sconces with professional restorations, both arms of double candelabra and center restored, to 10 1/4" high. **$123**

Wedgwood figural Trentham vase, England, 1873, modeled by Rowland Morris, polychrome enameled and modeled as two cherubs supporting vase on their backs, tools of agriculture applied to raised base, impressed mark, professional restorations to chips along top rim and to feet at either end of base, one end to foliate garland missing, cherubs stained, 10 1/2" high.............**$510**

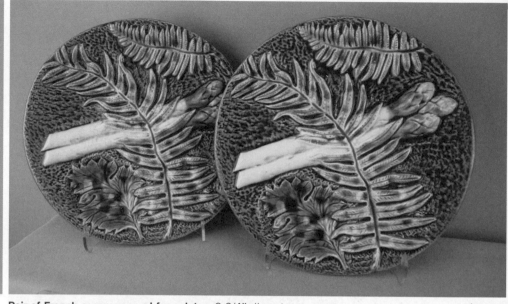

Pair of French asparagus and fern plates, 9 3/4" diameter. $484

Minton stag head sweetmeat dish, England, 1864, polychrome enamel decorated and modeled with circular dish set atop cornucopia-shaped stem terminating at stag head, all set on raised oval base, impressed marks, areas of antlers professionally restored, 4 1/4" high. $570

English two-section "Pug" humidor, dog with yellow collar with pink bow, glossy brown glaze, unmarked, perfect condition, 8" h. **$375**

Four English items, 19th century, footed oval tray with oval platter and two Wedgwood plates, largest 3" x 12-1/4" x 10-1/4"... **$313**

Old English jardiniere and pedestal depicting flowers growing from trees over dark tones, bottom of pedestal has impressed "ENGLAND" mark, late 19th to early 20th century, 15 3/4" x 19 1/2" diameter, pedestal 30" high x 14 1/4" diameter, overall 46" high. **$726**

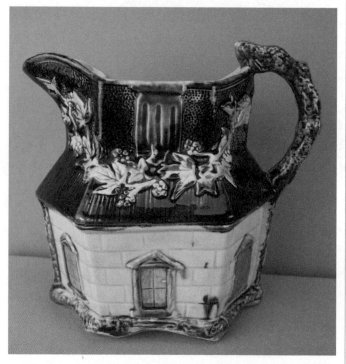

Cottage figural pitcher with rare cobalt rooftop, 8" high...... **$333**

Fielding wheat and daisy pewter top syrup pitcher, 5" high. **$272**

Shells and coral on waves pitcher,
  8" high **$575**

**Fielding shells and fishnet pitcher with
  coral handle,** hairline crack on spout,
  minor surface wear, 7" high. **$272**

**Fielding turquoise shells and fishnet pitcher
with coral handle,** base chip to underside,
6 1/2" high. **$303**

Brown picket fence cheese keeper, repair to
  handle and rim of base, 9 1/2"............. **$242**

French asparagus platter with rare cobalt ground, 14 1/2" long............................$393

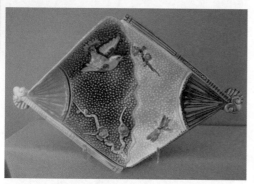

Eureka Pottery Co. bird and fan diamond-shaped tray, 16" long. $194

George Jones strawberry serving platter, 14 1/2" long. $514

Mottled unusual form teapot, 5" high. $194

Pond lily plate, 9 1/2" diameter. $303

Gustafsburg tall compote supported by three storks, overlapping leaf and bull rush top, 10 1/2" high x 10 1/4" diameter.....................**$272**

Two Continental center-pieces, 19th century, large oval bowl with bird decoration and bowl with satyr decoration, larger 6-1/2" x 20" x 11".......................... **$625**

Ceramic tobacco jar in form of bulldog in gentlemanly attire with pipe, German, late 19th century, impressed on bottom 6118 and 65, hairline along bottom, hairline from rim below arm with pipe, small chip on other arm's sleeve, 8" h. $270

Delphin Massier vase, rooster alongside corn husk, early 20th century, signed, 13-1/2" **$2,000**

Hugo Lonitz compote, figural fish base, 19th century, impressed mark, 6-1/2" x 5-3/4" dia... **$313**

Fielding fan and insect with scroll platter with turquoise pebble ground, good color, minor rim chip to back, 13" w. ....**$200+**

Wedgwood grape and vine punch set with large punch bowl, 10-1/2" dia., 6-1/2" t., and eight matching cups, strong color and detail to entire set, rare...**$1,500**

W. Schiller & Son jardiniere, circa 1900, 13" h. x 15" dia. **$175**

George Jones chestnut leaf tray with mottled center, hairline, 12" dia. ....**$400+**

Wedgwood ribbon and bow sauce dish, 7" w..**$150+**

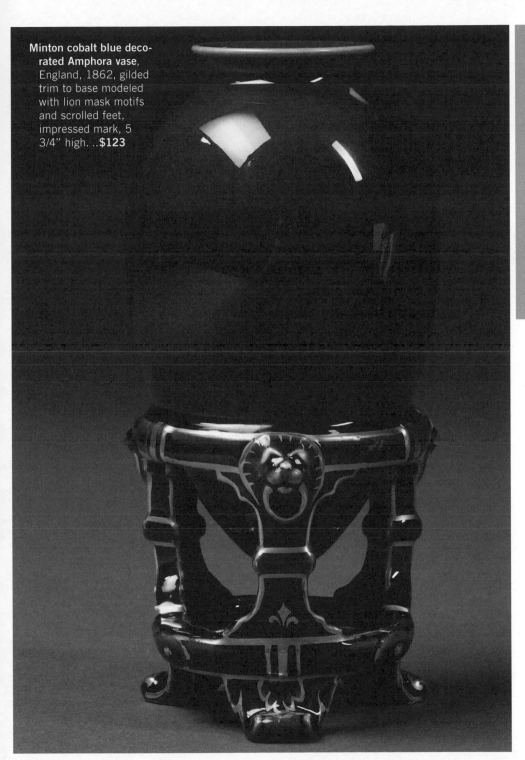

Minton cobalt blue decorated Amphora vase, England, 1862, gilded trim to base modeled with lion mask motifs and scrolled feet, impressed mark, 5 3/4" high. ...**$123**

MAJOLICA

Three English Wedgwood fish plates with raised decoration, 19th century, stamped Wedgwood, 8-3/4" dia. **$250**

English sardine box, rectangular form, 19th century, stamped Jones, 3-3/4" x 5-3/4" x 4-3/4". **$375**

Turquoise strawberry server with flowers and leaves, twig handle and attached cream and sugar bowls, good color, 10" d. .... **$225+**

Delphin Massier parrot perched on bamboo branch, early 20th century, signed, 14". $1,750

Wedgwood jardiniere on pedestal base, England, circa 1893, allover marigold-colored ground with molded body decorated in panels of floral urns, impressed marks, jardiniere 17" high, pedestal base 24 1/4" high. $1,200

English game dish, covered with quail on lid and sides, 19th century, 6" x 9-1/2" x 6-3/4"................... **$688**

George Jones calla lily jardiniere, England, late 19th century, decorated in low relief on textured roulette turquoise ground with yellow rim, impressed and pad mark, 10 1/2" high................**$300**

McCoy

THE FIRST MCCOY with clay under his fingernails was W. Nelson McCoy. With his uncle, W.F. McCoy, he founded a pottery works in Putnam, Ohio, in 1848, making stoneware crocks and jugs.

That same year, W. Nelson's son, James W., was born in Zanesville, Ohio. James established the J.W. McCoy Pottery Co. in Roseville, Ohio, in the fall of 1899. The J.W. McCoy plant was destroyed by fire in 1903 and was rebuilt two years later.

It was at this time that the first examples of Loy-Nel-Art wares were produced. The line's distinctive title came from the names of James McCoy's three sons, Lloyd, Nelson, and Arthur. Like other "standard" glazed pieces produced at this time by several Ohio potteries, Loy-Nel-Art has a glossy finish on a dark brown-black body, but Loy-Nel-Art featured a splash of green color on the front and a burnt-orange splash on the back.

George Brush became general manager of J.W. McCoy Pottery Co. in 1909. The company became Brush-McCoy Pottery Co. in 1911, and in 1925 the name was shortened to Brush Pottery Co. This firm remained in business until 1982.

Separately, in 1910, Nelson McCoy Sr. founded the Nelson McCoy Sanitary and Stoneware Co., also in Roseville. By the early 1930s, production had shifted from utilitarian wares to art pottery, and the company name was changed to Nelson McCoy Pottery.

Designer Sydney Cope was hired in 1934, and was joined by his son, Leslie, in 1936. The Copes' influence on McCoy wares continued until Sydney's death in 1966. That same year, Leslie opened a gallery devoted to his family's design heritage and featuring his own original art.

Nelson McCoy Sr. died in 1945, and was succeeded as company president by his nephew, Nelson McCoy Melick.

A fire destroyed the plant in 1950, but company officials—including Nelson McCoy Jr., then 29—decided to rebuild, and the new Nelson McCoy Pottery Co. was up and running in just six months.

Nelson Melick died in 1954. Nelson Jr. became company president, and oversaw the company's continued growth. In 1967, the operation was sold to entrepreneur David Chase. At this time, the words "Mt. Clemens Pottery" were added to the company marks. In 1974, Chase sold the company to Lancaster Colony Corp., and the company marks included a stylized "LCC" logo. Nelson Jr. and his wife, Billie, who had served as a products supervisor, left the company in 1981.

In 1985, the company was sold again, this time to Designer Accents. The McCoy pottery factory closed in 1990.

For more information on McCoy pottery, see *Warman's McCoy Pottery*, 2nd edition, by Mark F. Moran.

Green hanging planter basket, circa 1940s, 7" dia., 4-1/2" h................................... **$30**

Native American cookie jar, normal crazing, no chips or cracks, 11" h. **$210**

Vintage unmarked art pottery dog dish, circa 1945, "MAN'S BEST FRIEND HIS DOG," green, unmarked, good condition, two darkened tight hairlines, 2-1/2" h. x 7-1/2" dia. **$45**

Art pottery dog dish, blue mottled glaze, marked (incised) McCoy Made in USA, age appropriate wear, 3-1/4" h., 5" dia. top, 6-1/2" dia. base.............................. **$36**

Large Brush McCoy glazed stoneware jardinière, Amaryllis pattern, cream and green ivotint glaze, circa 1920s, glaze chip to rim, 9-1/2" h. x 11-1/2" dia. **$180**

Aqua and pink floral teapot, cream and sugar, circa 20th century, several fleabites and crack in sugar handle, 7" h. x 10" l. ... **$94**

MCCOY

Arts & Crafts pottery umbrella stand, Brush McCoy, cylindrical form, decorated with repeating stylized lotus stems in ivory glaze on brown reserve, 16-3/4" h. **$270**

Three vases in pink, no chips or damage, largest 9-1/4" h., 5-3/8" dia. **$30**

Covered butter dish in glossy green, 1960s, McCoy USA mark .... **$30-$40**

Covered casserole, 1940s, McCoy USA, 6-1/2" d. .... **$55-$65**

Cherries and Leaves charger in glossy yellow, mid-1930s, unmarked, 11-1/4" d. **$550-$650**

Strap pitcher in glossy burgundy, late 1940s, McCoy mark .... **$75-$85**

McCoy flowerpot, ribbed with rose design, stoneware, 1920s, unmarked, 4" h, 5-1/2" d. .... **$30+**

Ivy jardinière in brown and green, early 1950s, unmarked, also found in a brighter glossy tan and green with matching pedestal, 8" h. .... **$350-$450**

Flowerpot in a skyscraper design, detached saucer, 1930s-40s, found in other colors, unmarked, 9" h, 10-1/2" d. .... **$75+**

Jardinière in a ring-ware design, stoneware, 1930s, unmarked, 9" h, 10" d. opening..**$100+**

Two jardinières with applied leaves and berries, late 1940s, McCoy USA mark, 7-1/2" h................................**$200-$250 ea.**

Sunburst jardinière in a multicolored glaze, 1930s, unmarked, 6-3/4" h. .... **$50-$70**

MCCOY

Basket-Weave jardinière and pedestal, peach glaze, late 1930s, NM USA mark, 13" and 7-1/2" h.......................................**$250+ set**

Leaves and Berries jardinière and pedestal in matte brown and green; jardinière, 7-1/2" d.; pedestal, 6-3/4" h............**$225-$275/pair**

Ring ware covered butter or cheese crock, 1920s, shield mark "M." ....**$90-$110**

Five sizes of Stone Craft mixing bowls (called pink and blue) ranging in diameter from 7" to 14" (also a 5" size), mid-1970s, McCoy LCC mark........... **$225-$250 for complete set**

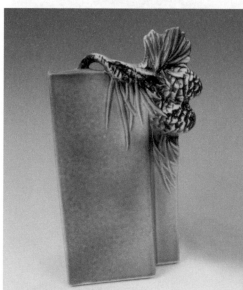

Pine Cone planter, mid-1940s, McCoy USA mark, 8" w., rare........................**$500-$600.**

Slightly larger planter, in rust glaze............ **$1,800-$2,000)**

Large fish planter, found in other colors, 1950s, McCoy mark, 12" l. ... **$1,200-$1,400**

Large centerpiece planter, 1950s, McCoy USA mark, found in other colors, 12" l....**$90-$110**

Hummingbird planter in green, late 1940s, McCoy USA mark, 10-1/2" w. ....**$125-$150**

Sand dollar vase in matte white, stoneware, 1940s, unmarked, also found in pastel colors, and brown and green .... **$250-$300, depending on color**

Swan planting dish in rustic ivory and turquoise, 1950s, McCoy USA mark, 8-1/2" h. ....**$700-$800**

MCCOY

Tall scroll vase in matte green (often found in glossy tan-brown), late 1940s, USA mark, 14" h. ....$150-$200

Floor vase, blue onyx glaze, 24" h, unmarked .... $700-$900

Blossomtime wall pocket in matte yellow, McCoy mark, 7-3/4" l. ...$90-$110

Fancy Lily Bud wall pocket in matte aqua, 1940s, incised McCoy mark, 8" l. ....$225-$250

Lily Bud pillow vase in glossy rose/pink, 1940s, NM USA mark, 7" high ....$90-$110

Shrimp vase in traditional colors, 1950s, McCoy USA mark, 9" h. ......$175+

Arrow Leaf vase in rustic glaze, McCoy mark, 10" high.................$125-$150

Three-sided ivy planter, 1950s, McCoy USA mark, hard to find, 6" high................ $400-$500

J.W. McCoy squat vase in a blended glaze, circa 1905, unmarked, 6" high. .... **$150+**

Bird on sunflower wall pocket, can also stand as planter, McCoy mark, came in a variety of glaze combinations, 6-1/2" h........ **$60-$75**

Leaves and Berries vase in matte brown and green, unmarked, 7" high .... **$80-$90**

Apple wall pocket in gold trim, 1950s, unmarked, 7" l. .... **$200-$225**

MCCOY

Ball pitcher with ice lip and four goblet-style tumblers in glossy burgundy, 1940s, unmarked.

Pitcher, 8 1/2" high .... $50-$60.

Tumblers, 5" high .... $25-$30 each

Cherries and Leaves serving bowl, two individual salad bowls, and two cups, all in glossy aqua, mid-1930s, unmarked, all very rare.

Serving bowl, 9" diameter .... $450-$550

Salad bowls, 5" diameter............................... $225-$275 each

Cups, 2-7/8" high .... $90-$110 each

Cucumber and "Mango" salt and pepper shakers with cork stoppers, 1950s, McCoy USA mark, 5 1/4" high...... $90-$110/pair

J.W. McCoy jardinière and pedestal in a Carnelian glaze, circa 1905, unmarked, overall 20 1/2" high. .... $400+

W.F. McCoy Stoneware two-gallon butter churn, 1850s, rare. No established value

Jardinière in a majolica glaze, stoneware, early 1920s, 9 1/2" high, 10 3/4" diameter..........**$150+**

Pine Cone teapot, creamer and sugar, 1950s, McCoy mark .... **$125-$150 set**

Pot and saucer (detached) in glossy burgundy, 1940s, unmarked, 9 1/2" high. ....**$125-$150**

Two square-bottom Ring ware mixing bowls in green and yellow, 1930s, shield mark with size inside (8" and 9", though they may actually be up to a half inch larger in diameter), also a pattern number (2, indicating the ring pattern)...**$150-$175 each**

Shoulder bowl in a windowpane pattern, 1920s, with shield mark and #4, 11" .....**$100-$125**

Large fish planter in pink, green and white, 1950s, McCoy USA mark, 12" l... **$1,200+**

Carriage with umbrella planter in traditional colors, cold paint in excellent condition, mid-1950s, McCoy USA mark, 9" high **$200+**

Garden Club vase in matte yellow, late 1950s, McCoy USA mark, 9 1/2" high ......**$150-$175**

Hunting dog planter in hard-to-find chartreuse glaze with black dog, 1954 McCoy mark, 12" wide, 8 1/2" high ....**$350-$450**

Three pigeon or dove flower holders (called "ladder pieces," so named because they were pictured in a early McCoy guide on a drying rack that was tiered like the steps of a ladder), 1940s, USA mark, 3 1/2" high ....**$100-$125 each**

Two pitcher flower holders, 1940s, NM USA mark, hand-painted in coral, 3 1/4" high...................................**$150-$200 each**

J.W. McCoy umbrella stand in the Wavy Tulip pattern, matte green glaze, circa 1915, unmarked, 20 3/4" high................ **$600-$700**

Butterfly cylinder vase with under-glaze decoration, 1940s, NM mark, 8" high.. **$350-$450**

Typical colors, coral, yellow, blue, or green .... **$60-$90**

Lily Bud divided planting dish in matte blue, 1940s, NM USA mark, 6 1/2" wide .... **$65-$75**

Triple bulb bowl in pink and black, 1950s, McCoy mark, 8" wide .... **$165-$185**

Cactus flower planter, three pieces, 1950s, marked 677 USA, 7" wide .... **$50+**

Meissen

KNOWN FOR ITS finely detailed figurines and exceptional tableware, Meissen is recognized as the first European maker of fine porcelain.

The company owes its beginnings to Johann Friedrich Bottger's 1708 discovery of the process necessary for the manufacture of porcelain. "Rediscovery" might be a better term, since the secret of producing hard paste porcelain had been known to the Chinese for centuries. However, Bottger, a goldsmith and alchemist, was the first to successfully replicate the formula in Europe. Soon after, The Royal Saxon Porcelain Works set up shop in Dresden. Because Bottger's formula was highly sought after by would-be competitors, in 1710 the firm moved its base of operations to Albrechtburg Castle in Meissen, Saxony. There, in fortress-like surroundings, prying eyes could be successfully deflected. And, because of that move, the company name eventually became one with its locale: Meissen.

The earliest Meissen pieces were red stoneware, reminiscent of Chinese work, and incised with Chinese characters. Porcelain became the Meissen focus in 1713; early releases included figurines and teasets, the decorations reminiscent of baroque metal. In 1719, after Bottger's death, artist J.J. Horoldt took over the firm's direction. His Chinese-influenced designs, which employed a lavish use of color and decoration, are categorized as chinoiserie.

By the 1730s, Meissen employed nearly 100 workers, among them renowned modelers J.G. Kirchner and J.J. Kandler. The firm became known for its porcelain sculptures; subjects included birds, animals, and familiar figures from commedia dell'arte. Meissen dinnerware also won acclaim; in earlier attempts, the company's white porcelain had only managed

Pair of fox head stirrup cups, 19th century, 3 1/4" high **$1,778**

to achieve off-white. Now, at last, there were dazzling white porcelain surfaces that proved ideal for the exquisite, richly colored decoration that became a Meissen trademark.

Following Horoldt's retirement in the mid-1700s, Victor Acier became Meissen's master modeler. Under Acier, the design focus relied heavily on mythological themes. By the early 1800s, however, Meissen's popularity began to wane. With production costs mounting and quality inconsistent, changes were instituted, especially technical improvements in production that allowed Meissen to operate more efficiently and profitably. More importantly, the Meissen designs, which had remained relatively stagnant for nearly a century, were refurbished. The goal: to connect with current popular culture. Meissen's artists (and its porcelain) proved perfectly capable of adapting to the prevailing tastes of the times. The range was wide: the ornate fussiness of the Rococo period; the more subdued Neoclassicism of the late 1700s; the nature-tinged voluptuousness of

Figure group depicting elegant woman in 18th century dress standing over cherub reading book, surrounded below by ladies-in-waiting and two girls, ovoid naturalistic base, late 19th/early 20th century, 12" high............................. **$6,463**

early 20th century Art Nouveau; and today's Meissen, which reinterprets, and builds on, all of these design eras.

Despite diligent efforts, Meissen eventually found its work widely copied. A crossed-swords trademark, applied to Meissen pieces from 1731 onward, is a good indicator of authenticity. However, even the markings had their imitators. Because Meissen originals, particularly those from the 18th and 19th centuries, are both rare and costly, the most reliable guarantee that a piece is authentic is to purchase from a reputable source.

Meissen porcelain is an acquired taste. Its gilded glory, lavish use of color, and almost overwhelmingly intricate detailing require just the right setting for effective display. Meissen is not background décor. These are three-dimensional artworks that demand full attention. Meissen pieces also often tell a story (although the plots may be long forgotten): a cherub and a woman in 18th century dress read a book, surrounded by a bevy of shepherdesses; the goddess Diana perches on a clock above a winged head of Father Time; the painted inset on a cobalt teacup depicts an ancient Dresden cathedral approached by devout churchgoers. Unforgettable images all, and all part of the miracle that is Meissen.

MEISSEN

Clock, figural, Rococo taste, tall case molded as cartouche applied with flowering garlands enclosing clock with white porcelain dial with Roman numerals, held by figure of seated goddess Diana, raised on tall waisted rocaille pedestal molded with winged head of Father Time above small putto petting Diana's dog, center hand painted with color vignette of couple in wooded landscape, scrolled feet, sides and back trimmed with gilt flowers, retailed by Tiffany & Co., New York City, mid-to-late 19th century, 15 1/2" high......................**$6,573**

Porcelain figurine titled "Duck Sale," marked on underside with gray M and impressed numbers 720 62, very good to excellent condition, 6 1/2" high x 6" wide......................**$830**

Four items, late 19th century, each polychrome enameled and gilded, including pair of figures of man and woman, each supporting floral garland, 6 1/4" high, 6 1/2" high; pair of covered urns with foliate festoons above figural landscape scenes, 5" high; crossed swords marks **$1,722**

Set of eight bird plates, 19th century, 8 1/2" diameter, together with two floral plates, 9 1/2" diameter **$652**

Reticulated floral bowl, 6" high, 10" diameter **$59**

Pair of porcelain vases, late 19th/early 20th century, scrolled snake handles, gilding to rim, handle terminals, lower body, and socle, crossed swords marks, 15 3/8" high **$984**

Four porcelain busts, circa 1900, each with blue crossed swords mark, comprising three allegorical of the seasons, one with single cancellation mark, incised model numbers and bust of Renaissance maiden, incised L17, 8 1/4" to 11" high **$2,750**

Three vases, circa 1900, each with underglaze blue crossed swords mark, flanked by serpent handles centered by floral sprays or bunches of fruit, largest with double cancellation and impressed A148/67, pair impressed or incised E153, tallest 19" high............................. **$1,250**

Pair of porcelain flower sellers, late 19th century, gilded and polychrome enamel decorated figures, man holding hat full of flowers, woman a basketful, each with underglaze blue crossed swords marks, 6 1/4", 6 5/8" high.............................. **$1,320**

Porcelain figural group, late 19th century, polychrome enamel decorated and gilded with figures of two boys supporting girl on stilts, all by sculpture of classical maiden, crossed swords mark, heavy losses to leaves and branches, restored to small scattered chips, basket on backside missing handle, 10 3/8" high............. **$1,920**

Pair of porcelain figures with garlands, late 19th century, each gilded and polychrome enamel decorated, man supporting garland atop his shoulders, woman holding garland across her chest, underglaze blue crossed swords marks, 6 3/8", 6 1/2" high................................ **$960**

Porcelain swan group, 19th century, gilded and polychrome enamel decorated, modeled as mother swan with two of her young, crossed swords mark, 4 5/8" high **$450**

Porcelain allegorical figural group, 19th century, gilded and polychrome enamel decorated, modeled as seated Cupid dressed in long coat and wearing hat and surrounded by three maidens, blue crossed swords mark, first quality mark, restorations to kneeling maiden's neck and arms, seated maiden's back of seat, cupid's legs, 7 1/4" high **$2,091**

Five porcelain figures, 19th century, each gilded and polychrome enamel decorated, including youth playing shuttlecock, 5 7/8" high; youth playing flute, 5 3/4" high; young girl feeding chickens, 4 5/8" high; young boy with barrel of grapes, 3 5/8" high; and maiden riding back of steer, 3 3/8" high; crossed swords marks **$1,968**

Group of Meissen porcelain tablewares, German, in Blue Onion pattern, three reticulated luncheon plates, six reticulated dessert plates, five reticulated bread plates, cup and saucer, and shaped rectangular platter with gilded rim, all with underglaze blue double crossed sword mark, except one bread plate marked MEISSEN within a circle, plus three Continental reticulated dessert plates, marked KS within a circle, platter has losses to gilding, platter 13-1/2" l. **$330**

Porcelain courting group, late 19th century, gilded trim with polychrome enameling to man and woman seated beneath tree, rabbit by their feet, underglaze crossed swords mark, first quality mark, loss and old repairs to numerous leaves, rabbit missing half of rear leg, restored to end of sword, 9 3/4" high **$1,320**

Hunter on horseback with dogs, German, late 19th century, marks: crossed swords, T 102, good condition with restoration to tail of one dog, 15-1/4" h. **$18,125**

Group of seven tablewares, German, in Blue Onion pattern, coffee pot, two lidded milk pots, two lidded jars, one with silver top, vinegar bottle and two-handled covered bowl with putto finial, all with blue underglaze crossed swords mark, except for coffee pot, which is marked MEISSEN under a cross, lidded bowl missing ladle with small chip to finial, repair to base of milk pot, tallest 7-1/2". $480

Pair of porcelain cobalt blue ground vases and covers, late 19th century, each with gilded scrolled foliage surrounding shaped cartouches, polychrome enamel decorated with courting figures on one side, floral bouquets on reverse, underglaze crossed swords marks, finial restored to one cover, 9 3/8" high...**$1,230**

Five porcelain figures, 19th century, each gilded and polychrome enamel decorated, including male youth, 7 1/4" high; woman with bird in apron, 7 1/8" high; posing dandy, 6 3/4"; man hiking, 7"; and harlequin and maiden dancing, 7"; crossed swords marks......................**$3,900**

MEISSEN

Figural perforated vase with lid, 19th century, some damage, 12-1/2" h...... $950

Porcelain figural group, late 18th/early 19th century, gilded and polychrome enamel decorated, modeled as farmer with cow and milkmaid, underglaze blue crossed swords mark, 7 3/8" high $1,140

Porcelain group of Abduction of Prosperpine, circa 1900, underglaze blue crossed swords mark with double cancellation, incised 1787, impressed 125 and black painted 57, 8" high $750

Porcelain lover's group, late 19th century, polychrome enameled and gilded model depicting man and woman in amorous pose, lamb by their side, crossed swords mark, first quality mark, restoration to woman's hand by lamb and to ribbons of man's hat, scattered chips to flowers and leaves, 7 1/2" high. $1,440

Tureen and platter, German, in Blue Onion pattern, lidded tureen and shaped oval platter with handles, both with underglaze blue crossed swords mark, tureen missing ladle, small chip to handle of platter, platter 20" l. **$510**

Porcelain group of Venus and attendants, centered by Venus seated in shell chariot riding a wave, surrounded by attendants in form of putti, dolphins, and mermaids, underglaze blue crossed swords with single cancellation, late 19th century, incised D81, impressed 68 and red painted 41, 8 1/2" high **$2,057**

Porcelain blue ground vase and cover, 19th century, bottle shape with gilded trim lines and decorated in white and black enamel with classical maiden on either side, underglaze blue crossed swords mark, 8 5/8" high ...**$1,968**

Malabar Lady and Malabar Man, late 19th century, marks to female: crossed swords, 1519, 12-1/2" h... **$3,750**

Group of 10 Meissen Blue Onion porcelain salts, German, two master salts surmounted by seated putti, two salts with shell-shaped bowls on scrolling feet, and six square salts, all with underglaze blue crossed swords mark, master salts incised with M129 style mark, largest 6" h......**$570**

MEISSEN

Porcelain figural courting group, late 19th century, polychrome enameled and gilded depiction of maiden centering male suitor, another kneeling by column with lovebirds in his hat, crossed swords mark, first quality mark, restoration to standing suitor's back hand, 12" high **$2,583**

Figural grouping, German, late 18th/early 19th century, 15" h. x 8-1/2" w............... **$500**

Leda and the Swan, German, late 19th century, marks: crossed swords, 433, some losses to top of toe on extended foot, floral garland, and tree leaves, 6-3/4" h. **$1,250**

Porcelain figural courting group, late 19th
century, polychrome enameled and gilded
model with three figures, maiden with
suitor, another maiden grieving by her
side, crossed swords mark, first quality
mark, restoration to bow in maiden's hat,
maiden's arm resting on shoulder of other
maiden, basket of flowers, fingers of hand
at basket, 12 1/4" high **$2,400**

**Porcelain blue onion three-tier cake plate
with figural woman with flowers finial,**
bottom with blue crossed swords mark
with number 2, circa 1860-1880, 21
1/2" high **$1,936**

Nine items with gilt and floral decoration,
19th/20th century: six round bowls, two-
handled rectangular bowl and square serving
tray, all marked, tray 16" sq. **$2,625**

Cup and saucer, cup 2" h. x 3" dia., saucer
5" dia. **$50**

◄ **Porcelain figural footed compote with applied floral decoration**, 19th/20th century, crossed swords mark, 19" x 14" x 11-1/2".................**$2,375**

▶ **Hand-painted porcelain urn covered with applied putti and large floral finial**, 19th century crossed swords mark, 24" x 12" x 9-1/2".......**$4,063**

Porcelain yellow ground vase and cover, early 20th century, gilded griffin head handles, polychrome enamel decorated oval cartouches with nude nymph to either side, underglaze crossed swords mark, slight hairline through figure on one side, 15 5/8" high **$923**

Gardener figure, German, 19th century, woman in 18th-century attire with basket of flowers, holding tool, standing beside rose-filled planter on circular base, marked with underglaze blue crossed swords, incised 122 on bottom, chip to rim of bonnet, minor losses to lace and flowers, missing blade of sickle, 8-1/2" h. **$900**

Pair of porcelain cobalt ground plates, 19th century, each with pierced floret and ringlet border and polychrome enamel decorated cartouches, one depicting Triumph of Bacchus, the other Renaud and Armide, titled in French, crossed swords marks, 9 1/8" diameter................. **$3,321**

Two porcelain figures from "The Senses" series, German, late 19th century, representing taste and smell, both with woman in 18th-century attire, seated at a table, one smelling a rose and the other enjoying a pastry, each marked with underglaze blue crossed swords, "taste" incised 127 on bottom, "smell" incised 42 on bottom, both groups with minor losses, tallest 5-1/2" h **$1,920**

Mettlach

CERAMICS WITH THE name Mettlach were produced by Villeroy & Boch and other potteries in the Mettlach area of Germany. Villery & Boch's finest years of production are thought to be from about 1890-1910.

Pate sur pate charger of Three Graces, #7052, 21" dia. **$590**

Cameo stein, #2652, 7" h. **$81**

Ornate punch bowl with colonial era scenes front and rear, two handles of fishlike creatures, basketweave designs and others in heavy white slip to body, impressed with Mettlach logo and notation "Gefnnachbildung, Seschutzi," 2088 and 98 with W in black slip and mark in green slip, one handle oversprayed, some staining to interior rim, 11-1/4" h. x 17" w..$200

Etched plaque #2361A, Wartburg Castle, mint condition, 17". **$403**

Etched plaque #2287, two cavalier knights shaking hands with verse, mint condition, 17". **$460**

Hofbrauhaus party stein, Mettlach #1909/1102 PUG, depicting people drinking at Hofbrauhaus, mint condition, half liter. **$207**

Hunter and verse stein, Mettlach #1526/597 PUG, mint condition, one liter. **$207**

Etched stein #1916, cavaliers drinking, Harvey Murphy replaced lid, body mint condition, 2-1/2 liters. **$460**

Newcomb College

THIS POTTERY WAS established in the art department of Newcomb College in New Orleans in 1897. Each piece was hand-thrown and bore the potter's mark and decorator's monogram on the base. It was always a studio business and never operated as a factory. Its pieces are, therefore, scarce, with the early wares eagerly sought. The pottery closed in 1940.

Sadie Irvine cabinet vase with willow leaves, 1933, marked NC/UE8/KS/SI, 3-1/2" x 3-1/2".......................... **$1,750**

Anna Frances Simpson small circular trivet with trumpet vine, 1924, marked NC/OC27/AFS, 4" dia................. **$750**

Sadie Irvine tall vase with pine trees and full moon, 1927, marked NC/SI/QP58/325/JM, 9-1/4" x 4"......... **$9,375**

NEWCOMB COLLEGE

Sadie Irvine transitional vase with magnolia blossoms, 1907, marked NC/JM/SI/BX67, 5-1/2" x 3-1/4". **$1,375**

Rare carved cabinet vase in oxblood glaze, 1932, marked NC/G1/TT38/JH/A, 2-3/4" x 3". **$1,625**

Henrietta Bailey rare seven-piece transitional tea set for two with pine trees, 1911, two teacups and saucers, teapot, sugar bowl, and creamer, all marked NC/HB/EI61, teapot 4" x 5-1/2". **$25,000**

Sadie Irvine candleholder with pink lilies at top and bottom, 1918, impressed with Newcomb College logo, shape 232, and 1918 date code JM35, incised with artist's monogram, most of original Newcomb Pottery label present, bruise at rim and small firing separation to bottom, 7" h. **$850**

Ada Wilt Lonnegan high glaze lidded creamer with incised and painted irises, lid incised with leaves, 1909, marked with Newcomb logo, date code for 1909 (DD 73), impressed initials of potter Joseph Meyer, and W for white clay body, excellent original condition, 4" h. **$3,200**

Joseph Meyer vase with gloss black glaze, impressed on base with Newcomb insignia, excellent original condition, 3" h. **$225**

Sadie Irvine vase with trumpet flowers, 1929, marked NC/236/RL24/SI, 7" x 3-3/4". **$2,750**

Henrietta Bailey vase with nicotina blossoms, 1917, marked NC/IY77/721A/HB, 4-1/4" x 4-3/4".................................. **$1,625**

Mazie Teresa Ryan early two-handled vase with jasmine, 1905, marked NC/M.T. RYAN/AT94, 4-1/2" x 4-1/2".............. **$3,500**

Sadie Irvine rare transitional scenic vase with tall pines and full moon, 1915, marked NC/HO8/SI, 8" x 3-1/2"......... **$3,625**

Sadie Irvine vase with carved and painted decoration of flowering vines, marked with Newcomb logo, date code for 1929 (RS 93), monogram of potter Jonathan Hunt, and incised monogram of artist, excellent original condition, no apparent crazing, 6-1/2" h. **$1,400**

Corinne M. Chalaron low bowl with stylized magnolia flowers, 1922, marked NC/JM55/CMC/
MQ35, 2-1/4" x 7"... **$1,063**

Anna Frances Simpson large scenic vase
with Spanish moss, live oaks and full
moon, 1922, marked NC/MO35/JM/
AFS/211, 11-1/4" x 6-1/4"...............**$11,875**

Henrietta Bailey transitional chamberstick
with paperwhites, 1911, marked NC/HB/
JM/T/EN24, 6-1/4" x 4-1/4"......... **$1,625**

Nippon

"NIPPON" IS A term used to describe a wide range of porcelain wares produced in Japan from the late 19th century until about 1921. It was in 1891 that the United States implemented the McKinley Tariff Act, which required that all wares exported to the United States carry a marking indicating their country of origin. The Japanese chose to use "Nippon," their name for Japan. In 1921 the import laws were revised and the words "Made in" had to be added to the markings. Japan was also required to replace the "Nippon" with the English name "Japan" on all wares sent to the United States.

Many Japanese factories produced Nippon porcelain, much of it hand-painted with ornate floral or landscape decoration and heavy gold decoration, applied beading and slip-trailed designs referred to as "moriage." Be aware that a number of Nippon markings have been reproduced and used on new porcelain wares.

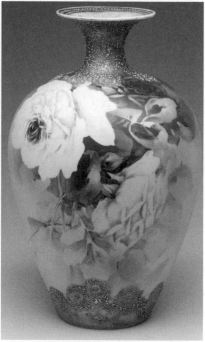

Floral vase, baluster form with two open handles at shoulder, hand painted with roses, blue maple leaf mark, first quarter 20th century, 13" h. **$431**

Floral vase, baluster form with everted lip, hand painted with roses, blue maple leaf mark, first quarter 20th century, 11" h. **$316**

Pair of floral vases, two-handle square baluster form with two open handles at shoulder and flared feet, raised moriage centering band of painted white dogwood flowers, green M-in-wreath marks, first quarter 20th century, 9-1/2" h. . **$316**

Painted urn decorated with Arabic scene, quarter-inch chip to one foot, wear to gold gilt, 17-3/4" h.................. **$830**

Plate with roses, 11" dia...**$236**

Scenic cobalt vase, square baluster form with two open handles at shoulder and flared feet, hand-painted scenic reserves on all four sides, applied red beaded grapes, green M in wreath mark, first quarter 20th century, 9-1/2" h. **$288**

Two decorated vases, each of flattened pillow form with two handles, smaller vase painted with irises, larger vase painted with Art Nouveau poppies and water lilies surrounding a reserve featuring swans on a lake, M-in-wreath marks, one blue and one green, first quarter 20th century, 8" and 10" h........................**$374**

Scenic vase, large two-handle tapering form hand painted with scenic reserve on both sides, extensive gilding, blue maple leaf mark, first quarter 20th century, 13" h.......................... **$161**

Whiskey jug with hand-painted European cottage scene, stopper needs new cork, 6" h.......... $100

Noritake

ALTHOUGH NORITAKE IS the long-recognized identifier for a particular brand of fine china, the firm began life in 1904 as Nippon Gomei Kaisha. The "Noritake" moniker came from the company's location in the village of Noritake, Japan. Because it was a geographic designation, the firm had to wait until the 1980s before receiving permission to officially register "Noritake" as a trade name.

Prior to the 1900s, Japan's "closed" society meant that relatively few domestically produced items found their way past the country's borders. Japanese artware was prized as much for its rarity as for its skillful execution. In the late 1800s, the easing of economic sanctions and growing interaction with the West meant that the rest of the world could appreciate the artistry of Japan.

Noritake was developed by Morimura Brothers, a distributorship founded in 1876. In its earliest years, Morimura operated as an exporter, bringing traditional Japanese giftware (paper lanterns, china, and a variety of decorative curio items) to buyers on American shores. The company eventually embraced the goal of producing a line of fine china dinnerware that, while Japanese-made, would prove irresistible in styling and execution to Western consumers.

Noritake dinnerware debuted in 1904. In 1914, when the product was deemed ready for a larger audience, exports began. The first Noritake pieces were hand-painted with extensive gold trim, both costly and time-consuming to produce. Additionally, much of the decorative work was farmed out to independent artisans throughout the region. Quality varied due to the varying skills of individual freelancers.

With the onset of mass production in the 1920s, Noritake was able to achieve consistency

Painted scenic bowl depicting landscape with cabin, trimmed in gilt with two handles, circa early 20th century, green leaf Noritake mark, 7" dia. x 2-1/4" h. **$48**

Hand-painted Art Deco porcelain covered dresser box depicting young woman with hand mirror, early 20th century, marked with green M-in-wreath backstamp, 3-3/4" dia. **$210**

Two hand-painted Art Deco porcelain cabinet plates, each depicting finely dressed young debutant with floral accents on turquoise luster ground, early 20th century, both marked with M-in-wreath backstamp, largest 8-3/4" dia. **$450**

Three-piece hand-painted Art Deco porcelain group, handled perfume bottle with harlequin figure (stopper absent), blue luster wall pocket with blown out fruits, and two-sided figural peacock posy vase, early 20th century, first and third marked with red M-in-wreath backstamps, wall pocket with green Paulownia made in Japan flower mark, largest 8" l. **$150**

in its output, expand productivity, lower costs, and increase brand name recognition.

From the 1920s until World War II, Noritake achieved its greatest prominence. The inventory fell into two overall categories: dinnerware and fancy ware. Dinnerware, as the name implies, encompassed products made specifically for the table—plates, bowls, tea sets, condiment holders, and the like. Fancy ware covered everything else, from wall pockets and vases to elaborately decorated display platters.

A major factor in Noritake's success was the Morimura brothers' early and aggressive use of advertising, cementing the brand in the minds of American buyers. Full-page Noritake ads graced major trade journals. Early on, the company also saw the value of such promotional efforts as premium tie-ins. During the 1920s, the Larkin Co., a New York mail-order distributor of various home and beauty products, offered buyers an assortment of Noritake china as a bonus when buying from the company's catalog. Among the most popular Larkin patterns was Azalea, still a favorite today.

The onset of World War II meant that, overnight, Noritake china was no longer available (or even welcome) in American homes. The company continued to produce china on a limited basis during the war, but only for domestic buyers.

During the American occupation of Japan (1945-1952), Noritake china became popular with servicemen stationed there; the company's increased production was one factor in assisting Japan along the road to economic recovery. The "Noritake China" name was, for a time, replaced with a more indeterminate "Rose China." The company indicated this was because the china was not yet at its pre-war level of quality; concerns about identifying the product too closely with a recent adversary may also have been a contributing factor.

In the years following the war, Noritake regained its previous worldwide reputation for quality. Whether lusterware of the 1920s, Art Deco stylings of the 1930s, or today's contemporary designs, Noritake porcelain reflects the artistic sensibilities of its creators, yet remains perfectly attuned to the specific cultural sensibilities of its intended audience.

George Ohr

GEORGE OHR, THE eccentric potter of Biloxi, Mississippi, worked from about 1883 to 1906. Some think him to be one of the most expert throwers the craft will ever see. The majority of his works were hand-thrown, exceedingly thin-walled items, some of which have a crushed or folded appearance. He considered himself the foremost potter in the world and declined to sell much of his production, instead accumulating a great horde to leave as a legacy to his children. In 1972 this collection was purchased for resale by an antiques dealer.

Spherical vase with folded rim, rare matte raspberry and emerald mottled glaze, 1897-1900, stamped G.E. OHR Biloxi, Miss., 6" x 6"...**$13,750**

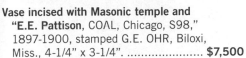

Vase incised with Masonic temple and "E.E. Pattison, COAL, Chicago, S98," 1897-1900, stamped G.E. OHR, Biloxi, Miss., 4-1/4" x 3-1/4". **$7,500**

Vase, thin-walled construction, "tortured" form, pumpkin colored high glaze, impressed on base Geo. E. Ohr, Biloxi, Miss., excellent original condition, 3-1/8" h.... **$1,600**

Large teapot with ear-shaped handle and snake spout, teal and brown sponged-on glaze, 1897-1900, stamped G.E. OHR, Biloxi, Miss., 6-1/2" x 9". **$10,000**

GEORGE OHR

Novelty spittoon inkwell, unusual green, oxblood, and amber glaze, 1892-1894, stamped GEO. E. OHR BILOXI, 1-1/2" x 3-1/2"... **$813**

Barrel-shaped vase of scroddled clay with amber and cobalt glaze, 1880s-1900s, hand-incised OHR, Biloxi, 5-1/4" x 4" ... **$1,250**

Curled bisque bank, 1897-1900, stamped G.E. OHR, Biloxi, Miss., 3-3/4" x 3-1/4"..... **$1,375**

Large bulbous vase, green, raspberry, cobalt, and yellow sponged-on glaze, 1897-1900, stamped G.E.OHR Biloxi, Miss., 7" x 4" **$3,250**

Cabinet vase with in-body twist, gunmetal glaze, circa 1897-1900, stamped G.E. OHR Biloxi Miss, 4-1/4" x 2-1/2". **$3,375**

White bisque vessel, 1898-1910, script signature, 3-1/2" x 4-1/2"..................... **$875**

"Burnt Baby" inkwell with snake, 1892-1894, unmarked, 3" x 2-3/4"............. **$1,875**

Bisque-fired vessel of scroddled clay, pinched, 1898-1910, script signature, 3-3/4" x 5-1/2"..... **$2,750**

Large unusual figural bisque bank, 1895-1896, stamped GEO. E. OHR BILOXI MISS., 5-1/2" x 3-1/2"................... **$2,000**

Bottle-shaped vase with curled handles and incised with leafy sprig, brown and gunmetal glaze, 1897-1900, stamped G.E. OHR, Biloxi, Miss., 5" x 4"... **$7,500**

Large bisque-fired vessel, in-body twist, folded rim, 1898-1910, script signature, 4-1/2" x 6-1/2". **$3,250**

Bisque-fired vase, pinched and lobed, 1898-1910, script signature, 5" x 6". **$3,750**

Overbeck

THE OVERBECK STUDIO pottery was founded by four sisters, Hannah, Mary Francis, Elizabeth and Harriet, in the Overbeck family home in Cambridge City, Indiana, in 1911. A fifth sister, Margaret, who worked as a decorator at Zanesville Art Pottery in 1910, was the catalyst for establishing the pottery, but died the same year. Launching at the tail end of the Arts and Crafts movement, and believing "borrowed art is bad art," the sister potters dedicated themselves to producing unique, quality pieces with original design elements, which often were inspired by the natural world. Pieces can also be found worked in the Art Nouveau and Art Deco styles, as well as unique figurines and grotesques. The studio used several marks through the years, including an incised "O" and incised "OBK," often accompanied by the artist's initials. The pottery ceased production in 1955.

Pink and purple billy goat with black accents, incised "OBK" logo, both horns have been broken at crown and glued back, 3-5/8" h. **$200**

Grotesque figure of wild dog in pink, green, blue, lavender and black, impressed with Overbeck symbol, small chips to front feet, 2" x 3-1/2".................................. **$180**

Grotesque figure of wild dog in pink, brown, blue, green and black, impressed with Overbeck logo, excellent original condition, 2-1/4" x 3-1/2"............................. **$325**

Grotesque figure of Dickensian lady colorfully dressed, impressed with Overbeck logo, excellent original condition, 3-1/2" h. **$140**

Grotesque figure of Southern Belle in dress with hoop skirt and broad-brimmed hat, blue, pink and white, impressed with Overbeck logo, excellent original condition, 4-1/4" h **$200**

Grotesque figure of member of choir wearing hat with white feature, holding hymnal, impressed on sole of right foot with Overbeck emblem, excellent original condition, 5-1/4" h. **$250**

Cockatoo pin, white bird backlit by green disc, impressed with Overbeck logo, excellent original condition, 2-1/2" l. **$190**

Grotesque figure of gentleman outfitted in pink morning coat, blue pants, blue cravat, and blue top hat, impressed with Overbeck logo, excellent original condition, 4-1/2" h. **$140**

Monochromatic vase with dozens of small clusters of flowers by sisters Elizabeth and Mary Frances Overbeck, incised marks include Overbeck logo and initials of two sisters, excellent original condition, 8-1/4" h. **$1,600**

Barnyard goose with large pink feet, neck outstretched, "OBK" logo incised beneath, tip of beak has glaze chip and perimeter of feet has some glaze nicks... **$300**

Petite figure of Southern Belle with blond tresses, dressed in flowered dress and matching hat, impressed with Overbeck symbol, excellent original condition, 1-7/8" h. **$180**

Skunk figure, impressed with Overbeck trademark, excellent original condition, 1-5/8" x 3-1/4"..................................... **$350**

Grotesque figure of champion pacer Single G, so named for G on forehead, marked on bottom with Overbeck Pottery ink stamp, excellent original condition, 2-1/4" x 3". Single G, who was born in Cambridge City, Indiana in 1910, had a 16-year career as a successful harness racer. He died in 1940 and is buried in Cambridge City. **$700**

Owens

OWENS POTTERY WAS the product of the J.B. Owens Pottery Co., which operated in Ohio from 1890 to 1929. In 1891 it was located in Zanesville and produced art pottery from 1896, introducing "Utopian" wares as its first art pottery. The company switched to tile after 1907. Efforts to rebuild after the factory burned in 1928 failed, and the company closed in 1929.

Three-piece tea set with metal mounts, 5-5/8" teapot, 4-1/4" sugar bowl and 4" cream pitcher, each impressed "J.B. Owens, Utopian, 1057," all with fine overall crazing, teapot with small chips at spout and tiny nicks below handles, sugar in excellent original condition, creamer with tiny nicks to two feet, each bears a sticker indicating it is "From the Collection of Frank L. Hahn," author of *Collector's Guide to Owens Pottery.* **$225**

Utopian vase formed of North Dakota clay (a partnership between Owens Pottery and North Dakota School of Mines), decorated with wild roses, impressed with Owens Utopian logo, shape 108, 2 and 8 and marked "ND" in slip near base to identify the source of clay, 5-7/8" h....................$110

Miniature Utopian handled vase decorated with a pair of yellow clematis, impressed "JB Owens Utopian, 866" on bottom, 3-1/4" h. **$160**

Feroza vase with molded jonquil design and brown metallic luster glaze, unmarked, excellent
original condition, 8-1/4" h. **$275**

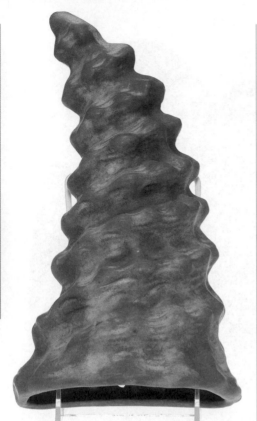

Wall pocket classified as "Green Ware,"
possibly part of Aqua Verde line, marked
only with incised number 1017, chipping
at hanger hole, minor nicks to back,
10-3/4" h..$200

**Soudaneze mug decorated with grapes
and leaves against mat black ground,**
impressed on base "Owens Soudaneze
X 235," excellent original condition,
4-3/4" h. $275

**Rare Utopian scenic vase showing heron
standing on one leg in a marsh with lotus
and cattail decoration by Mae Timberlake,**
impressed "J.B. Owens Utopian 798"
on bottom and initialed by artist on side,
14-1/8"...$1,300

R.S. Prussia

ORNATELY DECORATED CHINA marked "R.S. Prussia" and "R.S. Germany" continues to grow in popularity. According to the Third Series of Mary Frank Gaston's *Encyclopedia of R.S. Prussia* (Collector Books), these marks were used by the Reinhold Schlegelmilch porcelain factories located in Suhl in the Germanic regions known as Prussia prior to World War I, and in Tillowitz, Silesia, which became part of Poland after World War II. Other marks sought by collectors include "R.S. Suhl," "R.S." steeple or church marks, and "R.S. Poland."

The Suhl factory was founded by Reinhold Schlegelmilch in 1869 and closed in 1917. The Tillowitz factory was established in 1895 by Erhard Schlegelmilch, Reinhold's son. This china customarily bears the phrase "R.S. Germany" and "R.S. Tillowitz." The Tillowitz factory closed in 1945, but it was reopened for a few years under Polish administration.

"Ostriches" serving bowl, scalloped-rim mold 182, transfer-printed with two ostriches in a landscape, red and green wreath-and-star mark, late 19th/early 20th century, 9-3/8" dia. **$920**

Prices are high and collectors should beware of forgeries that sometimes find their way onto the market. Mold names and numbers are taken from Mary Frank Gaston's books on R.S. Prussia.

The "Prussia" and "R.S. Suhl" marks have been reproduced, so buy with care. Later copies of these marks are well done, but quality of porcelain is infe-rior to the production in the 1890-1920 era.

Collectors are also interested in the porcelain products made by the Erdmann Schlegelmilch factory. This factory was founded by three brothers in Suhl in 1861. They named the factory in honor of their father, Erdmann Schlegelmilch. A variety of marks incorporating the "E.S." initials were used. The factory closed circa 1935. The Erdmann Schlegelmilch factory was an earlier and entirely separate business from the Reinhold Schlegelmilch factory. The two were not related to each other.

Floral-decorated beverage items, 14, chocolate pot with five cups and saucers, three-piece tea set, pot lacking cover, all mold 501 with matching transfer-printed roses and bronze/gilt shoulder band, satin finish, unmarked, late 19th/early 20th century, pot 9-1/2" h. overall...**$518**

"Melon Boys" plate with decorative gold trim, 8-3/4", and ball-footed urn with Grecian women in a garden setting, closed ring handles, 4-3/8"; red back stamp logo on bottom of both pieces, wear to areas on each...$80

Floral-decorated chocolate set, nine pieces, pot with four cups and saucers, mold 82 transfer-printed with roses, red and green wreath-and-star marks, late 19th/early 20th century, pot 8-1/2" h. overall........................**$374**

Nine-piece demitasse set, floral decoration, pot 9-1/2" h., cups 2" h. **$295**

Scenic cake plate, "Icicle" mold 7 transfer-printed with Man in Mountain, sailboat and castle on cliff, red and green wreath-and-star mark, late 19th/early 20th century, 10-1/4" dia. ...**$375**

Floral-decorated tankard pitcher, "Iris Variation" mold 514 transfer-printed with floral bouquet, late 19th/early 20th century, unmarked, undamaged, 10" h. overall. Provenance: From the Rudolph Evers estate collection, Bridgewater, Virginia. **$184**

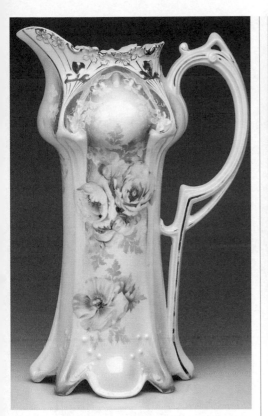

Floral-decorated tankard pitcher, mold 82 transfer-printed with poppies on both sides, red and green wreath-and-star mark, professional restoration to one foot, late 19th/early 20th century, 14" h. overall. Provenance: From the Rudolph Evers estate collection, Bridgewater, Virginia **$288**

Floral-decorated tankard pitcher, "Carnation" mold 526 transfer-printed with roses on both sides, red and green wreath-and-star mark, late 19th/early 20th century, undamaged except for light chip under base, 11" h. overall. Provenance: From the Rudolph Evers estate collection, Bridgewater, Virginia............. **$345**

Winter season serving bowl, eight-lobe form with scalloped and molded rim, center transfer-printed with woman in snowy landscape, pearlized finish with shadow star transfers, unmarked, late 19th/early 20th century, 10-1/2" dia..**$575**

Red Wing

VARIOUS POTTERIES OPERATED in Red Wing, Minnesota, starting in 1868, the most successful being the Red Wing Stoneware Company, organized in 1877. Merged with other local potteries through the years, it became known as Red Wing Union Stoneware Company in 1906 and was one of the largest producers of utilitarian stoneware items in the United States.

After a decline in the popularity of stoneware products, an art pottery line was introduced to compensate for the loss. This was reflected in a new name for the company, Red Wing Potteries, Inc., in 1936. Stoneware production ceased entirely in 1947, but vases, planters, cookie jars, and dinnerware of art pottery quality continued in production until 1967, when the pottery ceased operation altogether.

For more information on Red Wing pottery, see *Warman's Red Wing Pottery Identification and Price Guide* by Mark F. Moran.

White stoneware bail-handle butter crock with advertising, (cover missing), left, 7-1/4" t.
without handle, unmarked.. **$400+**

Sponge-decorated butter crock, with lid, 7" t., unmarked. ....$300+

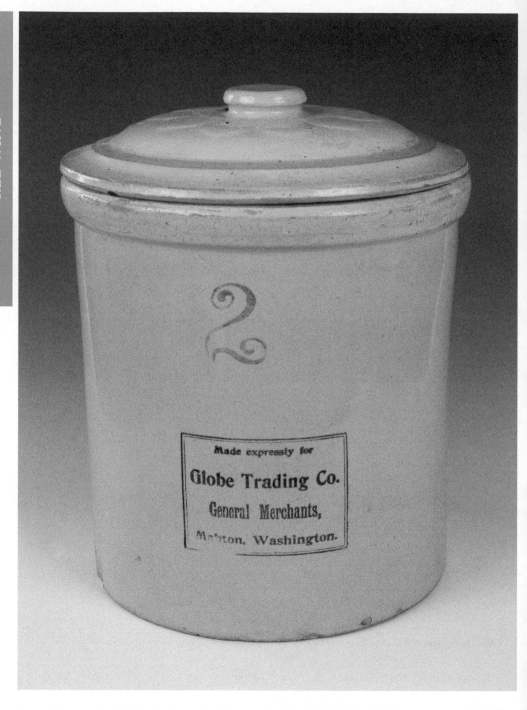

Two-gallon crock, with Washington advertising and original lid, 12" t. with lid....................$2,500

Close-up, hand-decorated butterfly and flower on a 20-gallon salt-glaze crock. .... **$2,000-$2,500, signed**

White stoneware advertising crocks, 6-1/4" and 6" t., unmarked. ....$900-$1,200 ea.

White stoneware advertising crocks, 5" and 3-3/4" t., unmarked. ....$900-$1,200 ea.

Blue and white covered butter crock in a daisy pattern,
left, 4-1/2" t. with lid, 5-1/2" dia. ....$400+

Blue and white bail-handle covered butter crock with advertising, 5-1/2" t. without handle. . **$500+**

Eighth-pint fancy jug, with
rare blue sponge decora-
tion, 2-3/4" t. ....**$1,800+**

Two-gallon white stoneware crock, with tilted birch leaves, 10" t., impressed mark, "Minnesota Stoneware Co. Red Wing, Minn." .... $70-$90

Three-gallon white stoneware crock, with tilted birch leaves and original lid, and rarely seen "Minnesota Stoneware Company" oval mark, 10-3/4" t. without lid; lid, 11" dia. ....**$900+**

Two-gallon crock, with tilted birch leaves and oval stamp with "Minnesota Stoneware Company" (spelled out, commonly found as "Co."), 12" t. with lid, otherwise unmarked. .... **$1,500+**

Four-gallon white stoneware crock, with birch leaves called "elephant ears," and original lid,
11-1/2" t. without lid... **$150+**

Five-gallon white stoneware crock, with oval and large wing, the most commonly found size for crocks and jugs...$70+

White stoneware 20-pound butter crock, with 4" wing, 7-1/2" t., 11-1/2" dia. .... **$1,000+**

White stoneware 20-pound butter crock, with hand-decorated numbers, a transitional mark
before stamping was regularly used, circa 1900, 8" t., 11-1/2" dia., raised mark on bottom,
"Minnesota Stoneware Red Wing, Minn." .... **$800-$1,000**

Transitional five-gallon crock, with hand-decorated blue-black number and "bowtie," circa 1900, the glaze on this crock is between white and tan, 13-1/4" t., unmarked ....$300+

Fifteen-gallon salt-glaze crock with cobalt decoration of "bowtie" and double leaves, circa 1890, 18-1/2" t., unmarked. (Collector Tip: The leaves seen here are precursors to the stenciled or stamped birch-leaf decoration used on white hand-thrown stoneware made just a few years later.) ....$800-$1,000

Ten-gallon crock, with Washington advertising that includes crockery. (Collector Tip: Strange as it may sound, it's unusual to find the word "crockery" on crockery.) .... **$1,500+ if perfect**

Eight-gallon transitional zinc-glaze crock, with stamped Minnesota oval and hand-decorated birch leaf .... **$3,500+**

Twelve-gallon salt-glaze crock, with large hand-decorated birch leaf pointing up............ **$2,500**

Stoneware bread crock in glossy green glaze, also found with matte Brushed Ware surface, and in tan; lid missing, 11" t., 14" dia., rare. ....**$2,800+ (as is)**

with lid .... **$4,000+**

Ten-pound butter crock with Osage, Iowa, advertising, 6-3/4" t., otherwise unmarked. **$1,500**

Three brown-top mini jugs two, with advertising and one a souvenir, each 4-1/4" t., found
unmarked and with raised "R.W.S.W. Co." ....$250+ ea.

with a high range of $800, depending on markings

White stoneware bail-handle jugs in three sizes, with advertising; from left,
6", 10" and 7-1/2" t. .... $300-$400 ea.

1915 Potters Excursion shoulder jug one gallon, 11" t... $7,000+

Two one-gallon white stoneware shoulder jugs with cobalt trim, with narrow and wide mouths, 11" and 10-1/4" t., both marked on bottom, "Minnesota Stoneware Co. Red Wing, Minn."**$375-$450 ea.**

Two white stoneware shoulder jugs one, with elaborate advertising for a Chicago liquor store.

Left, 7-1/2" t., with rare mark, "Minn. S. Co. Red Wing, Minn."...$70+

Right, 8-3/4" t., unmarked ....$300-$500

Two white stoneware shoulder jugs, with advertising; left, 10-1/2" t.; right, 8-1/2" t... **$275-$350 ea.**

Two brown-top stoneware jugs, with small red wings; left, half gallon, 9" t.; right, one gallon, wide mouth, 10-1/2" t..**$150-$225 ea.**

Half-gallon shoulder jug, with Cannon Falls, Minn., advertising, 8-1/2" t., impressed bottom mark, "Minnesota Stoneware Co. Red Wing, Minn." ....**$500+**

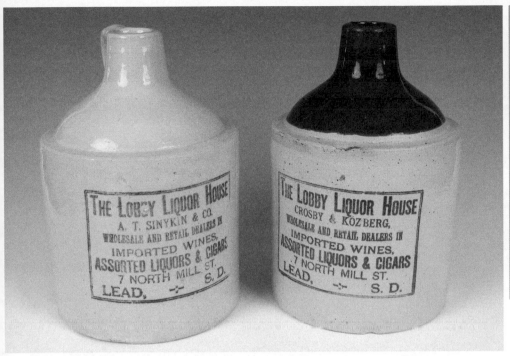

Two half-gallon shoulder jugs, one with a white top and one brown, late 19th and early 20th century, with advertising for the same liquor store in Lead, S.D., but identifying different owners, each 8-3/4" t.

White ....$500-$600

Brown..$600-$800

White stoneware refrigerator jars, three sizes, with cobalt trim, each has a raised, footed base so that the same size jars could be stacked, seen here in diameters of 4-3/4", 5-3/4", and 6-3/4". ...... **$250-$350 ea.**

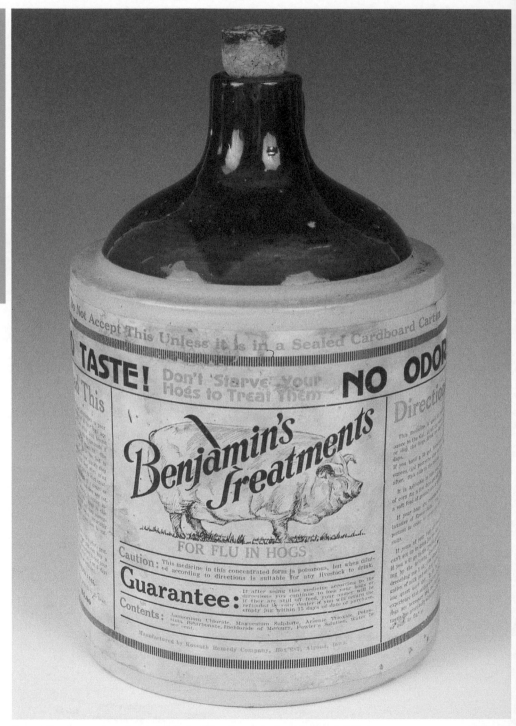

One-gallon brown-top stoneware jug, with rare original paper label, 11" t. ....$300+

Three-gallon salt-glaze "beehive" jug with elaborate "3" and stylized leaf, circa 1890, with glaze drippings known as "turkey droppings," 14" high, unmarked. **$2,000**

Five-gallon white stoneware "beehive" two-handle jug, with advertising, 17" high, rare. **$4,000**

Four-gallon salt-glaze churn, with cobalt decoration of "lazy 8" and "tornado," circa 1890, and cover in Albany slip glaze, 16" high, unmarked. ....$800-$900

Sponge-decorated paneled mixing bowls, complete set of seven, in diameters of 5", 6-1/4", 7-1/2", 8", 9", 10" and 11", unmarked except for impressed size number

5" .... **$500+**

Other sizes.... **$125-$300 ea.**

Blue and white "Greek Key" stoneware mixing bowls, complete set of seven, in sizes ranging from 6" to 12" dia., unmarked.

6" to 10" size..$125+ ea.

11" and 12" size... $250-$300 ea.

Lion planter No. 917, 13" long, also raised mark, "Red Wing USA." $400

Wide-mouth, brown-top one-gallon jug left, with raised star on bottom, 10" t. ....$75+

Dome-top one-gallon jug, with unglazed top, with raised letters, "Wm. R. Adams Microbe Killer," 10-1/2" t., unmarked..$325+

Sponge-decorated yellow ware bowls; left, two sizes, with advertising, 1930s, 7-1/2" and 5-1/2" dia.; right, Saffron Ware covered casserole with advertising, 7-1/2" dia. without handles, ink-stamped, "Red Wing Saffron Ware." .... **$300-$400 ea.**

Blue and white stoneware pitcher and basin with raised lily; pitcher, 10-1/2" t.; basin, 15-1/2" dia., unmarked..**$1,200+ set**

Sponge-decorated pitchers, three sizes, two with advertising; left, with cherry band, 8-1/2" t., $1,800+; center, 9" tall, $400+; right, squat jug, with advertising inside, "Compliments of Farmers Co-op Creamery Association—Hull, Iowa," 6-1/2" tall.................................... **$1,500+.**

Red (pink) and blue banded ribbed stoneware mixing bowls, complete set of eight, in sizes ranging from 4-1/4" to 12" diameter, unmarked.. **$90-$110 ea.**

Sand jar with lily and cattail motif, made for both Red Wing and RumRill, No. 106, 15" t., unmarked...**$800+**

Three-gallon churn-form store advertisement, with "elephant ears," with original churn cover, 14 3/8" high including lid. **$7,500**

Two-gallon churn with Utah advertising, otherwise unmarked, 12 5/8" high.......................**$4,000**

Rooster vases in Fleck Zephyr Pink, two sizes, No. 1438 (Collector Tip: Also found marked No. M1438), designed by Charles Murphy, 9-3/4" and 14" t...**$200+ ea.**

Cow and calf in bisque, small base, 5" long, 4 1/4" high **$3,000**

Two stoneware eggs, showing face of child emerging from one side and child's bare bottom emerging from other side, each also has vent hole, each 1 3/4" long. ....**$900 each**

Decorator Line footed oval bowl No. M3017, 13 1/2" wide...$225

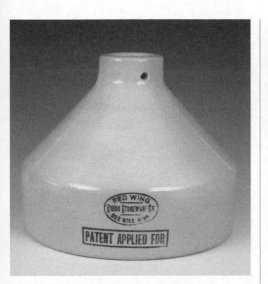

White stoneware Christmas tree holder,
rarely found in colored glaze,
8 1/2" high. **$800**

Hotel-size spittoon, with blue sponge
decoration, 6" high x 9 1/2"
diameter.. **$2,000**

**Four-gallon white stoneware water cooler
without gallon mark**, lid impressed 3W,
12 3/4" high without lid, lid 9 1/2"
diameter.................................. **$800-$1,000**

**Unusual three-gallon stoneware ice
water cooler**, in a glaze between tan
and white, Albany slip interior, 11 3/4"
high... **$900-$1,250**

Figure of a centaur No. 1123, in Bronze-Tan Engobe with yellow and black decoration, 9 1/4" high **$1,000**

Planter figure of centaur, No. 914, in glossy bronze, 12" high. **$1,200**

**Statue titled "Woman in the Hand" No.
1178**, designed by Charles Murphy,
1942, one of only three known,
12" high. **$4,000**

**"Woman with Two Tubes" double bud vase No.
1175**, designed by Charles Murphy, 1942, 10
1/2" high. ....**$1,200-$1,500 in these colors**

**Baseball batter and catcher figurines
designed by Charles Murphy**, Nos. 1176
and 1177, batter holds wooden bat, 8"
and 7" high. .... **$600 each**

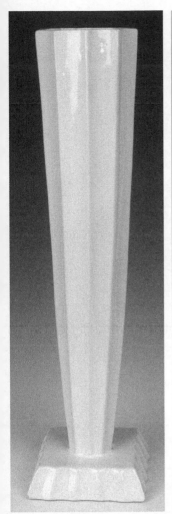

Vase No. 165, early
1930s, 18" high....... **$500**

"Cherub" Brushed Ware vase in "cement" finish, also found
in green, No. 131, ink-stamped in circle: "Red Wing Union
Stoneware Co.—Red Wing, Minn.," 12" high. **$550**

"Rocket" vase in Orange and Bay glaze (also called Scarlet and Bay), No. 425, 8 1/2" high, rare. **$650**

Lamp base No. 806, (based on No. 200 vase) in Nokomis glaze, 9 1/2" high. .... **$800-$1,200**

Vase No. 3019 in burnt orange crystalline glaze, designed by Charles Murphy, raised mark, "Red Wing U.S.A. 3019," 13" high x 13" diameter.................... **$500**

Candlesticks No. 233C in Nokomis glaze, part of console set with Bowl No. 233, each 7" high............................ **$1,000 pr.**

Sponge-decorated umbrella stand, 17-3/4" tall, unmarked.................................. **$1,800-$2,200**

Belle Kogan planter called "The Nymphs," No. B2500, part of the "Deluxe Line," 16-1/2" w. x 6-3/4" t. ....**$180+**

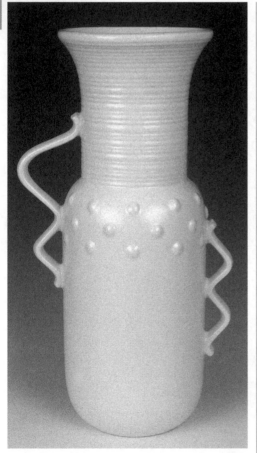

Vase No. 1212, 1940s, 16" high..............**$450**

Floor vase No. 145, in a glaze called "Ripe Wheat," 15" t. ....**$550+**

Redware

RED EARTHENWARE POTTERY was made in the American colonies from the late 1600s. Bowls, crocks, and all types of utilitarian wares were turned out in great abundance to supplement the pewter and handmade treenware. The ready availability of the clay, the same used in making bricks and roof tiles, accounted for the vast production. The lead-glazed redware retained its reddish color, although a variety of colors could be obtained by adding various metals to the glaze. Interesting effects occurred accidentally through unsuspected impurities in the clay or uneven temperatures in the firing kiln, which sometimes resulted in streaks or mottled splotches.

Redware pottery was seldom marked by the maker.

Pennsylvania redware spaniel bank, attributed to George Wagner, 6-3/4" h..............**$1,541**

Pennsylvania redware bank, dated 1862, with dog finial and manganese splotching, inscribed on base AP 1862 PLM, 5-1/2" h. **$4,266**

Chester County, Pennsylvania redware crock, late 19th/early 20th century, inscribed Henry Schofield, 7-3/4". **$889**

Miniature Pennsylvania redware pie plate with yellow slip clef decoration, 19th century, 4-3/8" dia. **$1,007**

Pennsylvania redware charger with yellow slip wavy line decoration, 19th century, 10-3/4" dia. **$790**

Southeast Pennsylvania redware covered bowl with extensive slip star and tulip decoration, circa 1800, 5" h. x 8-1/2" dia. **$5,214**

Pennsylvania redware colander with slip band and zigzag decoration, 19th century, 3-3/4" h. x 8-3/4" w. **$2,607**

Pennsylvania redware loaf dish, with slip wavy line decoration, 19th century, 9-1/2" l. x 12-3/4" w **$1,304**

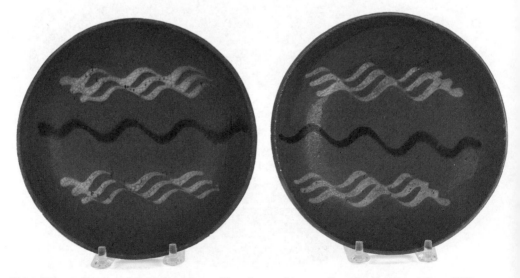

Pair of Pennsylvania redware pie plates, with yellow and brown slip wavy line decoration, 19th century, 6-7/8" dia... **$1,541**

Pennsylvania redware bird rattle,
19th century, attributed to
William Maize, New Berlin,
Union County, Pennsylvania,
3" h. **$1,778**

York County, Pennsylvania redware figure of seated dog clutching basket of fruit, 19th century, attributed to Jesiah Shorb, West Manheim Township, York County, Pennsylvania, 4-1/4" h............................. **$4,029**

Pennsylvania redware pie plate with slip tulip decoration, 19th century, attributed to Dryville Pottery, 8-1/2" dia. **$1,896**

Pennsylvania redware pie plate, with green slip X decoration, 19th century, 8-1/4" dia. **$711**

Pennsylvania redware pie plate with slip tulip decoration, 19th century, 8" dia. **$2,370**

Pennsylvania redware wall pocket with manganese splash decoration, 19th century, 7-1/2" h. x 5-1/4" w **$267**

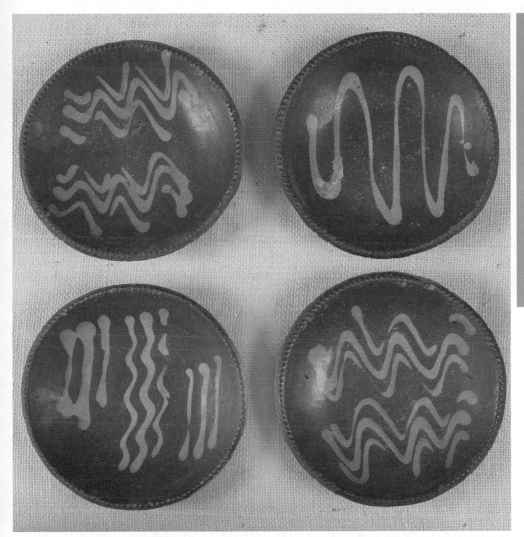

Four Pennsylvania slip decorated redware plates, mid-19th century, 7-1/4" dia. $948

American redware pie plate with yellow slip ABC, 19th century, 10" dia.................................$889

Rockingham Wares

THE MARQUIS OF Rockingham first established an earthenware pottery in the Yorkshire district of England around 1745, and it was occupied afterwards by various potters. The well-known mottled brown Rockingham glaze was introduced about 1788 by the Brameld Brothers and became immediately popular. It was during the 1820s that the production of true porcelain began at the factory, and it continued to be made until the firm closed in 1842. Since that time the so-called Rockingham glaze has been used by various potters in England and the United States, including some famous wares produced in Bennington, Vermont. Very similar glazes were also used by potteries in other areas of the United States including Ohio and Indiana, but only wares specifically attributed to Bennington should use that name.

Inkwell, figural, modeled as a woman reclining asleep on an oblong rockwork base, yellowware with overall mottled dark brown Rockingham glaze, several old edge chips, reportedly made by the Larkin Bros. Company, Newell, West Virginia, ca. 1850-80, 3 7/8" h. **$101**

Jug, advertising-type, figural, model of a walking pig, impressed on the rear "Bieler's Ronny Club," yellowware with a mottled brown Rockingham glaze, original white porcelain stopper marked "Brookfield Rye Bieler," reportedly from Cincinnati, Ohio, ca. 1880-1900, 9 1/2" l., 5 1/4" h **$1,232**

Flask, flattened ovoid shape tapering to a fluted neck & ringed mouth, molded on one side with the American Eagle & on the other with a morning glory vine, dark brown Rockingham glaze, No. G11-19, several old glaze chips, ca. 1840-60 .... **$308**

Model of a lion, recumbent animal raised on a deep rectangular base, mottled dark brown glaze, restoration to minor surface roughness along base, ca. 1860, 6 3/4 x 9" **$303**

Rogers (John) Groups

CAST PLASTER AND terra cotta figure groups made by John Rogers of New York City in the mid- to late 19th century were highly popular in their day. Many offer charming vignettes of Victorian domestic life or events of historic or literary importance, and those in good condition are prized today.

"The Traveling Magician," an old man & a small boy seated below a raised stand with the magician who pulls a rabbit out of a top hat, a young tambourine girl asleep beside the platform, titled on the front, base marked "Patented Nov 27, 1877," some restoration with new patina, 23" h. **$3,565**

"The Council of War," President Lincoln seated reading a document & flanked by General Grant & Secretary of State Stanton, version with Stanton wiping his glasses over Lincoln's shoulder, patent-dated 1868, some minor chips, 24" h **$2,645**

"The Council of War," President Lincoln seated reading a document & flanked by General Grant & Secretary of State Stanton, patent-dated 1868, flaking to the surface & very minor chips, 24 1/2" h.... **$1,955**

"Rip Van Winkle on The Mountain," figure of Rip holding his rifle & holding back his dog & standing over a mountain gnome with a keg on his knee, old repaint with some restoration, 9 x 9 1/2", 21" h. ... **$460**

"Parting Promise," the figure of a young man about to start on a journey standing & placing an engagement ring on her finger, molded title on the front of the oval base "Provenance," some surface chipping around base, 22" h... **$633**

"Is It So Nominated in The Bond?," a scene from Shakespeare's "The Merchant of Venice," including Antonio Bassanio, Portia & Shylock, some restoration with a new patina, 12 1/2 x 19 1/2", 23" h **$288**

"The Wounded Scout," a standing black man in ragged clothes supporting a wounded Union soldier, round base, some chipping & restoration, 8 1/2" d., 22 3/4" h.................. **$690**

"Rip Van Winkle Returned," figure of Rip in ragged clothes standing in the gateway of his ruined old homestead, new patina, some restoration, 8 x 9", 21" h...**$518**

Rookwood

MARIA LONGWORTH NICHOLS founded Rookwood Pottery in 1880. The name, she later reported, paid homage to the many crows (rooks) on her father's estate and was also designed to remind customers of Wedgwood. Production began on Thanksgiving Day 1880 when the first kiln was drawn.

Rookwood's earliest productions demonstrated a continued reliance on European precedents and the Japanese aesthetic. Although the firm offered a variety of wares (Dull Glaze, Cameo, and Limoges for example), it lacked a clearly defined artistic identity. With the introduction of what became known as its "standard glaze" in 1884, Rookwood inaugurated a period in which the company won consistent recognition for its artistic merit and technical innovation.

Rookwood's first decade ended on a high note when the company was awarded two gold medals: one at the Exhibition of American Art Industry in Philadelphia and another later in the year at the Exposition Universelle in Paris. Significant, too, was Maria Longworth Nichols' decision to transfer her interest in the company to William W. Taylor, who had been the firm's manager since 1883. In May 1890, the board of a newly reorganized Rookwood Pottery Co. purchased "the real estate, personal property, goodwill, patents, trade-marks... now the sole property of William W. Taylor" for $40,000.

Under Taylor's leadership, Rookwood was transformed from a fledgling startup to successful business that expanded throughout the following decades to meet rising demand.

Throughout the 1890s, Rookwood continued to attract critical notice as it kept the tradition of innovation alive. Taylor rolled out three new glaze lines—Iris, Sea Green and Aerial Blue—from late 1894 into early 1895.

At the Paris Exposition in 1900, Rookwood cemented its reputation by winning the Grand Prix, a feat largely due to the favorable reception of the new Iris glaze and its variants.

Over the next several years, Rookwood's record of achievement at domestic and international exhibitions remained unmatched.

Throughout the 1910s, Rookwood continued in a similar vein and began to more thoroughly embrace the simplified aesthetic promoted by many Arts and Crafts figures. Production of the Iris line, which had been instrumental in the firm's success at the Paris Exposition in 1900, ceased around 1912. Not only did the company abandon its older, fussier underglaze wares, but the newer lines the pottery introduced also trended toward simplicity.

Unfortunately, the collapse of the stock market in October 1929 and ensuing economic depression dealt Rookwood a blow from which it did not recover. The Great Depression took a toll on the company and eventually led to bankruptcy in April 1941.

Rookwood's history might have ended there were it not for the purchase of the firm by a group of investors led by automobile dealer Walter E. Schott and his wife, Margaret. Production started once again. In the years that followed, Rookwood changed hands a number of times before being moved to Starkville, Mississippi, in 1960. It finally closed its doors there in 1967.

Rookwood Marks

Rookwood employed a number of marks on the bottom of its vessels that denoted everything from the shape number, to the size, date, and color of the body, to the type of glaze to be used.

COMPANY MARKS

1880-1882
In this early period, a number of marks were used to identify the wares.

1. "ROOKWOOD" followed by the initials of the decorator, painted in gold. This is likely the earliest mark, and though the wares are not dated, it seems to have been discontinued by 1881-1882.
2. "ROOKWOOD / POTTERY. / [DATE] CIN. O." In Marks of American Potters (1904), Edwin AtLee Barber states, "The most common marks prior to 1882 were the name of the pottery and the date of manufacture, which were painted or incised on the base of each piece by the decorator."
3. "R. P. C. O. M. L. N." These initials stand for "Rookwood Pottery, Cincinnati, Ohio, Maria Longworth Nichols," and were either painted or incised on the base.
4. Kiln and crows stamp. Barber notes that in 1881 and 1882, the trademark designed by the artist Henry Farny was printed beneath the glaze.
5. Anchor stamp: Barber notes that this mark is "one of the rarest."
6. Oval stamp.
7. Ribbon or banner stamp: According to Barber, "In 1882 a special mark was used on a trade piece... the letters were impressed in a raised ribbon.
8. Ribbon or banner stamp II: A simpler variation of the above stamp, recorded by Herbert Peck.

1883-1886
1. Stamped name and date.
2. Impressed kiln: Appears only in 1883.

1886-1960
Virtually all of the pieces feature the conjoined RP monogram. Pieces fired in the anniversary kilns carry a special kiln-shaped mark with the number of the anniversary inside of it.

1955
A diamond-shaped mark that reads: "ROOKWOOD / 75th / ANNIVERSARY / POTTERY" was printed on wares.

1960-1967
Occasionally pieces are marked "ROOKWOOD POTTERY / STARKVILLE MISS"; from 1962 to 1967 a small "®" occasionally follows the monogram.

DATE MARKS

Unlike many of their contemporaries, Rookwood seems very early on to have adopted a method of marking its pottery that was accurate and easy to understand.

From 1882-1885, the company impressed the date, often with the company name, in block letters (see 1883-86, No. 1).

Although the date traditionally given for the conjoined RP mark is June 23, 1886, this marks the official introduction of the monogram rather than the first use.

Stanley Burt, in his record of the Rookwood

at the Cincinnati Museum noted two pieces from 1883 (Nos. 2 and 3) that used the monogram. The monogram was likely designed by Alfred Brennan, since it first appears on his work.

From 1886 on, the date of the object was coded in the conjoined "RP" monogram.

1886: conjoined "RP" no additional flame marks.

1887-1900: conjoined "RP" with a flame added for each subsequent year. Thus, a monogram with seven flames would represent 1893.

1900-1967: conjoined "RP" with 14 flames and a Roman numeral below the mark to indicate the year after 1900. Thus, a monogram with 14 flames and the letters "XXXVI" below it signifies 1936.

CLAY-TYPE MARKS

From 1880 until around 1895, Rookwood used a number of different colored bodies for production and marked each color with a letter code. These letters were impressed and usually found grouped together with the shape number, sometimes following it, but more often below it.

The letter "S" is a particularly vexing designation since the same initial was used for two other unrelated designations. As a result, it is particularly important to take into account the relative position of the impressed letter.

R = Red

Y = Yellow

S = Sage

G = Ginger

W = White

O = Olive

P = From 1915 on Rookwood used an impressed "P" (often found perpendicular to the orientation of the other marks) to denote the soft porcelain body.

SIZE AND SHAPE MARKS

Almost all Rookwood pieces have a shape code consisting of three or four numbers, followed by a size letter. "A" denotes the largest available size, "F" is the smallest. According to Herbert Peck, initial designs were given a "C" or "D" designation so that variations could be made. Not every shape model, however, features a variation in every size.

GLAZE MARKS

In addition to marking the size, shape and year of the piece, Rookwood's decorators also used a number of letters to designate the type of glaze to be used upon a piece. Generally speaking, these marks are either incised or impressed.

"S" = Standard Glaze to be used. (Incised.)

"L" = Decorators would often incise an "L" near their monogram to indicate that the light variation of the Standard Glaze was to be used. (Incised.)

"SG" = Sea Green Glaze to be used.

"Z" = from 1900-1904 designated any piece with a Mat Glaze. (Impressed.)

"W" = Iris Glaze to be used.

"V" = Vellum Glaze to be used; variations include "GV" for Green Vellum and "YV" for Yellow Vellum.

OTHER MARKS

"S" = If found away from the shape number, this generally indicates a piece that was specially thrown at the pottery in the presence of visitors. (Impressed.)

"S" = If this precedes the shape number than it denotes a piece that was specifically thrown and decorated from a sketch with a corresponding number. Because of the size and quality of pieces this letter has been found on, this probably signifies a piece made specifically for an important exhibition.

"X" = Rookwood used a wheel ground "x" to indicate items that were not of first quality. There has been some suggestion that decorators and salespersons might have conspired to "x" certain pieces that they liked, since this designation would reduce the price. Since there are a number of items that appear to have been marked for no apparent reason, there may be some truth to this idea. Unfortunately, as this idea has gained credence, many pieces with obvious flaws have been listed as "marked x for no apparent reason," and collectors should be cautious.

Generally, the mark reduces the value and appeal of the piece. Peck describes a variation of the "x" that resembles an asterisk as indicating a piece that could be given away to employees.

"T" = An impressed T that precedes a shape number indicates a trial piece.

s = These shapes (crescents, diamonds, and triangles) are used to indicate a glaze trial.

"K1" and "K3"= c. 1922, used for matching teacups and saucers

"SC"= Cream and Sugar sets, c. 1946-50

"2800"= Impressed on ship pattern tableware

SOME LINES OF NOTE

AERIAL BLUE: Commercially, this line was among the least successful. As a result, there are a limited number of pieces, and this scarcity has increased their values relative to other wares.

BLACK IRIS: This line is among the most sought after by collectors, commanding significantly more than examples of similar size and design in virtually any other glaze. In fact, the current auction record for Rookwood—over $350,000—was set in 2004 for a Black Iris vase decorated by Kitaro Shirayamadani in 1900.

IRIS: Uncrazed examples are exceptionally rare, with large pieces featuring conventional designs commanding the highest prices. Smaller, naturalistically painted examples, though still desirable, are gradually becoming more affordable for the less advanced collector.

PRODUCTION WARE: This commercial and mass-produced artware is significantly less expensive than pieces in most other lines.

STANDARD GLAZE: These wares peaked in the 1970s-1980s, and the market has remained thin in recent years, but regardless of the state of the market, examples of superlative quality, including those with silver overlay, have found their places in the finest of collections.

WAX MAT: This is among the most affordable of the hand-decorated lines.

Maria L. Nichols, two-handled Limoges-style vase, Cincinnati, 1882, stamped 1882/MLN with anchor, 10 1/2" x 6 3/4"...$1,750

▶ **Limoges-style whiskey jug with clouds**, grasses and fired on gold, thought to be the work of Maria Longworth Nichols in 1882, marks include Rookwood in block letters, date and initials MLN in black on bottom appear to be fired on, restoration to handle, 8 1/4" high................. **$2,000**

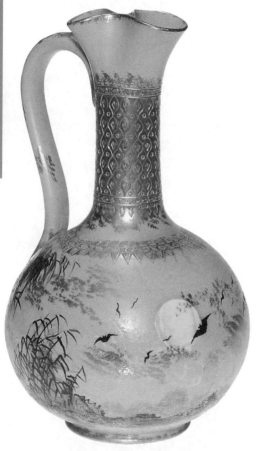

Dull Finish ewer decorated by Rookwood's founder, Maria Longworth Nichols, in 1882, incised design around top and bottom of vessel with spooky landscape showing bats flying through a sky illuminated by full moon with somber landscape below, impressed Rookwood in block letters with date, shape number 101 and Y for yellow clay body, incised with Nichols' monogram, handle looks professionally and invisibly reattached to body, 12 1/8" high............................ **$1,300**

Gardenware Faience statue depicting young lad grasping fountain, sitting on grapes and leaves, impressed on base "Rookwood Faience 3062 Y," 19 1/4" high .. **$1,800**

Dull Finish pitcher with butterflies, A. R. Valentien, 1886, impressed Rookwood symbol with date, shape 308 X, and Y for yellow clay, incised with artist's monogram, professional restoration to rim and upper portion of handle where it attaches to body, 19 3/4" high. **$1,500**

Wax Mat lamp vase decorated by John Dee Wareham, Clydesdale horse, trees and grasses, done in 1938 allegedly for Augustus Busch of Anheuser Busch Brewing Co., impressed Rookwood insignia, date and S to indicate Special shape, Wareham's cypher in blue slip, factory sticker indicates this is a Decorated Wax Mat with original price of $50; cast hole to bottom of vessel, without crazing and in excellent original condition, 14" high. Accompanying newspaper article indicates vase was made for "Gussie" Busch (1899-1989), whose brewery utilized Clydesdal horses to pull beer wagons during parades. **$1,000**

Standard Glaze pillow vase decorated in 1897 by William P. McDonald, portrait of gentleman, purportedly that of Judson Harmon, governor of Ohio from 1909 to 1913 and Attorney General under Grover Cleveland, when this portrait was done; impressed Rookwood logo with date and shape 707 X, incised with McDonald's monogram, fine crazing and some scratches, 11 5/8" high. **$1,200**

Wax Mat vase with Greek key pattern, designed by Wilhelmina Rhem, 1945, flame mark XLV/ 6696/WR, 11-1/2" x 9". **$1,000**

Ed Diers, scenic Vellum plaque, "Mountain Stream," Cincinnati, 1917, flame mark XVII/V and original price, mounted in original frame (painted), 8 1/2" x 11".....................................**$8,125**

Pair of Union Terminal bookends, designed by Arthur Conant, cast in 1933 and covered with Ivory Mat Glaze, impressed Rookwood symbol, date and shape 6378, uncrazed with fine detail, excellent original condition, 4 1/2" x 7"...**$6,250**

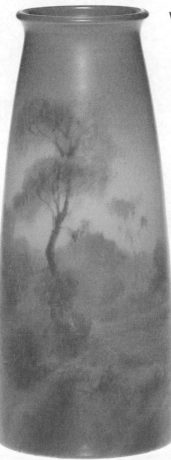

Vellum landscape vase decorated by Fred Rothenbusch in 1916, trees above misty valley, impressed Rookwood symbol, date, shape 1660 D, and V for Vellum, incised with Rothenbusch's monogram, fine overall crazing, 9 5/8" high **$1,200**

Standard Glaze ewer decorated in 1888 by Kataro Shirayamadani with dragon stretching around shoulder of vessel, impressed Rookwood symbol with date, shape number 62, and an S for sage clay body, incised with L for Light Standard Glaze, Japanese script signature, light crazing and restoration to chip beneath spout, 9 1/8" high. This ewer was decorated during Shirayamadani's second year at Rookwood **$1,300**

Large Standard Glaze plaque, Old Master style, by Grace Young in 1903, depicting two Dutch gentlemen seated at a table, after a similar work by Jan de Bray, impressed on rear with large Rookwood insignia, date and shape X 1188 X, incised "After de Bray" and with Young's monogram, pinpoint burst glaze bubbles, oversprayed, 10" x 14 3/8". **$3,500**

Rookwood advertising sign with dark blue rook perched on branch with green leaves and name of pottery, made in 1915, impressed on back with Rookwood insignia, date and shape 1622, minor edge and corner chips, 4 1/4" x 8 1/2". **$5,250**

Tall Black Opal Glaze vase decorated in 1925 by Lorinda Epply, trailing flowers, impressed Rookwood symbol, date and shape 2785, incised with Epply's monogram, uncrazed with restoration to drill hole in base, minor glaze burn to shoulder, 13 5/8" high. **$1,500**

Vellum vase decorated in 1924 by Fred Rothenbush, tree-lined lake around circumference of vase, impressed Rookwood symbol, date and shape 1356 E, excellent original condition without crazing, two tiny glaze skips at base, 7 1/2" high. **$1,600**

Spanish water jug crafted by Albert Valentien in 1883, impressed designs around top and near bottom of vase, painted scene with large beetle and dragonfly in treed landscape, fired-on gold, impressed Rookwood name in block letters, date, shape 108, kiln mark, Y to indicate yellow clay, incised with artist's monogram, no crazing, tiny "in-the-making" indentations around foot, 9" high. $2,100

Dull Finish vase decorated by A.R. Valentien in 1884, incised patterns in bands around top and bottom, glazed gold, central portion of vessel encircled with landscape of birds flying above Oriental grasses, impressed Rookwood in block letters with date, shape 162 B, and a Y to indicate yellow clay, incised with artist's cipher, 10 1/2" high..**$2,200**

Dull Finish flat-sided jug decorated by Edward Pope Cranch in 1884, one side with quartet of owls perched on branch, opposite side with trio of buzzards on branches, incised and outlined in black against brown ground, impressed Rookwood in block letters, date, shape number 85, G to indicate ginger clay, artist's last name, without crazing, fine original condition, 6 1/2" high. **$2,100**

Elegant Iris Glaze scenic vase with sailboats seen through tall trees, done in 1911 by Kataro Shirayamadani, people visible in boats with peach-colored sky, marks include Rookwood logo, date, shape number 1652 B, impressed V, wheel ground X and incised cypher of artist, un-crazed, several small glaze flaws at base account for X, professionally and invisibly restored, 14" high. **$9,750**

Vellum landscape plaque painted by Carl Schmidt in 1919, stream flowing between two wooded banks, trees reflected in water with hills in background, impressed Rookwood symbol and date, typewritten label identifying work as "Evening Glow, C. Schmidt," Rookwood circular paster on backing, fine, overall crazing, excellent original condition, original frame, 9 3/8" x 12 1/4"...**$5,000**

Porcelain covered box decorated by Sara Sax in 1930, stylized flowers and geometric details in Art Deco tradition, impressed on base with Rookwood symbol, date, shape 6205 and fan-shaped esoteric mark, artist's monogram in black slip, no crazing, excellent original condition, 5" high. x 7" x 4 1/2". **$2,300**

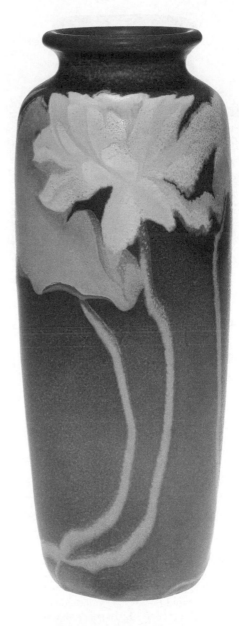

Rare Standard Glaze full-length portrait of geisha by Grace Young in 1900, woman stands with fan in her right hand, marks include Rookwood logo, date, shape number 907 D and incised monogram of Young, faint crazing, excellent original condition, 10 1/4" high **$7,750**

Painted Mat vase decorated by Harriet Wilcox in 1904, lotus flower stems and pads against dark background, impressed Rookwood symbol, date and shape 904 C, Wilcox's monogram in black slip, no crazing, excellent original condition, 12 1/4" high **$12,500**

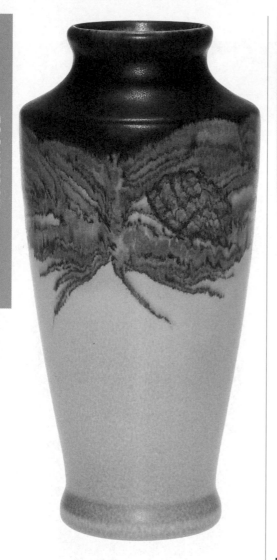

Decorated mat glaze vase, produced by
Elizabeth Lincoln in 1923, pine boughs
with cones around circumference of vessel, impressed Rookwood symbol, date
and shape number 1920, monogrammed
by artist in black slip, uncrazed, excellent
original condition, 9 3/8" high............ **$1,200**

**Limoges-style vase decorated by Albert
Valentien in 1883**, two storks on front
and another on back, standing in marshy
terrain with grasses and trees, fired-on
gold, impressed Rookwood in block letters, date, G for ginger clay, kiln mark on
bottom, signed by artist in slip on side,
restoration to foot, some wear to gilding,
28 1/4" high. **$3,000**

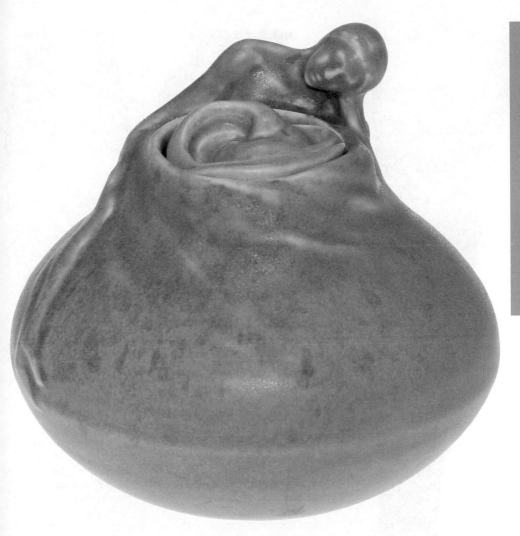

Three-piece inkwell modeled by Anna Valentien in 1902 with nude draped around opening, mat green glaze, impressed with Rookwood insignia, date and shape 156 Z, incised with artist monogram, ink cup has chip to one edge, tiny nick to interior edge that supports ink cup, both unseen when lid is in place, 4 1/4" high... **$1,200**

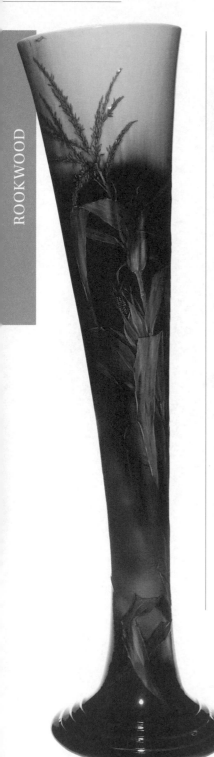

Rookwood Scenic Vellum vase painted in 1928 by E.T. Hurley, areas of water bracketed by birch trees with stands of timber in background, marks include Rookwood logo, date, shape number 614 C, incised V for Vellum glaze, Hurley's incised intitials, uncrazed, 13" high, accompanying original Rookwood sales brochure with a sticker from William Kendrick's Sons Jewelers in Louisville, retailer from whom consignor's family purchased vase in late 1920s. **$5,000**

Dull Finish vase decorated in 1887 by A.R. Valentien, bird seated on tree branch looking upward, impressed with Rookwood monogram, which indicates date, shape 30 B and an "S" for sage clay, incised with artist's symbol, excellent original condition, 12" h. **$750**

◄ **Tall Standard Glaze vase decorated by A.R. Valentien in 1890 with "Waving Corn" design from base to rim**, impressed Rookwood emblem, date, shape 292 XX, and W for white clay body, incised L for Light Standard Glaze and artist's monogram, restoration at rim and to two small nicks at side, completely oversprayed, 40" high. **$1,600**

Yellow Vellum vase decorated with yellow chrysanthemums on brown ground by Lorinda Epply in 1929, impressed Rookwood symbol, date, shape 546 C, and V for Vellum, incised with Y for Yellow Vellum, artist's monogram, uncrazed, excellent original condition, 9 5/8" high. **$2,000**

Decorated mat glaze vase encircled with white and blue irises against brick red ground, work of John Wesley Pullman in 1929, impressed Rookwood symbol, date and shape 900 B, artist's monogram in black slip, great original condition with no crazing, 10 1/2" high. **$2,600**

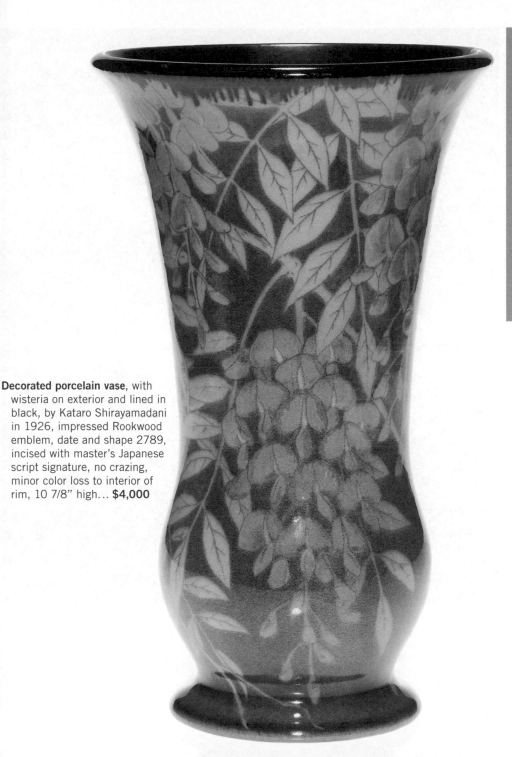

Decorated porcelain vase, with wisteria on exterior and lined in black, by Kataro Shirayamadani in 1926, impressed Rookwood emblem, date and shape 2789, incised with master's Japanese script signature, no crazing, minor color loss to interior of rim, 10 7/8" high... **$4,000**

Rare Dull Finish plaque decorated by M. A. Daly in 1896 with portrait of cavalier, done in Old Master style, reverse of plaque bears incised menu for 1896 meeting of Cincinnati Art Club, proferring "Cream of Celery Soup, Olives, Pickles, Broiled Quails (sic), Stewed Potatoes, Roquefort and Camembert Cheese and Coffee"; signed "M.A. Daly '96" in lower right corner of front and incised "MENU C.A.C. 1896" along with menu components on back, without crazing and in excellent original condition in wooden frame, 6 3/8" x 4 1/2"...................**$2,600**

Iris Glaze vase decorated by Carl Schmidt in 1905 with mushrooms encircling vessel, impressed Rookwood symbol, date and shape 900 E, incised with W for white (Iris) glaze, Schmidt's monogram, fine, overall crazing, excellent original condition, 8 7/8" high. **$3,200**

Standard Glaze cache pot, decorated by Ed Abel in 1893 with wildflowers front and rear, impressed with Rookwood symbol, which indicates date, shape 519 and a "W" for white clay body, incised with artist's monogram, fine light crazing, excellent original condition, 5-1/2" h. **$300**

Dull Finish vase decorated in 1886 by Albert Valentien, two small birds flying around branch of tree, band of gold encircling vessel at shoulder, impressed Rookwood in block letters, with date, shape 117 C and a "Y" to indicate yellow clay body, excellent original condition, 8-1/4" h...**$500**

Dull Finish (Smear Glaze) pitcher decorated by Albert Valentien in 1884 in Chaplet style, incised clouds and flowers, clouds outlined in gold and colored brown, impressed Rookwood in block letters, date, a "G" for ginger clay and a kiln mark, Cincinnati Art Museum numbers in red, artist monogram in black slip, excellent original condition, 8-1/8" h. This item sold as Lot 281 in the historic Glover Collection Auction in 1991..........**$700**

Rare Decorated Porcelain scenic vase constructed by Arthur Conant in 1921, thatch-roofed cottage near gnarled cherry trees with pink blossoms beneath blue sky, impressed Rookwood symbol, date and shape 925 C, incised with Conant's monogram, beautiful original condition with no crazing, 10 1/2" high......................**$6,750**

Ballerina flower holder designed by Louise Abel, cast in 1923, Mat gray green glaze with some crystals, impressed with Rookwood logo, date and shape 2538, wheel ground X, two tiny glaze nicks at base, 6-7/8" h. **$180**

Perfume jug decorated by Harriet Wenderoth in 1882 with carved flowers and leaves, green high glaze, impressed Rookwood in block letters, with date, shape 61 and a kiln mark, incised with artist's mark, light crazing, excellent original condition, 4-3/4" h. **$250**

Early Standard Glaze cream pitcher decorated by Martin Rettig in 1885 with a butterfly on one side and Oriental grasses on the other, impressed Rookwood in block letters, with date, shape 79 and an "S" for sage clay body, incised with Rettig's cipher, fine overall crazing, excellent original condition, 3" h. **$250**

Calendar holder made during the 1920s, Mat blue glaze, impressed only with Rookwood symbol, excellent original condition, accompanied by original perpetual calendar insert, 6-3/4" h. **$425**

Rare Rookwood production vase designed by Shirayamadani, produced in 1910, green over brown mat glazes, embossed lotus blossoms and flowers with egret perched on one pad, marks include company logo, date and shape number 1354, excellent original condition with no crazing, 11" high. **$1,100**

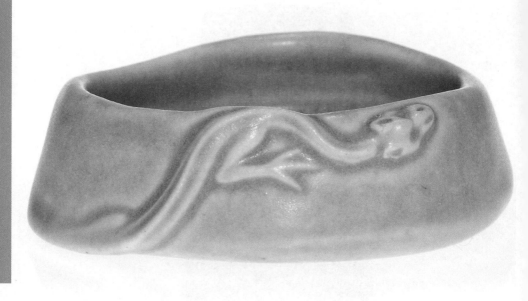

Mat green bowl with lizard crawling up side, Shirayamadani design, cast in 1904, impressed with Rookwood symbol, date and shape 630 Z, excellent original condition, 1" x 3". $325

Petite dragon bowl designed by Shirayamadani, cast in 1905, yellow Mat Glaze with some red hazing, impressed with Rookwood logo, date and shape 1080, excellent original condition with small, stray glaze spot, 1" x 3". $425

Decorated Mat Glaze vase by Lisbeth Lincoln in 1925, large chrysanthemums, impressed
Rookwood symbol, date, shape 614 B, triangular-shaped esoteric mark, artist's monogram in
black slip, no crazing, excellent condition, 14 7/8" high. **$2,000**

ROOKWOOD

Rare Iris glaze plaque depicting four-masted ship near Kennebuck, Maine, by Sturgis Laurence in 1903, large ship sailing past domed-shaped island while other vessels, tiny on horizon, sail and steam past, plaque is signed SL in lower left corner and marked on back with large Rookwood logo, date, notation X1168X, and incised notation "Mouth of Kennebuck Sturgis Laurence," uncrazed, 1/8" nick at top edge of tile, most likely factory, 10 1/8" x 14 3/8" **$23,000**

Dull Finish vase with incised leaves by Nettie Wenderoth, circa 1881, incised with artist's monogram and notation Rookwood Pottery in script, decoration outlined in gold, the name Collins and a monogram, both in gold slip, are also on base, excellent original condition, 7" h. **$300**

Rookwood Butterfat glaze vase painted by Janet Harris in 1931, possible repeating pattern of elephants, gray glaze, marks include Rookwood logo, date, shape number 6098 and Harris's monogram in black slip, uncrazed, 4 5/8" high. $1,100

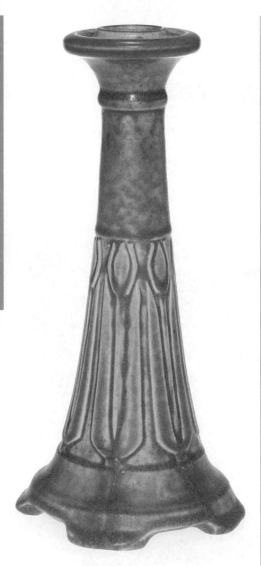

Designed Crystal vase decorated by Flora King in 1946 with horse standing in field, impressed with Rookwood symbol, date and shape 6292 C, incised with number 252 and King's initials, overall crazing, excellent original condition, 7-1/2" h...... **$475**

Production candlestick encircled with tulips, cast in 1910, brown over green Mat Glaze, impressed with Rookwood symbol, date, a "V" for Vellum body, and shape number 1830, small chip at base, 10" h.. **$150**

Standard Glaze tyg decorated by Matt Daly in 1894 with portrait of a laughing man on front and woven basket on rear, impressed with Rookwood symbol, date, shape 659 and a "W" for white clay, incised with artist's monogram, fine, light crazing, overspray indicative of restoration, 8" h. **$300**

Decorated mat glaze vase with tall plants with red flowers going around vessel, by Lisbeth Lincoln in 1922, impressed Rookwood symbol, date and shape 614 F, artist's monogram in black slip, no crazing, excellent original condition, 6 3/4" high **$1,300**

Dull Finish lidded box decorated by Albert Valentien in 1882 with beetles flying around Oriental style branches with gold accents, impressed Rookwood in block letters, with 1882 date, shape 21 and a "Y" for yellow clay body, artist's monogram in black slip, label identifying this as lot 0976 from historic Glover Collection Auction in June, 1991, line to lid and crazing confined to interior, 3" x 5"........ **$500**

Glaze effect vase made in 1939, crystalline green over brown high glaze, impressed with Rookwood logo, date and an "s" to indicate special shape, fine original condition, 5" h. **$650**

Early vase decorated by Alfred Laurens Brennan in 1885, bird in flight above Oriental grasses, Limoges style, impressed Rookwood in block letters with date, shape 126 C and an "R" for red clay, incised with Brennan's monogram, fine light crazing, excellent original condition, 9-1/2" h **$300**

Standard Glaze ewer decorated by William McDonald in 1891, with hawthorn blossoms, impressed with Rookwood symbol, which provides date, shape 527 D, and a "W" for white clay, incised with an "L" for Light Standard Glaze and artist's monogram, fine overall crazing, 10" h...................... **$400**

Limoges style pitcher decorated in 1885 by Albert R. Valentien, trio of birds flying beneath clouds and above Oriental grasses, impressed Rookwood in block letters with date, shape number 56, small kiln mark, a "G" for ginger clay, incised with decorator's monogram, fine light crazing, restoration to chip at rim, 9-1/2" h............ **$400**

Pelican ash receiver cast in 1930, blue and tan Mat Glaze, impressed with Rookwood symbol, date, shape 6149 and fan-shaped esoteric mark, excellent original condition, 4-1/8" x 6-1/8". **$350**

Rookwood architectural faience tile depicting a sailing ship, impressed Rookwood Faience 1177 Y, fine original condition with light crazing and a couple of pinpoint burst glaze bubbles, 6" x 6", oak frame..... **$400**

Squat jewel porcelain vase with horses, designed by Jens Jensen, 1933, flame mark XXXIII/S/ artist's cipher, 4-1/4" x 5-1/2". **$875**

Dull Finish vase dated 1882, incised with vines, leaves and berries by a decorator with initials M.E.B., impressed Rookwood in block letters, date, number 68 3 and a "C" and incised with artist's initials, excellent original condition, 7-3/4" h......**$275**

Rare Aerial Blue scenic vase of shepherdess holding her staff as she watches over her flock, by William P. McDonald in 1894, impressed with Rookwood insignia, date, shape 721 C and Aerial Blue mark, number 273 encased between two crescent moons, incised with McDonald's monogram, very fine light crazing, vase of blue clay, readily visible on bottom, 5 1/2" high. **$3,000**

Rare and important Modeled Mat or carved Painted Mat vase done by Albert Valentien in 1900, two brightly colored irises in relief carved and painted by artist, marks include Rookwood logo, date, shape number 909 C and Valentien's full signature, uncrazed, 8 5/8" high. **$11,000**

Decorated Mat Glaze vase with vine with blueberries and green leaves, the work of Sallie Coyne in 1925, impressed with Rookwood logo, date and shape 907 F, Coyne's monogram in black slip, excellent original condition with some tiny color misses at base, stray color spot, 7-3/4" h........................**$350**

Rookwood porcelain scenic vase painted by Arthur Conant in 1918, white peonies on one side and red sparrow opposite, crosshatching surrounds collar, interior lined in salmon color, hints of water beyond reddish ground, marks include Rookwood logo, date, shape number 243 E, sideways P for porcelain body, incised monogram of Conant, uncrazed, 6 5/8" high **$2,500**

Vellum glaze scenic vase painted by Fred Rothenbusch in 1922, forest with small house with red roof, lit windows, stars above, marks include Rookwood logo, date, shape number 546 C, impressed V for Vellum glaze body, incised monogram of artist, faint crazing 9 3/4" high...................... **$2,600**

Standard Glaze portrait of Native American maiden done in 1898 by Artus Van Briggle, young girl with shoulder-length hair, marks include Rookwood logo, date, shape number 786 D, star-shaped mark, incised initials of artist, minor glaze scratches and very faint crazing, 8" high.....................**$8,000**

Early Standard Glaze cruet, circa 1886-1888, decorated with flowering branch of rose bush, white clay body, bottom has been ground so no marks remain, light crazing and some small grinding chips at base, 5-3/4" h. **$180**

Rare Deco style ashtray featuring a fish lying across bowl resting its snout on a wall, a Shirayamadani design, cast in 1936, ivory Mat Glaze, impressed with Rookwood logo, date and shape 6554, single burst glaze bubble at top of wall, 2-1/4" x 5-3/4"..... **$170**

Dull Finish ewer decorated by Martin Rettig in 1884, bird flying above trees, impressed Rookwood in block letters with date, shape 101 A and a "G" for ginger clay, incised with artist's monogram, excellent original condition, 11-3/8" h.......... **$500**

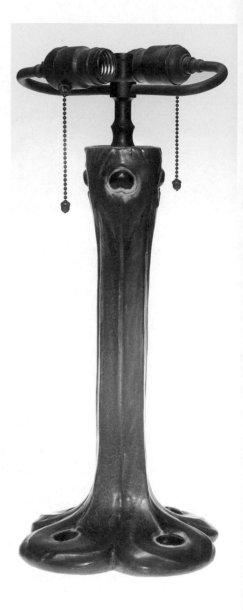

Dull Finish ewer decorated by M.A. Daly in 1887 with bough of flowering magnolias, impressed with Rookwood logo, which indicates date, shape 806 A, and 7 A, designating a type of white clay, with an "S" to indicate Daly's preference for Smear Glaze (dull finish) and his monogram, both in slip, some crazing, restoration at rim and where the handle attaches to neck, 23-1/4" h................... **$800**

Early carved and painted mat glaze lamp, peacock feather design on four lobes, carved and painted by Anna Valentien in 1904, impressed Rookwood symbol, date and shape 1047, artist's monogram in black slip, original fittings, nick to one edge, 15" high...................... **$2,000**

Standard Glaze vase decorated by Harriet Wilcox in 1898 with dandelions against shaded gold to brown ground, impressed with Rookwood monogram, which indicates date, shape 583 D and an esoteric mark, incised with Wilcox's initials, fine light crazing, excellent original condition, 8-1/2" h. $650

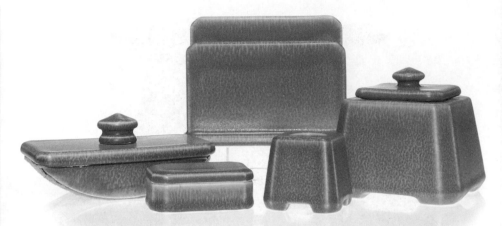

Five-piece desk set consisting of 4" x 5" letter holder, 3-1/8" inkwell with liner, 1" x 2-3/4" lidded box, 2-1/4" x 5" blotter roller, and 1-7/8" unknown item, each impressed with Rookwood logo and shape 2747, each dated 1924 except for last piece dated 1925, all in excellent original condition, each covered with speckled brown glaze. **$375**

Standard Glaze vase decorated by Sallie Coyne in 1900 with buckeyes, impressed with Rookwood symbol, which indicates date shape 762 C, incised with artist's monogram, fine overall crazing, excellent original condition, 5-1/2" h. **$500**

Standard Glaze teapot decorated by Lisbeth Lincoln in 1902 with yellow daffodils, base impressed with Rookwood symbol, date and shape 771 B, incised with Lincoln's monogram, fine overall crazing, chip to inner portion of lid from which cracks emanate, none visible with lid in place, 9-3/4" h. **$275**

Seated elephant paperweight, designed by Shirayamadani, cast in 1945, Wine Madder glaze, impressed with Rookwood logo, date, and shape 6490, tiny glaze bubbles at base, 3-3/4". **$200**

Jens Jensen Wax Mat vase with yucca plants in heavy glazes on opposing sides, painted at Rookwood in 1943, squeeze bag wavy lines run vertically up each side, marks include company logo, date, shape number 2194 and incised monogram of artist, 9-3/8" h. **$450**

Figure of a colonial woman, cast in 1946, uncrazed green high glaze, impressed with Rookwood symbol, date and shape 6907, wheel ground X to base, excellent original condition, 7-1/2" h. **$110**

Z line stoppered whiskey jug with incised decoration, made in 1904, Mat Green glaze, impressed with Rookwood symbol, date and shape 765 BZ, wheel ground X, 9-1/4" h. ... **$450**

ROOKWOOD

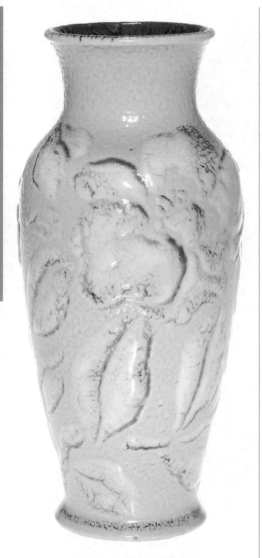

Butterfat Glaze vase decorated by Wilhelmine Rehm in 1945 with flowers, Butterfat Glaze in white over brown, lined in mottled brown, impressed with Rookwood logo, date and shape 6868, incised with number 7085 and Rehm's monogram, excellent original condition, 9" h. **$375**

Dull Finish vase decorated in 1885 by Matthew Daly, trio of turtles at shoreline, impressed Rookwood in block letters and with date and shape 241, incised with Daly's mark, 1-1/2" x 3/8" chip at rim, which has been glued into place, 13-1/4" h. **$650**

Standard Glaze mug decorated by Matt Daly in 1889 with a pair of frogs in tutus, impressed
with Rookwood logo, which indicates date, shape 422 and an "S" for sage green clay, incised
with Daly's monogram, restoration to line at rim, 5-7/8" h...**$850**

Kitten paperweight designed by David Seyler, cast in 1943, crystalline blue Mat Glaze that permits portions of white body to show through, impressed with Rookwood logo, date and shape 6661, excellent original condition, 1-1/4" x 3-3/4"......... **$400**

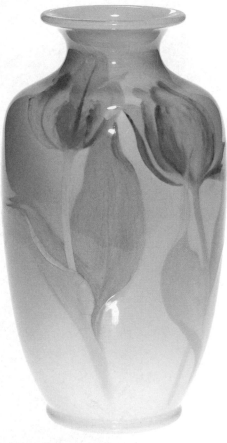

Cat paperweight designed by Louise Abel, cast in 1946, chartreuse high glaze, impressed with Rookwood logo, date, shape 6182, and designer's mold monogram, overall crazing, excellent original condition, 6-3/4". **$200**

Iris Glaze vase decorated with yellow tulips, the work of Sara Sax in 1893, impressed with Rookwood symbol, which indicates date, partial shape number and Sax's monogram, incised with a "W" to indicate white (Iris) glaze, crazing, drill hole to bottom, which removed part of shape number and has been plugged, 8-1/8" h. **$550**

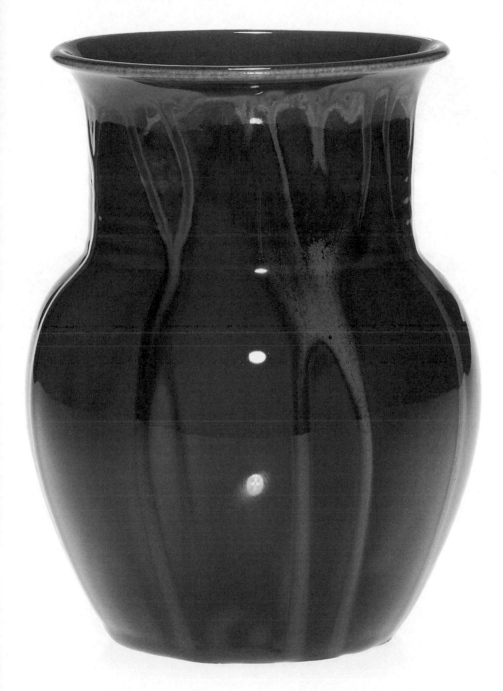

Coromandel Glaze vase made in 1932, glossy red tinted aventurine glaze with metallic gray dripped from rim, impressed with Rookwood logo, date and shape 6315, excellent original condition, 6-1/4" h...**$550**

Panther figure designed by William McDonald, Mat black glaze, no marks visible, excellent original condition, 2-3/8" x 6-1/4"........$400

Porcelain vase decorated by Lorinda Epply in 1931 with stylized flowers and glaze dripping over rim and covering interior, impressed with Rookwood logo, date and shape 2254 E, with Epply's monogram in black slip, excellent original condition, 4-1/2" h. x 5-1/4" dia. $700

Mat Glaze lamp deeply incised with designs by Rose Fechheimer in 1906, lamp with olive green glaze with brown highlights, some panels colored in darker green by artist, impressed with Rookwood symbol, date and shape 822 A, signed on side with an "F" in a box, an alternative cipher for Fechheimer, lamp base in excellent original condition, contemporary mica shade, ceramic portion 11-3/8" h. $750

ROOKWOOD

Five-sided pencil holder, each side panel showing a rook seated beneath a branch, cast in 1912, green Mat Glaze with red highlights, impressed with Rookwood symbol, date and shape 1795, excellent original condition, 4-5/8" h................... **$350**

Dull Finish ewer decorated by Martin Rettig during first half of 1880s with chrysanthemums, incised with Rettig's monogram and an "S" to indicate Smear Glaze (Dull Finish), impressed with shape number 101 A and 7 W for a type of white clay, fine original condition with a small color miss on handle, 10-1/2" h.... **$400**

Mat Glaze card tray lightly modeled with flower and swirls, flower in pink against green ground, the work of Anna Valentien in 1904, impressed with Rookwood symbol, date, shape 689 Z and experimental designation X 1206 X, with artist's monogram in black slip, excellent original condition with mild peppering, 1/2" x 5-5/8". **$200**

Porcelain lidded coffee pot with spout stopper, decorated by Arthur Conant in 1933 with scene of wild hog peering through reeds, impressed Rookwood symbol, date and shape 6330, pot, lid and stopper in excellent original condition, 11 1/2" high **$4,200**

ROOKWOOD

Early Rookwood production piece described as "Persian Pitcher," made in 1882, cobalt blue high glaze with two angular handles, marks include Rookwood in block letters, date, shape number 26 and "W" for white clay, excellent original condition, 11-3/4" h. **$500**

Mahogany Glaze vase decorated by Kataro Shirayamadani in 1889 with trumpet vines, impressed with Rookwood insignia, which discloses date, shape number 488 D and an "R" for red clay, incised with Shirayamadani's Japanese script signature, fine overall crazing, restoration at rim, 14-1/2" h. (Mahogany Glaze is formed by the application of Standard Glaze onto red clay body.) **$950**

Rookwood Vellum vase with carved and stylized peacock feathers done in 1905 by Sara Sax, marks include company logo, date, shape number 942 E, impressed "V," incised "V" for Vellum glaze, impressed monogram of artist, faint crazing and tight half-inch line at rim, 4-3/4" h. **$375**

Pair of Dolphin candlesticks, cast in 1919, Mat green glaze, each impressed with Rookwood symbol, date and shape 2464, excellent original condition, 11-1/4" h. **$475**

Modeled Mat vase featuring lotus flowers, carved by Rose Fechheimer in 1906, green Mat Glaze, impressed with Rookwood logo, date and shape 942 D, incised with artist's monogram, excellent original condition, 6-3/8" h. $900

Pair of Rookwood lamps cast in 1937, Coromandel Glaze, impressed with Rookwood logo, date and shape 6311, excellent original condition, original fittings present but lamps need to be rewired, ceramic portion 7-3/8" h...**$800**

Rose Medallion & Rose Canton

THE LOVELY CHINESE ware known as Rose Medallion was made through the past century and into the present one. It features alternating panels of people and flowers or insects, with most pieces having four medallions with a central rose or peony medallion. The ware is called Rose Canton if florals and birds or insects fill all the panels. Unless otherwise noted, our listing is for Rose Medallion ware.

Punch bowl, deep rounded sides with colorful alternating panels of flowers & Oriental figures, late 19th c., 15" d., 6" h **$1,668**

Punch bowl, rounded deep & flaring shape, decorated inside & out with large alternating panels of flowers & Oriental figures, second half 19th c., 11 1/2" d., 4 3/4" h. **$1,150**

Teapot, cov., small round raised foot supporting the deep rounded lower body with a sharply angled gently angled shoulder centering the low flat mouth fittled with a high domed cover, ornate C-scroll handle & serpentine spout, the sides & cover decorated with alternating panels of colorful flowers or Chinese figures, mid-19th c., 8 1/4" h.......... **$1,093**

Vase, 24" h., floor-type, Rose Medallion, decorated with large panels with figures alternating with floral panels, the tall trumpet neck flanked by gold applied Foo dog & dragon handles, late 19th c **$1,150**

Plates, 9 3/4" d., Rose Mandarin, each with the same border with brilliant blue fretwork, pink flowers & baskets on a dark mustard yellow iridescent ground, each with a detailed figural center scene, one showing women & children in a courtyard, the other with a man brandishing a sword at a woman, minor wear, pr.. **$460**

Platter, 14 x 17", oval, the border in the rare kissing carp motif alternating with blue & green scrolls, the center decorated with a detailed figural scene with 26 figures including children, courtiers with large necklaces & a man holding a sceptre, faint orange peel glaze, minor wear to gilt accents **$1,955**

Vase, palace-style, 35 1/2" h., 13 1/2" d., wide cylindrical body with the rounded shoulder tapering to a large waisted neck with a widely flaring flattened rim, the neck with large figural Foo dog & ball handles, each side of the body & neck decorated with large panels with scenes of numerous people in buildings, detailed floral background & gold trim, one under rim chip, 19th c ... **$2,300**

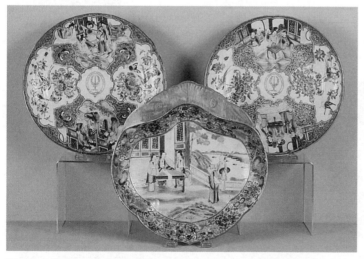

Plates, 9 5/8" d., armorial Rose Medallion, each decorated with alternating panels of exotic birds & butterflies & groups of figures, the panel separated by bars with tiny florals & a butterfly, an orange armorial crest in the center, slight wear, one with short hairline, the other with small filled-in rim chips, pr **$575**

Rosenthal

THE ROSENTHAL PORCELAIN manufactory has been in operation since 1880, when it was established by P. Rosenthal in Selb, Bavaria. Tablewares and figure groups are among its specialties.

Vase, cov., 12 1/4" h., temple jar form with tapering ovoid body with short cylindrical neck supporting a domed flanged cover with a knob finial, black ground decorated with a silver overlay design of a large bird of paradise flying over an intricate flower highlighted in orange & white, marked, ca. 1936..........**$575**

Vase, 9 7/8" h., cylindrical, all white molded with a stylized leaf design, marked "Rosenthal Germany - Cuno Fischer - Studio Line," ca. 1963........................**$115**

Roseville

ROSEVILLE IS ONE of the most widely recognizable of potteries across the United States. Having been sold in flower shops and drug stores around the country, its art and production wares became a staple in American homes through the time Roseville closed in the 1950s.

The Roseville Pottery Co., located in Roseville, Ohio, was incorporated on Jan. 4, 1892, with George F. Young as general manager. The company had been producing stoneware since 1890, when it purchased the J. B. Owens Pottery, also of Roseville.

The popularity of Roseville Pottery's original lines of stoneware continued to grow. The company acquired new plants in 1892 and 1898, and production started to shift to Zanesville, just a few miles away. By about 1910, all of the work was centered in Zanesville, but the company name was unchanged.

Young hired Ross C. Purdy as artistic designer in 1900, and Purdy created Rozane—a contraction of the words "Roseville" and "Zanesville." The first Roseville artwork pieces were marked either Rozane or RPCO, both impressed or ink-stamped on the bottom.

In 1902, a line was developed called Azurean. Some pieces were marked Azurean, but often RPCO. In 1904 at the St. Louis Exposition, Roseville's Rozane Mongol, a high-gloss oxblood red line, captured first prize, gaining recognition for the firm and its creator, John Herold.

Many Roseville lines were a response to the innovations of Weller Pottery, and in 1904 Frederick Rhead was hired away from Weller as artistic director. He created the Olympic and Della Robbia lines for Roseville. His brother Harry took over as artistic director in 1908, and in 1915 he introduced the popular Donatello line.

By 1908, all handcrafting ended except for Rozane Royal. Roseville was the first pottery in Ohio to install a tunnel kiln, which increased its production capacity.

Frank Ferrell, who was a top decorator at the Weller Pottery by 1904, was Roseville's artistic director from 1917 until 1954. A Zanesville native, Ferrell created many of the most popular lines, including Pine Cone, which had scores of individual pieces.

Many collectors believe Roseville's circa 1925 glazes were the best of any Zanesville pottery. George Krause, who had become Roseville's technical supervisor, responsible for glaze, in 1915, remained with Roseville until the 1950s.

Company sales declined after World War II, especially in the early 1950s when cheap Japanese imports began to replace American wares, and a simpler, more modern style made many of Roseville's elaborate floral designs seem old-fashioned.

In the late 1940s, Roseville began to issue lines with glossy glazes. Roseville tried to offset its flagging artware sales by launching a dinnerware line—Raymor—in 1953. The line was a commercial failure.

Roseville issued its last new designs in 1953. On Nov. 29, 1954, the facilities of Roseville were sold to the Mosaic Tile Company. For more information on Roseville, see *Warman's Roseville Pottery*, 2nd edition, by Denise Rago.

ROSEVILLE

Bottom Marks

There is no consistency to Roseville bottom marks. Even within a single popular pattern like Pine Cone, the marks vary.

Several shape-numbering systems were implemented during the company's almost 70-year history, with some denoting a vessel style and some applied to separate lines. Though many pieces are unmarked, from 1900 until the late teens or early 1920s, Roseville used a variety of marks including "RPCo," "Roseville Pottery Company," and the word "Rozane," the last often with a line name, i.e., "Egypto."

The underglaze ink script "Rv" mark was used on lines introduced from the mid-to-late teens through the mid-1920s. Around 1926 or 1927, Roseville began to use a small, triangular black paper label on lines such as Futura and Imperial II. Silver or gold foil labels began to appear around 1930, continuing for several years on lines such as Blackberry and Tourmaline, and on some early Pine Cone.

From 1932 to 1937, an impressed script mark was added to the molds used on new lines, and around 1937 the raised script mark was added to the molds of new lines. The relief mark includes "U.S.A."

All of the following bottom mark images appear courtesy of Adamstown Antique Gallery, Adamstown, Pennsylvania.

Impressed mark on Azurean vase, 8" h.

Raised mark on a Bushberry vase.

Ink stamp on a Cherry Blossom pink vase, 10" h.

Wafer mark on a Della Robbia vase, 10-1/2" h.

Gold foil label and grease pencil marks on an Imperial II vase, 10" h.

Impressed mark on an Iris vase.

Ink stamps on a Wisteria bowl, 5" h.

Impressed marks on a Rozane portrait vase, 13" h.

Experimental Geranium vase with pink flowers on front and incised "Geranium Flowers white pink rose" on back, marked "Flower 58 washed 168 8-34-103" in black grease pencil on bottom, excellent original condition, 9" high.................. **$2,400**

Tall rare Della Robbia vase with wild roses and cut-out rim, circa 1910, raised Rozane Ware seal, incised artist's signature on bottom and initials on side, 15 1/2" x 6" **$43,750**

Experimental Bittersweet vase decorated on front with vining flowers for which line was named, incised on back "Bittersweet Open shells yellow orange Berries—Red Leaves—Lt. Green," excellent original condition, 9". **$2,200**

Large Rozane Dark vase decorated by Arthur Williams, full-length figure of man in classical garb, impressed Rozane 954 RPCo 1 and cross on bottom, signed A Williams on side, overall crazing, small glaze bubbles and small firing separation on bottom, 21" high $1,000

Della Robbia vase with stylized poppies done by artisan with initials "KO," four carved flowers and many seed pods encircle vase, marked with artist's initials on side, shape 27 in Della Robbia line, light overall crazing, excellent original condition, 14 1/4" high ...$9,750

Olympic vase on three feet, three full-length classical women with repeating bands around rim and foot, unmarked, red color with overspray, 13 1/8" high $1,200

Dealer advertising sign, 1940s, Roseville script mark in yellow matte against pink matte background, excellent original condition, 4 5/8" x 7 3/4" **$1,000**

Olympic tankard titled "Triptolemos and the Grain of Wheat," three classic Greek figures with repeating bands at top and base, marked in black on bottom "Rozane Pottery Triptolemos and the Grain of Wheat," excellent condition with minor scratches, 11" high **$2,000**

Blackberry faceted bowl, most of original Roseville sticker on bottom, excellent condition, 3 3/4" high x 10" wide **$200**

Tourist vase depicting tourists on country road in red car, wide dark bands, unmarked, some crazing and two glaze bubbles, fine original condition, 12 3/8" high **$1,100**

Fudji vase in several shades of blue, unmarked, excellent original condition, 7 3/4" high **$2,600**

Scarce Mongol vase, circa 1904, with recreation of ancient Chinese blood red glaze, raised Rozane Ware wafer with Mongol wing, old sticker that is illegible, sticker from White Pillars Museum in Norwich, Ohio, certificate verifying vase was part of Purviance Collection at White Pillars, shallow scratches, 10 7/8" high **$1,500**

Lamp with raised flowers and foliage in high glaze combination of turquoise, yellow, and pink over matte bronze glaze, original fittings, replaced double sockets and cord, metal base marked "Davrt, NY," excellent condition, ceramic portion 8" high **$600**

Futura Bamboo Leaf ball vase, shape 387-7", Roseville Pottery foil label on bottom, overall crazing, 7 1/2" **$400**

ROSEVILLE

Rare Aztec jardiniere and pedestal, circa 1915, artist's cipher on pedestal, 35 1/2" x 16" overall.................... **$1,875**

Carnelian I two-handled vase with dark blue over light blue matte glazes, shape 339-15", marked with RV inkstamp, regular crazing, some tiny glaze bursts, 15" high......................... **$200**

Rozane Mongol vase with copper red glaze, raised Rozane Mongol wafer, few short scratches, 10 7/8" high **$2,000**

Futura Purple Crocus vase, shape 429-9", unmarked, professional restoration to chip at base **$700**

Azurean vase decorated by Walter Myers with two fish observed through low hanging branch of flowering tree, impressed on bottom with large B, smaller B, and shape number 898, signed "W. Myers" by artist on foot, fine crazing and two pinpoint size nicks at base, 12 5/8" high **$1,700**

Rosecraft Panel vase with nudes poised in four panels, glaze separation on rim and small clay bumps on one nude, stamped "Rv" on bottom, 10 1/4" high **$500**

Imperial II vase in green and orange, shape number 476-8, unmarked, excellent original condition, uncrazed, 8 1/4" high **$650**

Wincraft buttress floor vase, shape 289-18" with pink tulips front and back, raised marks, good condition, 18 1/2" high......................... **$325**

Carnelian II spherical vase in turquoise with silver-like mottling on shape 441, excellent condition, 8" x 9" **$450**

Pauleo vase in mottled two-tone blue matte glaze on tall form, incised number 234 on bottom, restoration to small glaze nicks on foot ring, 17 3/4" high. **$700**

Azurean pitcher decorated with flower and berry design, perhaps by Claude Leffler, impressed on bottom RPCo 937 F 1 and bearing artist monogram to right of handle, fine crazing, 3-1/2" h. **$300**

ROSEVILLE

Early Velmoss jardiniere with embossed leaves and flowers, unmarked, minor scuffs on surface, 9 5/8" high x 13" diameter.. **$375**

Florentine II sand jar with panels of clustered flowers, marked with raised "Roseville USA" and shape 297, overall crazing and some minor chips at base, 16 1/2" high **$100**

Rare Egypto oil lamp base consisting of three elephants with riders providing support for font area, marked with Rozane Ware Egypto wafer seal on bottom, older restoration to large chip on flat base, 10 1/2" high... **$1,000**

Pair of tall slender candlesticks in blueberry glaze, one with triangle black Roseville sticker, excellent condition, 15" high **$225**

Imperial I floor vase, excellent condition, 15 1/2" high **$325**

Rozane vase with two handles, English spaniel on vessel, decorated by Claude Leffler, impressed on base "Rozane 826 RPO 3 A B" and signed "C.L. Leffler" in slip on foot, overall crazing, two glaze bubbles, several chips at base, 21" high **$600**

Early Rozane jardiniere and pedestal with garlands of flowers against stippled backdrop, open glaze pop at inside bottom, early number mark on bottom, excellent condition, 30 1/4" high (combined) **$425**

Aztec vase with small white flowers and decorative piping applied with pastry bag, gray-blue ground, marked with R on foot, two small chips at base, one glazed over, 10-3/4" h **$200**

Ming Tree floor vase with branch handles, shape 585-14", raised marks, repair to chip on rim, 14 1/2" high **$250**

Rozane Royal Dark vase with life-size red and yellow irises painted by Josephine Imlay, signed by artist on side, marked with Roseville Rozane Ware wafer seal on bottom, completely oversprayed indicating some sort of professional repair, 15 5/8" high **$325**

**Crystalis oil lamp vase on Egypto form of three elephants with riders that form support for oil
font holder**, reddish orange Crystalis glaze covers inside and outside of vase, large crystals
visible on flatter surfaces, marked with Rozane Ware Egypto wafer seal, restoration to small
base chip, 10 5/8" high..**$2,900**

Handled Baneda vase, shape 596 in green overlaid in blue with panel displaying orange pumpkins and yellow flowers on green vines, beneath is gold foil Roseville sticker, shape number in red crayon, perfect condition, 9-1/4" h................... **$600**

Azurean vase, shape 892-8-1/2", decorated with pansies, impressed Azurean in block letters, shape 892 and RP Co., light crazing and some glaze inclusions on neck, 8-3/8" h. **$375**

Azurean vase, shape 955-17, peonies, impressed with shape number, RPCo 1, some restoration at rim, oversprayed, tight spider to base, crazing, 17-1/4" h. **$350**

Fuchsia vase in green, shape 904-15", impressed Roseville 904-15, some restoration at the rim, 15-1/2" h. **$140**

Azurean humidor decorated with pipe and matches, impressed RPCo, F, 897 and 2, lid and base oversprayed, tight line at rim, crazing, 5-1/4" h. **$150**

Carnelian II scroll-handled vase in pink with variations of green, excellent condition, 10-1/4" h. $225

Blackberry vase, shape 576-8", unmarked, fine original condition, mold and color appear average, 8" h. $325

Large Crystalis vase with two handles and orange crystalline glaze, marked with Rozane Ware wafer seal, restoration to rim chips, 11-1/8" h. $400

Dealer advertising sign, 1930s Art Deco style, mat pink glaze, marked Roseville on front, excellent original condition, 2" x 6-1/4". $700

Creamware smoking set consisting of lid crested by match holder and base with jar for tobacco fused to ashtray base, tobacco jar encircled by decal that shows an Indian smoking a pipe, unmarked, overall crazing, tight line at rim of jar, tight firing line to interior side, bruise at rim of lid, 7" h. ... $300

Iris vase in blue, impressed Roseville 929-15", excellent original condition, 15-1/4" h.. **$350**

Pauleo vase in red metallic luster glaze, marked with number 130 in black slip, excellent original condition, 14" h. **$500**

Fudji vase, circa 1906, garnished with enameled yellow flowers front and rear on bisque ground, marked with green Fujiyama ink stamp, minor staining, 6" h. **$300**

Vase covered with organic mat green glaze, impressed with a "C" on bottom, 12" h. **$170**

Imperial I wall pocket, shape 1222-9", unmarked, excellent original condition, 10-1/8" h. **$200**

Laurel vase, shape 674, mustard brown glaze, black highlights, marked with number 5 in black slip below base, excellent original condition, 9" h. **$400**

Imperial II vase in blues and yellows, shape 484-11, black paper label, excellent original condition, crystals in glaze, 11-1/4" h.. **$650**

Early pitcher, each side decorated with two tulips, one pink and white, the other pink and yellow, attributed to L. Metzberger, a decorator and molder at Roseville, marked "LM" on bottom in slip, 7-3/8" h........... **$325**

Dealer sign bearing the name Roseville Pottery, gray green mat glaze with brown showing through in places, marked only on front of sign, chips to two corners, 4-1/4" x 9-1/4"..................................... **$800**

Egypto inkwell with lid, encircled with classical molded design and covered with fine mat green glaze, marked with raised Rozane Egypto wafer, excellent original condition, 3-3/4" h. **$500**

Futura "Sand Toy" bowl, shape 189-4-6", un-marked, tiny nick at base, 4-1/8" x 5"..... **$300**

Matt Green covered bowl, cover acting as flower holder and covered with matt green glaze, unmarked, small chip to rim of bowl, which is covered when the top is in place, 3-5/8" x 7-1/4" w. **$110**

Pine Cone bowl in blue, shape 632-3", lightly impressed with Roseville logo and shape number and marked D 8 in blue slip, fine original condition, 3"......... **$110**

Earlam sand jar, 1930s, foil label, 14-1/2" x 11-1/2". **$2,125**

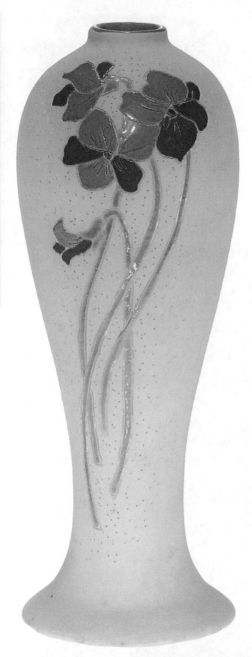

Rosecraft Panel Nude fan vase in green, each side depicting a different female nude posing with scarves in Art Nouveau tradition, marked with blue Rv inkstamp, excellent original condition, 8" h. **$500**

Rozane Woodland vase with two enameled flowers on bisque-like ground, raised Rozane Woodland disc, excellent original condition, 8-7/8" h. **$400**

Rozane Royal Dark letter holder decorated by Tot Steele, raised Rozane Ware Royal wafer and signed Steele on side, crazing and two small base chips, 3-5/8" x 4-3/4". **$80**

Rosecraft Panel Nude vase in brown, four panels each depicting a female nude in Art Nouveau style, unmarked, small chip to underside of rim, 10-1/2" h. **$500**

Wisteria vase, shape 637-6-1/2", Roseville silver foil sticker, sticker from retailer Fowler, Dick and Walker, Inc., number 637 in orange crayon, excellent original condition, 6-1/2" x 8-1/2". **$600**

Rozane Dark ewer covered with silver overlay, impressed on base Rozane 930 RPCo. 4 and marked JW in black slip, fine crazing, 4-5/8" h. **$200**

Poppy ewer, shape 880-18", mat pink, impressed with Roseville logo and shape number and marked with a B in blue slip, fine original condition, 18-1/4" h.. **$325**

Royal Capri vase with gold finish, shape 578-7", marked with stylized R, U.S.A. and the shape number, excellent original condition, little or no wear, 7-3/8" h. Original advertising piece shows the vase is covered with "22 carat stippled gold." **$190**

Rozane Royal Light vase decorated by Lillie Mitchell, blackberry vines, marked with raised Rozane Ware wafer seal partially effaced, indicating a "second," impressed 7 L and signed by artist in slip on side, fine, light crazing and some minor roughness at base, 12-1/4" h. **$325**

Mara vase in colorful iridescent glaze, marked with impressed number 13, excellent original condition with two minor scratches, 5-3/8" h. **$950**

Rozane Woodland vase decorated with flowers in autumnal colors on bisque-like ground, unmarked, some staining, 13" h. **$750**

Rozane Royal Light vase with orchid, 1900s, Mae Timberlake, raised Rozane Ware, royal seal, artist's signature to body, 10-1/2" x 3".... **$625**

Rozane vase with portrait of goat, impressed Rozane RPCo on base, no artist mark visible, oversprayed and deteriorating, few glaze bubbles, crazing, 8-1/4" h $150

Pillow vase with fluted rim and two handles, decorated by Fred Steele with a vignette depicting two English spaniels, impressed on base Rozane 88 RPCo 4 and signed "F Steele" by artist to lower left of picture, fine crazing, some restoration at rim evidenced by overspray, chip to foot ring not visible from side, 9" x 11-1/4". $400

Rozane Royal Light vase decorated with red clover, Rozane Royal wafer seal and impressed with numbers 36 and 4, heavy dark crazing to lower portion of base, 11" h.......................... $200

Rozane Dark vase decorated by Arthur Williams, portrait of Native American male in profile, unmarked, bearing a sticker from White Pillars Museum, overall crazing, restoration from middle of vase to base, 13-3/4" h. ... $800

Rozane vase decorated by Arthur Williams with portrait of a man done in Old Masters style, impressed on base Rozane, 212 RPCo X, signed on side near base by artist, fine crazing, burst glaze bubble toward rear of vase, 13" h. $650

Quaker humidor en-circled by 2" wide red band with repeating pattern of two Quaker men in tricornered hats and white wigs, trimmed with black piping, unmarked, base has crazing, lid does not, 5-1/2" h. **$200**

Rare vase with iris design covered with black luster glaze, unmarked, oversprayed, pinhead-size glaze bubbles, light crazing, possibly part of Rozane line dating from first decade of 20th century, 14" h. **$350**

Two Woodland vases with tulips, ca. 1905, both with Rozane Ware medallion, 9-1/4" h. and 13-1/4" h..................... **$1,250**

Royal Bayreuth

GOOD CHINA IN numerous patterns and designs has been made at the Royal Bayreuth factory in Tettau, Germany since 1794. Listings below are by the company's lines, plus miscellaneous pieces. Interest in this china remains at a peak and prices continue to rise. Pieces listed carry the company's blue mark except where noted otherwise.

Among the important reference books in this field are *Royal Bayreuth - A Collectors' Guide* and *Royal Bayreuth - A Collectors' Guide - Book II* by Mary McCaslin.

Bowl, 10 1/2" d., gently scalloped rim with four shell-molded gilt-trimmed handles, three-color roses .... **$800-$1,100**

Plaque, pierced to hang, "tapestry," round with a scroll-molded gilt-trimmed border, center portrait of woman leaning on horse, 9 1/2" d ....**$700-$850**

Vases, 3 1/8" h., 2 5/8" d., squatty bulbous lower body below the tall tapering sides ending in a ringed neck & flanked by loop handles, one with scene of Dutch boy & girl playing with brown dog & the other with scene of Dutch boy & girl playing with white & brown dog, green mark, pr.... **$50-$150**

Tomato creamer & cov. sugar bowl, creamer 3" d., 3" h., sugar bowl 3 1/2" d., 4" h., pr .... **$75-$100**

Vase, 2 3/4" h., miniature, a thin footring & swelled bottom ring below the gently flaring sides with a scalloped rim, tiny gold rin handles at the bottom sides, two-color roses.**$106**

Box, cov., square, desert scene decoration on cover, Arabs with camels on background colors of pink & brown, unmarked, 2 x 2 1/2", 1 3/4" h. .... **$50-$75**

Berry set: 10" d. master bowl & six berry dishes; round with deep lobed sides decorated in the center with a cluster of large pink roses & scattered small roses around the sides, very minor flake on one small bowl, the set **$230**

Creamer, with scene of goats in snow .... **$100-$200**

Dresser tray, rectangular, with gently ruffled rim, decorated with depiction of Little Boy Blue sleeping in haystack **$400-$550**

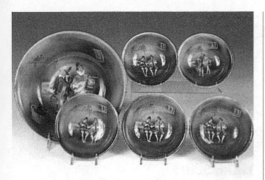

Berry set,9 3/4" d. bowl & five 5" d. sauce dishes; Peasant Musicians decoration, 6 pcs.. **$350-$450**

Box, cov., heart-shaped, decorated with scene of two brown & white cows & trees in pasture, green & yellow background, unmarked, 2 x 3 1/4", 1 1/2" h..... **$75-$100**

Dresser tray, rectangular with rounded corners, scene of boy & three donkeys in landscape, 8 x 11"........................ **$150-250**

Cake plate, decorated with snowy scene & two polar bears, gold trimmed scalloped border.................................. **$1,500-$2,000**

Cheese dishes, miniature, decorated with scenes of cattle, each .... **$450-$550**

Creamer, figural water buffalo, black & white .... **$125-$200**

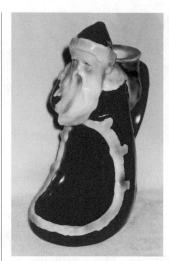

Model of woman's shoe, old fashioned high-button shoe in silver tapestry design, 5" l., 3 1/2" h ... **$2,000-$2,500**

Hatpin holder, model of a penguin, in red, white & grey, signed ..... **$600-$800**

Candleholder, figural, Santa, very rare .... **$8,000-$10,000**

Hair receiver, cov., "tapestry," small gold scroll feet & low squatty rounded body with a fitted low cover with a small ruffled center opening, decorated with a scene of swans on a lake, 4" d ..... **$200-$300**

Pitcher, tankard, 6 7/8" h., 3 3/4" d., orange inside top, classical figures on black satin ground, gold bands with black & white geometric design around neck & base ..... **$175-$200**

Chocolate pot, cov., tall tapering cylindrical body with a rim spout, long gold leaf-scroll handle, inset domed cover with knob finial, color scene of a boy with three donkeys, 8 1/2" h **$230**

Pitcher, 3 1/2" h., 2 1/4" d., scene of musicians, one playing bass & one with mandolin, unmarked ...... **$50-$75**

Pitcher, water, jug-type body with applied handle, set-in spout, portrait "tapestry" decoration of 18th c. lady in plumed hat .... **$750-$900**

Pitcher, water, bulbous body with scene of fisherman standing in boat against wooded backdrop, flaring neck & spout, applied handle .... **$400-$500**

Pitcher, 2" h., miniature advertising piece with scene of "sanatorium grounds" on front, angled handle .... **$150-$250**

Pitcher, 3 1/8" h., 2 3/8" w., squared waisted body with short, wide spout & angled gilt handle, scene of Arab on horse ....**$100-$150**

Pitcher, water, 6 1/2" h., in the form of a perched butterfly, in shades of green, deep pink & light blue, handle in the form of a stem with leaves............. **$5,500-$7,500**

Stein, with pewter hinged top, decorated with scene of stag swimming away from hunting dogs, 6" h.................................... **$400-$500**

Tea set: child's, cov. teapot, cov. sugar, creamer, two plates, & two cups & saucers; ovoid bodies, each piece decorated with a scene of children playing, the set .... **$700-$800**

Vase, baluster-form body with decoration of red & blue parrots & pink flowers, trumpet neck, short pedestal on disc foot, side handles with images of human faces where they attach to body .... **$400-$425**

Tray, decorated with scene of girl with geese, molded rim with gold trim, 9 x 12 1/4" .... **$350-$500**

Vase, 9 1/2" h., peacock decoration, openwork on neck & at base, ornate scroll handles, lavish gold trim .... **$600-$725**

Pitcher, 3 1/4" h., 2" d., decorated with Cavalier scene, two Cavaliers drinking at a table, grey & cream ground, unmarked............ **$50-$75**

Pitcher, 5 1/4" h., figural, Santa Claus, pack on back serves as handle ...... **$3,500-$4,500**

Royal Copley

ROYAL COPLEY WAS a trade name used by the Spaulding China Company of Sehring, Ohio, during the 1940s and 1950s for a variety of ceramic figurines, planters and other decorative pieces. Similar Spaulding pieces were also produced under the trade name "Royal Windsor," or carried the Spaulding China mark.

Dime stores generally featured the Royal Copley line, with Spaulding's other lines available in more upscale outlets.

The Spaulding China Company ended production in 1957, but for the next two years other potteries finished production of its outstanding orders. Today these originally inexpensive wares are developing a dedicated collector following thanks to their whimsically appealing designs.

Advisor for this category is Donald-Brian Johnson, an author and lecturer specializing in Mid-Twentieth Century design.

Blackamoor Man & Blackamoor Woman, kneeling, 8 1/2" h., pr............................. **$100-$120**

Hummingbird on flower,
blue or red & white
bird, red flower, green
leaves form base, blue
bird brings higher price,
5 1/4" h.............. **$50-$75**

Girl on Wheelbarrow,
7" h. .... **$50-$55**

**Horse Head with Flying
Mane,** 8" h.......... **$35-$55**

**Oriental Boy & Oriental
Girl,** standing, 7 1/2" h.,
pr....................... **$35-$55**

Dog with Raised Paw,
7 1/2" h .... **$70-$80**

Airedale, seated, brown &
white, 6 1/2" h.... **$40-$45**

Kitten and Book,
6 1/2" h .... **$45-$55**

Ribbed Star, all-white,
"Royal Windsor" sticker,
4 3/4" h. .... **$35-$40**

Palomino Horse Head,
6 1/4" h. .... **$50-$60**

Dancing lady, wearing hat & long full-skirted dress, one hand holding her hat in place while wind blows at her dress, four colorations, unmarked, 8" h., each ...... **$135-$150**

Gadwells drake & duck, Game Bird series, signed "A.D. Priollo" on base, Royal Windsor mark, series consists of Gadwells, Teals & Mallards, Gadwells & Teals are hardest to find, sizes vary, pr........ **$150-$250**

Kittens, black & white with red bow at neck, sitting, one looking up & one looking down, one shown on left is harder to find, 8" h., each .... **$75-$85**

Hen & rooster, black & white with red trim, green base, 7" h. & 8" h., pr .... **$200-$225**

Kingfishers, one on leaf base with wings extended, the other flying downward, blue, rose or yellow, blue is hardest to find, rose pairs are hard to match, 5" h., pr., each ......**$100-$150**

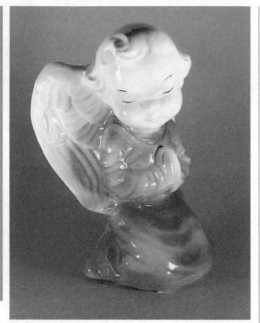

Angel, large, kneeling, blue robe, 8" h... **$70-$85**

Spaniel Pup with Collar, 6" h.............**$40-$45**

Clown, 8 1/4" h. ....**$120-$145**

Kitten on Cowboy Boot, 7 1/2" h.........**$65-$70**

Doe & Fawn Head, rectangular log-form
planter, 5 1/4" h.............................**$50-$60**

Dog in Picnic Basket, 7 3/4" h............**$80-$90**

Fancy Finch on Tree Stump, red, white &
black bird perched on brown leafy branch
beside white planter, 7 1/2" h........ **$90-$100**

Elf and Shoe, 6" h.............................**$60-$70**

Angel on Star, white relief figure on creamy
yellow ground, 6 3/4" h...................**$30-$40**

Rooster on wheelbarrow, 8" h ....**$100-$125**

Siamese cats, two, one sitting & one recumbent, white with black trim, blue eyes, green or rust woven basket, green is more desirable, 8" h., each.......... **$175-$200**

Stuffed Animal Dog, white & brown, 5 1/2" h .... **$70-$80**

Poodle, reclining, white with black nose & eyes, 8" l .... **$80-$90**

Royal Dux

THIS FACTORY IN Bohemia was noted for the figural porcelain wares in the Art Nouveau style it exported around the turn of the 20th century. Other notable figural pieces were produced through the 1930s. The factory was nationalized after World War II.

Vase, 20 1/2" h., 11 1/2" d., Art Nouveau style, footed wide squatty base section below the tall gently tapering upper body tapering to a wide cupped rim, molded down the sides & around the base section with re-alistic leaves & blos-soms with undulating loop handles down the sides, dusted black finish & gold trim, pink triangle & impressed numbers, late 19th - early 20th c **$518**

Figure of a bather, the semi-nude young maiden seated on a rockwork base, in naturalistic colors, signed with the applied pink triangle mark, early 20th c., 21" h ... **$3,335**

Figures, peasant man & woman, he standing wearing a wide-brimmed hat, gold shirt & brown pants & holding a bag over one shoulder & a net in the other, on a round naturalistic base with stump & chain she wearing a short-sleeved blouse & vest & long deep red dress with one hand holding up her gold apron full of apples & a jug over her arm, on a matching rounded base, pink triangle & im-pressed triangle marks with numbers, 20" & 22" h., pr **$720**

Figure group, a large cream-colored bull being held on a rein by a standing farmer wearing a hat, long-sleeved sheet, pants & boots, on a naturalistic rectangular base, decorated in dark gold, pink triangle mark & impressed number, late 19th - early 20th c., 13" l., 11" h **$748**

Vases, 12" h., figural, a large cylindrical molded tree trunk form, one applied with a the figure of a boy playing a lyre & the other with the figure of dancing girl with a lamb, cream ground with heavy gold trim, pink triangle marks & impressed numbers, late 19th - early 20th c., pr **$408**

Vases, 11" h., figural, each with a block-form base supporting a short stone block pedestal topped with a tall column forming a vase, one mounted in front with the figure of a standing maiden wearing a tight-fitting robe with wide sleeves, her hands behind her head; the other mounted with the figure of a young shepherd with a cap, animal skin outfit & playing the pipes of Pan, decorated in shades of reddish brown, dark mustard yellow & cream, applied pink triangle marks, facing pair **$431**

Lamp, figural table model, the oblong base enclosed in a brass frame & mounted with the model of a large creamy white work horse carrying a removable young farm boy wearing a cap, shirt & rolled up pants, trimmed in dark gold, pink triangle mark & impressed "1602," metal upright at back with electric fitting & decorated creamy silk shade, early 20th c., figure 12" l., 14" h ... **$690**

Figure group, an Arab man wearing a hood & flowing robes seated atop a tall walking camel, a half-naked young boy below struggling with two large bags, decorated in shades of deep red, brown, tan, cream & gold, pink triangle & Made in Czechoslovkia marks on base, 6 x 14", 18" h **$480**

Mirror, figural table-type, an upright oval beveled edge mirror set along one side with a curved flower & vine support raised on a tree trunk base, a tall classical maiden standing to the side wearing long deep red robes, squared dished base, pink triangle mark, late 19th - early 20th c., base 16" w., overall 17" h.....................**$1,323**

Center piece, figural, in the form of a large open conch shell raised on a large coral branches, an Art Nouveau sea nymph seated on one end of the shell, painted in pale shades of green, creamy yellow & brown, applied pink triangle mark, early 20th c., 12" h.............................. **$776**

Royal Vienna

THE SECOND FACTORY in Europe to make hard paste porcelain was established in Vienna in 1719 by Claud Innocentius de Paquier. The factory underwent various changes of administration through the years and finally closed in 1865. Since then, however, the porcelain has been reproduced by various factories in Austria and Germany, many of which have also reproduced the early beehive mark. Early pieces, naturally, bring far higher prices than the later ones or the reproductions.

Vases, cov., 13 3/4" h., a stepped molded high square plinth base attached to a slender tapering pedestal supporting a flaring urn-form body with an angled shoulder & short flaring neck flanked by angular long gold handles, a tapering pointed cover with pointed gold finial, ruby & gold ground, the body h.p. with a continuous scene of youths drinking, eating, playing cards & singing reserved on a richly gilt-seeded ground, ornate leaf & scroll decoration on the lower body, neck, cover & plinth base, gilt & blue border bands, blue Beehive mark, titled in German under the base, late 19th c., pr.................. **$5,040**

▶ **Vases**, cov., 45" h., the high octagonal base with a flaring foot supporting a large bulbous ovoid body on a ringed pedestal, the tapering neck flanked by ornate arched & looping gold dragon handles, the domed cover with two figures, a man & a woman dressed as Classical warriors, the main body of each painted on each side with colorful scenes of Achilles, Diana, Hector or Thetis, the body & base in deep maroon trimmed with elaborate gilt scrolls & leaf designs & bands of white & gold bands, the pedestal base decorated with four panels showing Classical scenes in color alternating of maroon panels with elaborate gilt scrolling, late 19th c., blue shield marks, one handle possibly reattached, the other with minor professional repairs, pr **$43,475**

Vases, 7 5/8" h., tall slightly tapering squared body with a rounded shoulder & short cylindrical neck with rolled rim, short gold scroll handles from rim to shoulder, ruby ground, each centered by an oval reserve h.p. with a color bust portrait of Napoleon or Josephine, each within a raised gold border below a trellis & diaper cartouche, the back decorated with an octagonal turquoise 'jeweled' panel of scrolling leaves above ribbon-tied floral garlands, red Beehive mark, early 20th c., pr. **$3,360**

Charger, round, h.p. with a romantic mythological scene of a pretty maiden seated on a garden bench beside a fountain & playfully scolding Cupid who has broken his bow, an orb at her feet, artist-signed, within a pink velvet & giltwood frame, early 20th c., 11" d **$2,400**

Tray, oval, the center h.p. with a large rectangular panel showing a classical view allegorical of the Triumph of the Arts & Science, depicted as a gathering of classical figures supporting emblems of knowledge, attended by putti among clouds, supporting white classical portrait roundels, the outer dark green ground ornately decorated with leafy scrolls & trellis, artist-signed, blue Beehive mark, late 19th c., 16 1/2" l. **$3,120**

Plate, 9 5/8" d., portrait-type, Art Nouveau taste, the center painted with a bust profile of a lovely young brunette maiden wearing an off-the-shoulder robe, the wide gently scalloped border in pale green accented with deep maroon reserves decorated overall with ornate gold scrolls, flowers & spider webs, artist-signed, titled in German on the back, impressed crowned "PF" mark, late 19th - early 20th c **$1,800**

Vase, 5" h., ovoid body tapering to a slender neck with a flaring rim, gilt openwork vine-like gold handles from the center neck to shoulder, a large gold oval enclosing a color portrait of a young maiden with brown hair, background in pale shaded green with ornate gilt decoration, artist-signed, marked on the base "Germany - Sincerity - 3666," tiny flat nick on the rim **$575**

Royal Worcester

THIS PORCELAIN HAS been made by the Royal Worcester Porcelain Co. at Worcester, England, from 1862 to the present. Royal Worcester is distinguished from wares made at Worcester between 1751 and 1862, which are referred to only as Worcester by collectors.

Plates, 10 1/2" d., each h.p. with a detailed landscape with a castle in the distance, shaped gold rim band, puce printed crowned monogram mark, date cypher for 1930, set of 12 ....$5,400

Vase, 4 3/8" h., a small lobed & flaring gilt-trimmed foot below the spherical reticulated yellow ground body with a creamy shoulder decorated with delicate gilt scrolls & four small gilt lug handles, a short flaring ringed & reticulated neck, attributed to George Owen, puce printed crowned monogram mark, ca. 1891.... **$9,600**

Demitasse cups & saucers, cobalt blue
ground, each printed & enriched around
the rim with a flowering rinceau vine
above a stepped geometric gilt band, the
interiors & wells decorated in gilt, puce
printed monogram mark, date cyphers for
1903, original box, set of 12 .... **$1,800**

Charger, round, in the Persian taste, ivory
ground, the center pierced with a quatrefoil panel decorated in three-tone gold
with scrolling vines & enameled flower
blossoms in coral, white & turquoise, a
matching pierced border band, puce
printed crowned mark, date cypher for
1880, 11 1/4" d.............................. **$1,200**

Figures, a male & female Middle Eastern water carrier, she standing with a jar on her
shoulder pouring into a large bowl below,
he standing with holding a jar in one hand
& pouring into a large bowl below, each
decorated in green, tan & gold on an ivory
ground, modeled by James Hadley, Shape
No. 594, ca. 1891, artist-signed & printed
marks, each with gilt wear, one liner with
rim chip, 17" & 17 3/4" h., pr **$881**

Figures, a standing male & female in
peasant costume, she holding a small keg
& he holding a scythe, a tree trunk vase
behind each, the old ivory ground decorated in shades of gold, tan, green & red,
modeled by James Hadley, ca. 1888,
printed & impressed marks, 13 3/4" &
14" h., pr **$999**

Candelabra, figural, designed with a round rockwork base supporting the figure of a young peasant girl seated in the fork of two tree trunks the continue up to form the leaf-molded candle sockets, h.p. delicate hues of green, brown & roses, late 19th c., 9" h **$345**

Ewer, a small rounded pedestal base supporting the large ovoid body tapering to a tall slender neck with a long upright & arched spout, ornate scroll & leaf handle, ivory ground decorated around the sides with a fancy gold floral swag design with further gold on the neck, handle & base, ca. 1899, 13 1/4" h................. **$382**

Ewer, bulbous lower body tapering to a slender cylindrical neck with gold-trimmed rim with small spout, the ivory textured ground h.p. with colorful leafy floral branches, a large gold coiling salamander handle down the side, signed on base with the green mark, late 19th c., 11 1/4" h.....**$575**

Figure of Diana, titled "The Bather Surprised," the standing semi-draped goddess with three-tone metallic robe resting on a tree stump, raised on a canted rectangular gold base, gilt crowned monogram mark, date cypher for 1919, 23 1/8" h.....**$1,920**

ROYAL WORCESTER

Plates, 10 5/8" d., commemorative, yellow ground ornately decorated with delicate gilt scrollwork issuing flaming torches, the center h.p. in color with a tight floral bouquet, the back with a presentation inscription dated 1927, gilt printed crowned marks, set of 12 .... **$2,400**

Plates, 10 5/8" d., ruby & ivory ground, the wide border decorated with ornate gilt scrollwork issuing flaming torches, the further ornate gold on the ivory band surrounding the central reserve of a tight bouquet of colorful flowers, puce printed crowned monogram mark, date cypher for 1909 .... **$1,440**

Plate, 7 7/8" d., the wide reticulated sides with a honeycomb design in blue trimmed with gold dots, a narrow outer & inner solid band in pink with white & turquoise jewel-ing, the solid center with a lightly embossed gilt landscape, printed mark, attributed to George Owen, dated 1882 .... **$16,450**

Figures, modeled as Kate Greenaway-style young man & maiden each holding a basket, a tree trunk base behind each, decorated in shades of green, blue, brown & gold, Shape No. 880, printed mark, ca. 1890, 9 3/4" h., pr. **$588**

Tea set: cov. teapot, open sugar bowl, creamer & cup & saucer; each with a gilt rim & raised gilt dots to a blue glazed honeycomb pierced body, white & turquoise jeweled borders over pink bands, printed & raised marks, attributed to George Owen, dated 1878, teapot 4 1/2" h., the set...**$28,200**

Vases, 6 3/4" h., gently swelled cylindrical reticulated body tapering to a short cylindrical gold neck, a pierced central unique band with a unique pierced design flanked by finer honeycomb bands in pale blue with gilt jeweling, upper & lower border bands enameled & jeweled with a zig-zag design, attributed to George Owen, dated 1892, printed mark, pr..**$21,150**

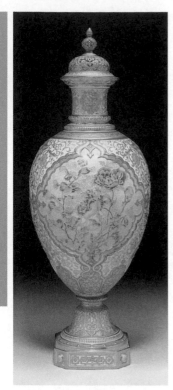

Vase, cov., 21 3/4" h., in the Persian taste, ivory ground, a square foot with angled corners supports the bell-form stem & tall ovoid body tapering to a ringed cylindrical neck with flaring rim topped by a domed & pierced cover with a pierced ball-form finial, the front & back of the body with quatrefoil panels h.p. with large chrysanthemums in shades red & green trimmed in gold, joined at the sides by rosettes & acanthus leaf panels among delicate elaborate leafy scrolls, the lower body & socle base with conforming beaded strapwork lappets, iron-red crowned monogram mark, mark of retailer Davis Collamore & Co., New York City, ca. 1880 .... **$4,800**

Vase, 6 5/8" h., footed spherical reticulated body tapering to a slender, ringed reticulated neck with gold trim & a flaring top, long scrolled serpent handles trimmed in gold from the neck to the shoulders, glazed in pale blue & buff & trimmed with raised gilt dots, Shape No. 871, attributed to George Owen, ca. 1900, printed mark.................... **$31,725**

Vase, 8 1/2" h., pate-sur-pate, footed tapering ovoid body with a wide cupped rim, double loop vine handles down the neck, blue ground finely h.p. in white slip & hand-tooled with a blossoming branch of cinquefoil blossoms & leaves, the back with an insect in flight, Royal China Works mark of Grainger's Worcester, date letter for 1893.................... **$2,400**

Vase, 9 3/4" h., Sabrina Ware, tall ovoid body with a short flared neck, decorated in dark blue & white with a landscape with white cranes wading in a marsh with large trees in the distance, marked "Royal Worcester England - Sabrina Ware - 2472" **$805**

Vase, 9" h., a low round reticulated foot supporting the large spherical reticulated body tapering to an ornately pierced tall slender trumpet neck, ornate red-stained male mask head handles on the shoulder, gilt decoration with large pierced medallions on a wide pale blue center band, Shape No. 1552, attributed to George Owen, dated 1894, printed mark................ **$30,500**

Vase, 10 3/8" h., a small pedestal foot supporting the large spherical body with a tall slender waisted neck, ivory ground with polychrome enamel floral bouquet on the side, bordered in translucent bluish grey, printed mark, ca. 1900, missing cover, gilt rim wear................................ **$147**

Vases, 4 1/4" h., spherical finely reticulated body with blue glazed honeycomb bands flanking a buff-stained band, raised on a lobed flaring foot with gold trim, the solid shoulder molded with four lug handles with gold trim, flaring & ringed cylindrical neck with gold trim, attributed by George Owen, Shape No. 1257, printed marks, ca. 1891, pr **$15,250**

Rozart Pottery

GEORGE AND ROSE Rydings were aspiring Kansas City (Missouri) potters who, in the late 1960s, began to produce a line of fine underglaze pottery. An inheritance of vintage American-made artware gave the Rydings inspiration to recreate old ceramic masters' techniques. Some design influence also came from Fred Radford, grandson of well-known Ohio artist Albert Radford (ca. 1890s-1904). Experimenting with Radford's formula for Jasperware and sharing ideas with Fred about glazing techniques and ceramic chemistry led the Rydings to a look reminiscent of the ware made

Vase, 15" h., Rozart Royal, with eagle in landing position on front, Rose Rydings **$345**

by turn-of-the-century American art pottery masters such as Weller and Rookwood. The result of their work became Rozart, the name of the Rydings' pottery.

Many lines have been created since Rozart's beginning. Twainware, Sylvan, Cameoware, Rozart Royal, Rusticware, Deko, Krakatoa, Koma and Sateen are a few. It is rare to find a piece of Rozart that is not marked in some way. The earliest mark is "Rozart" at the top of a circle with "Handmade" in the center and "K.C.M.O." (Kansas City, Missouri) at the bottom. Other marks followed over the years, including a seal that was used extensively. Along with artist initials, collectors will find a date code (either two digits representing the year or a month separated by a slash followed by a two-digit year). George signs his pieces "GMR," "GR," or "RG" (with a backwards "R"). Working on Twainware, Jasperware and Cameoware in the early years, George has many wheel-thrown pieces to his credit. Rose, who is very knowledgeable about Native Americans, does scenics and portraits. Her mark is either "RR" or "Rydings." Four of the seven Rydings children have worked

Ewer, sgraffito mouse design, Rose Rydings, 10" h **$255**

in the pottery as well. Anne Rydings White (mark is "Anne" or "AR" or "ARW") designed and executed many original pieces in addition to her work on the original Twainware line. Susan Rydings Ubert (mark is "S" over "R") has specialized in Sylvan pieces and is an accomplished sculptor and mold maker. Susan's daughter Maureen does female figures in the Art Deco style. Becky (mark is "B" over "R"), now a commercial artist, designed lines such as Fleamarket, Nature's Jewels, and Animals. Cindy Rydings Cushing (mark is "C" over "R" or "CRC") developed the very popular Kittypots line. Mark Rydings is the Rozart mold maker.The Rozart Pottery is still active today. Pottery enthusiasts are taking notice of the family history, high quality and reminiscent beauty of Rozart. Its affordability may soon cease as Rozart's popularity and recognition are on the rise.

Sign, for Rozart Pottery dealer, "Rozart Pottery" in script, with base, Copper-verde glaze, 5 1/2" l ..**$125**

Model of duck, on base **$82**

Mug, advertising Gatsby Days Excelsior Springs, Missouri, May 1998, with picture of woman in old-fashioned picture hat on front, 3 1/2" h............ **$56**

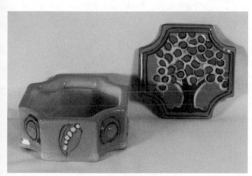

Box with lid, Arts & Crafts style, quatrefoil shape with image of tree painted on lid and various decorations about sides of box, George Rydings, 6" w.................... **$212**

Letter holders, rectangular, with various designs painted on front, limited edition, 4 1/2" h., 6 1/2" l., each **$75**

Vase, 7 1/2" h., pillow shape with bird on branch on front, Cindy Cushing.............. **$150**

Vase, 14 1/2" h., with Indian portrait on front, Becky White **$290**

Satsuma

THESE DECORATED WARES have been produced in Japan since the end of the 18th century. The early pieces are scarce and high-priced. Later Satsuma wares are plentiful and, with prices rising, are also becoming highly collectible.

Vase, 29" h., 10" d., floor-type, tall slightly tapering body with a slightly bulbed base band with three cut-outs, the angled shoulder tapering to a cylindrical neck, the neck & shoulder decorated with diaper panels & stylized florals, the upper body divided into a band of large arched panels each h.p. with a different flower plant, the lower body decorated with various geometric designs & floral panels, all in shades of gold, tan, rose red & light blue, 19th c **$390**

Vase, 9 1/4" h., a flared round foot with gold geometric bands below the large bulbous ovoid body with a flat closed rim flanked by gold lion head & ring shoulder handles, the sides h.p. with large oval panels filled with Geisha wearing gold-trimmed robes in a landscape with a lake & trees in the distance, the other side with an oval panel decorated with Rakans, signed, raised on an ornate high squared & footed bronze stand, late 19th c .. **$588**

Vases, 9 1/2" h., 4 1/2" d., footed ovoid six-sided body with a short flaring neck, the sides decorated with groups of Buddhist saints in color with heavy gold trim, figural elephant shoulder handles, painted chop mark on the base, probably late 19th c., pr**$259**

Vase, 16 1/4" h., a large ovoid body tapering to a wide trumpet neck, a decorative gold base band, the sides h.p. with wide deep orange ground decorated with large h.p. flowering peony trees & butterflies in white, gold, brown & light blue, the shoulders with a gold molded drapery design, the neck decorated with a band of large gold Mon emblems below a narrow paneled rim band, ca. 1900 ... **$441**

Teapot, cov., footed squatty spherical body with a wide shoulder centered by a tall cylindrical neck fitted with a small domed cover, a long gold dragon wrapped around the base of the neck with the neck & head forming the spout & the arched tail forming the handle, the creamy background h.p. with exotic birds among colorful flowering plants in shades of red, blue, white & purple with heavy gold trim, black & gold chop mark on the base, late 19th - early 20th c., 6 3/4" h **$1,006**

Saturday Evening Girls

SATURDAY EVENING GIRLS (Paul Revere) pottery was established in Boston, Massachusetts, in 1906, by a group of philanthropists seeking to establish better conditions for underprivileged young girls of the area. Edith Brown served as supervisor of the small "Saturday Evening Girls Club" pottery operation, which was moved, in 1912, to a house close to the Old North Church where Paul Revere's signal lanterns had been placed. The wares were mostly hand decorated in mineral colors, and both sgraffito and molded decorations were employed. Although it became popular, it was never a profitable operation and always depended on financial contributions to operate. After the death of Edith Brown in 1932, the pottery foundered and finally closed in 1942.

Flaring bowl painted with tulips in cuerda seca, circa 1925, Paul Revere Pottery medallion/ PRP/?MD/11-2-?, 3" x 7-1/2"...**$1,000**

Cream pitcher depicting white rabbit on either side and the name Joan Audrey Carlson in a band beneath, marked with Paul Revere Pottery circular paper label, excellent original condition, 4-1/4" h......................**$375**

Vase painted with lotus in cuerda seca, circa 1925, Paul Revere Pottery medallion, 6-1/2" x 3-1/2"..................**$2,125**

Albina Mangini plate and pitcher with running rabbits, "Caroline"s Plate," 1913, signed AM/
SEG/10/13/December 25, 1913, 4-1/4" x 4-1/2", plate 7-3/4" dia. **$2,125**

Fannie Levine, Sara Galner, 1914, chamberstick with Greek key pattern and faceted paperweight with swan, both signed and dated, 2" x 6", 2-1/2" sq... **$1,188**

Sèvres

SOME OF THE most desirable porcelain ever produced was made at the Sèvres factory, originally established at Vincennes, France, and transferred, through permission of Madame de Pompadour, to Sèvres as the Royal Manufactory about the middle of the 18th century. King Louis XV took sole responsibility for the works in 1759, when production of hard paste wares began. Between 1850 and 1900, many biscuit and soft-paste pieces were made again. Fine early pieces are scarce and high-priced. Many of those available today are late productions. The various Sèvres marks have been copied, and pieces in the "Sèvres Style" are similar to actual Sèvres wares but not necessarily from that factory.

Pair of gilt-bronze-mounted porcelain urns and covers, France, circa 1900, each with multicolored lustre borders and central cartouches of allegorical subjects with landscapes on reverse, nymph handles, signed under covers, 17 1/4" high **$11,070**

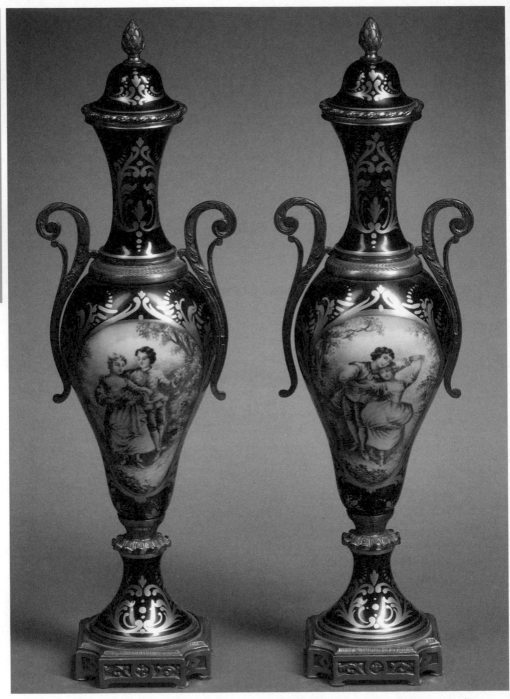

Pair of bronze-mounted porcelain urns, France, circa 1900, each with dark cobalt ground, gilt trim, and oval medallions, polychrome enamel decorated with cartouche of lovers to one side, cottage landscapes on reverse, 16" high **$492**

Pair of jeweled porcelain cabinet portrait plates, 19th century, with matching cobalt blue rims, enamel decorated with reserves of flowers and classical motifs, with gilt accenting and white, turquoise, and red jeweling, inner rim with flower garland wrapped in ribbon, each painted in center with portrait roundel in red jeweled surround, one depicting Pierre Corneille, the other Embegirde Femme de Pharamond, identified and with factory marks on reverse, 9 1/2" diameter **$2,829**

French enameled portrait urn, late 19th to early 20th century, depicting shepherd courting young girl, signed J. Missant lower right of painting, cobalt ground with scrolled floral gilt accents, 11 3/4" high x 13 3/4" wide............ **$1,815**

Vase with crystalline glaze with large blue crystals on cobalt surface along with splashes of mustard and turquoise, made in 1902, marked with triangular logo featuring S and date, excellent original condition, 9 1/4" high **$500**

Porcelain vase made in 1910 with crystalline glaze, featuring large blue crystals and smaller ivory crystals, brass mounts at top and bottom, attached to brass stand, marked with triangular logo showing S and date within, excellent original condition, 10" high ... **$400**

French gilded bronze and porcelain urn depicting courting couple in landscape scene with yellow ground, 19th century, signed lower right of painting, blue double "L" with "S" and "L," 26 1/2" high x 13" wide **$2,420**

French porcelain sculpture depicting man holding hat, standing near stool, bottom has blue double L mark with A (used circa 1753 but possibly made as late as 19th century), 13" high **$424**

Pair of French porcelain six-arm candelabrum, 19th century, each with hand-painted scenes of courting couples and landscapes, signed A. Daret, each scene surrounded by cobalt ground, mounted on gilded bronze lion base with scrolled floral arms, each approximately 25 5/8" high... **$1,331**

Pair of gilded French bronze and porcelain five-arm candelabrum, each with cobalt porcelain body with hand-painted landscape and courting couple scenes, 19th century, each approximately 27 1/4" high x 12 1/2" diameter **$2,178**

Pair of French porcelain cobalt ground urns depicting man and woman with floral scenes, 19th century, dore bronze rim mount with handles and base, each approximately 8 7/8" high. Provenance: From the estate of Count and Countess Claes-Eric de Lewenhaupt of Sweden................................... **$787**

Porcelain Napoleonic military plate with gilded border, 19th century, artist signed Swebach, dated 1812, 9" diameter **$1,375**

Two cups and one saucer, French, 19th century, largest: cup 3" high, saucer 5" diameter **$750**

Porcelain hand-painted box with top depicting woman with cherub, 19th century, signed "Rolle" lower left hand corner, body depicting floral bouquets with pink ground, bottom holds blue Sèvres double L mark with red Chateau des Tuilieres mark, 5 5/8" high x 9 1/2" long x 6 1/4" deep....**$726**

Pair of green urns with ormolu, late 18th/early 19th century, 10 1/4" **$1,100**

SÈVRES

French porcelain mounted centerpiece bowl with figural cherub bronze-doré six-armed candelabra frame, 19th century, front of bowl has hand-painted scene depicting young family, verso depicts floral bouquet, oval hand-painted porcelain portrait plaque of aristocratic woman on front of base, crafted scrolled leaves, latticework and floral garlands, 31 1/2" high x 25 1/4" long x 14 3/4" deep..................**$12,100**

Vase with mottled blue high glaze and gold trim at top and bottom, circa 1892-1893, stamped on base S 92 within oval and with Dore' a Sèvres 93 logo, initials JT in green slip, excellent original condition, 9 1/2" high **$160**

Cup with lid and saucer, 18th/19th century, 6" x 6 1/2" **$750**

Large figure of fish in brown with gilded accents, marked with Sèvres France M-N-F logo, chip to right rear corner of the plinth, 9 1/4" high x 17 1/2" long **$275**

Three porcelain Napoleonic military plates with gilded borders, 19th century, one artist signed L. Moreau, script signature M. Imple de Sèvres, each 9 3/8" diameter **$2,375**

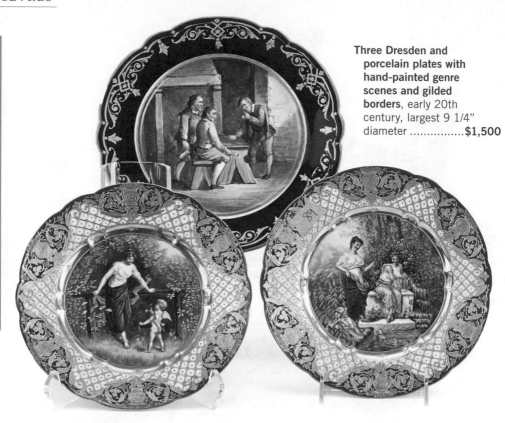

Three Dresden and porcelain plates with hand-painted genre scenes and gilded borders, early 20th century, largest 9 1/4" diameter $1,500

Crystalline vase with mushroom-colored crystals on green surface dripped over cobalt, 1919, Sèvres ink stamp with date, gold colored holder, excellent original condition with two mounting holes drilled to bottom of vase to attach it to holder, ceramic portion 6 7/8" high..................$600

Four porcelain items, 19th/20th century: covered center bowl with gilt and floral decoration, pair of covered urns, and lidded urn with rams head handles, all marked, tallest 16 1/2"....**$625**

Pair of French urns, cobalt blue and gold decorated, 19th century, 22 1/2" x 9 1/2" **$1,900**

Shawnee

THE SHAWNEE POTTERY Company of Zanesville, Ohio, opened its doors for operation in 1936 and, sadly, closed in 1961. The pottery was inexpensive for its quality and was readily purchased at dime stores as well as department stores. Sears, Roebuck and Co., Butler Bros., Woolworth's and S. Kresge were just a few of the companies that were longtime retailers of this fine pottery.

Shawnee U.S.A.

Shawnee Pottery Company had a wide array of merchandise to offer, from knickknacks to dinnerware, although Shawnee is quite often associated with colorful pig cookie jars and the dazzling "Corn King" line of dinnerware. Planters, miniatures, cookie jars and Corn King pieces are much in demand by today's avid collectors. Factory seconds were purchased by outside decorators and trimmed with gold, decals and unusual hand painting, which makes those pieces extremely desirable in today's market and enhances the value considerably. Shawnee Pottery has become the most sought-after pottery in today's collectible market.

Vase, miniature, 2 1/2" h., embossed stagecoach scene, found in burgundy, green & cobalt blue, marked "U.S.A." **$125-$150**

Vase, miniature, 2 1/2" h., embossed spinning wheel, found in burgundy, green & cobalt blue, marked "U.S.A." ... **$125-$150**

Bank-cookie jar, figural Winnie Pig, chocolate or butterscotch base, marked "Patented: Winnie Shawnee 61 U.S.A." 10 1/2" h .... **$350-$375**

Bank, figural Howdy Doody riding a pig, marked "Bob Smith U.S.A.," 6 3/4" h...... **$500-$576**

Ashtray, figural kingfisher, parrot, bird, fish, terrier or owl, marked "U.S.A.," dusty rose, turquoise, old ivory, white or burgundy, 3" h., each...................... **$55-$65**

Bank, figural bulldog, 4 1/2" h., unmarked....................................**$150-$175**

Creamer, White Corn line, airbrushed & gold trim, marked "U.S.A.," 4 3/4" h ..... **$95-$125**

Clock, Pyramid shape, copper-clad Medallion finish, with pink or copper face, marked "951 Kenwood U.S.A.," 7 1/2" h ... **$95-$125**

Creamer, ball-type, Dutch style, decorated with tulip & blue around neck, marked "U.S.A.," 4 1/4" h .... **$175-$200**

Creamer, ball-type, Dutch style, decorated with red feather, marked "U.S.A. 12," 4 1/2" h ....**$100-$125**

Dealer's display sign, figural Spanish dancers, "Valencia" embossed across base, tangerine glaze, 11 1/4" h ....**$400-$450**

Cookie jar-ice bucket, cov., figural elephant, pink, marked "Shawnee U.S.A. 60" or "Kenwood U.S.A. 60".........**$95-$100**

Cigarette box, cov., embossed Indian arrowhead on lid, rusty brown, marked "Shawnee," 3 1/4 x 4 1/2"..**$475-$525**

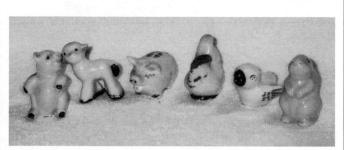

Figurine, miniature, model of a 2 3/8" h. bear cub, 2 1/4" h. standing lamb, 2 1/4" h. standing pig, 2 1/8" h. rooster, 1 3/4" h. baby bird or 2 1/2" h. bunny with ears down, bright white or old ivory, unmarked, each ....**$15-$25**

Canister, cov., squared shape with rounded corners, pale blue with colorful fruit decal, marked "U.S.A.," 7" h ....**$35-$45**

Figurine, miniature, model of 2 3/8" h. tropical fish, 3" h. bunny on haunches, 2 3/4" h. circus horse, 2 1/2" h. seated terrier or 2" h. fish, bright white or old ivory, unmarked, each ....**$15-$25**

Coffeepot, cov., Valencia line, tangerine glaze, 7 1/2" h ....**$95-$125**

Cookie jar, cov., figural Smiley Pig, shamrock decoration, marked "U.S.A.," 11 1/4" h .... **$150-$200**

Cookie jar, cov., figural Winnie Pig, with green collar, marked "Patented Winnie U.S.A.," 11 3/4" h .... **$175-$200**

Creamer, figural Smiley Pig, decorated with embossed peach flower, marked "Patented Smiley U.S.A.," 4 1/2" h .... **$55-$75**

Pitcher, 7 3/4" h., figural Smiley Pig, pink & blue flower decoration, marked "Patented Smiley U.S.A." .... **$75-$85**

Creamer, Lobster Ware, satin charcoal grey or Van Dyke brown, figural lobster handle, marked "U.S.A.," 4 1/2" h .... **$75-$85**

Planter, model of a bicycle built for two with man & woman riders dressed in Gay Nineties style, gold trim, marked "Shawnee U.S.A. 735," 6" h......................... **$75-$100**

Teapot, cov., figural Granny Ann, lavender apron with gold trim & floral decals or peach apron with blue & red trim with gold trim & floral decals, marked "Patented Granny Ann U.S.A.," each ...... **$250-$275**

Lamp base, figural Puppy, brown on cream base, unmarked, 4 3/4" h................ **$65-$75**

Planter, model of a fox & bag, marked "U.S.A.," 4 1/2" h .... **$50-$65**

Teapot, cov., figural Elephant patt., green, bright blue or yellow glaze, marked "U.S.A.," 6 1/2" h., each .... **$165-$225**

Planter, model of an angel fish, marked "U.S.A.," found in yellow, flax blue, old ivory & pink, 8 1/2" h .... **$55-$65**

Range set: tall flattened & tapering salt & pepper shakers & flattened, domed sugar bowl/grease jar; Sahara line, Medallion copper-clad finish with blue or pink base on sugar bowl, sugar marked "Kenwood U.S.A. 997," sugar 3 1/2" h., shakers 5 1/2" h., the set......................... **$65-$75**

Sugar bowl-grease jar, cov., Fruit & Basket patt., with gold trim, marked "Shawnee U.S.A. 81," 5 1/2" h........... **$125-$175**

Teapot, cov., figural Tom the Piper's Son, white body with h.p. trim or airbrushed in blues & reds, marked "Tom the Piper's Son patented U.S.A. 44," 7" h., each .... **$65-$75**

Teapot, cov., figural Cottage, marked "U.S.A. 7," 5 1/2" h .....**$375-$450**

Teapot, cov., figural Elephant with burgundy, green & brown h.p. on white ground, marked "U.S.A.," 6 1/2" h ....**$225-$275**

Teapot, cov., figural Tom the Piper's Son, airbrushed matte reddish orange & greenish yellow with gold trim, marked "Tom the Piper's Son Patented U.S.A. 44".......**$325-$375**

Shelley China

MEMBERS OF THE Shelley family were in the pottery business in England as early as the 18th century. In 1872 Joseph Shelley formed a partnership with James Wileman of Wileman & Co. who operated the Foley China Works. The Wileman & Co. name was used for the firm for the next fifty years, and between 1890 and 1910 the words "The Foley" appeared above conjoined "WC" initials.

Beginning in 1910 the Shelley family name in a shield appeared on wares, although the firm's official name was still Wileman & Co. The company's name was finally changed to Shelley in 1925 and then Shelley China Ltd. after 1965. The firm changed hands in the 1960s and became part of the Doulton Group in 1971.

At first only average quality earthenwares were produced, but in the late 1890s new shapes and better quality decorations were used.

Bone china was introduced at Shelley before World War I, and these fine dinnerwares became very popular in the United States and are increasingly popular today with collectors. Thin "eggshell china" teawares, miniatures and souvenir items were widely marketed during the 1920s and 1930s and are sought-after today.

Vase, 4 3/4" h., simple baluster form with short flat mouth, Crested Ware, white ground with the color coat-of-arms of a town in England .... **$25-$30**

Teapot, cov., Dainty Big Floral Shape, Capper's Strawberry patt. No. 2396, from the Seconds group, 1959 .... **$200-$300**

Jardiniere, Art Nouveau style, rounded foot tapering to a slender pedestal flanked by slender S-curve legs supporting a wide squatty bulbous bowl with a widely flaring rim, in shades of brown, blue, white & green, No. 3567, Wileman & Co., ca. 1900..**$300-$400**

Pin dish, round with widely flaring fluted sides, Marguerite patt., 4 3/4" d ..... **$45-$50**

Teapot, cov., Princess Shape, Poppies, orange patt. No. 12227, Floral style, from the Best Ware group, 1933, teapot only ..... **$350-$550**

Luncheon set (trio), cup & saucer & dessert plate; Fluted shape, Rose, Pansy, Forget-me-not patt., 3 pcs ....**$75-$90**

Cup & saucer, Crocus patt., Eve Shape, #11971, Art Deco style, ca. 1930, the set .... **$225-$275**

Teapot, cov., Dainty Shape, Thistle patt. No. 13829, from the Best Ware group, 1955 .... **$200-$300**

Tea set: cov. teapot, open sugar bowl, creamer, cup & saucer, rimmed soup plate & sandwich plate; Dainty Blue patt., the set .... **$775-$800**

Tea set, cov. teapot, open sugar bowl, creamer & six cups & saucers; Diamonds patt., Mode shape, very rare Art Deco design, the set.................................. **$4,000**

Luncheon set (trio), cup & saucer & dessert plate; Vogue shape, Horn of Flowers patt., 3 pcs... **$225-$250**

Tea set: cups & saucers, open sugar, creamer, cake plate & more; Art Deco style, Blue Lines & Bands patt., 21 pcs............... **$3,000**

Teapot, cov., Queen Anne Shape, Blue Iris patt. No. 11561, Floral style, from the Best Ware group, 1919, various sizes, each.. **$300-$400**

Teapot, cov., Shell Shape, Wileman & Co., patt. No. 5137, introduced in 1891 .... **$500-$600**

Vase, 7 1/2" h., footed wide gently flaring sides with a flattened shoulder to the short widely flaring neck, Crane patt., burnt orange ground with blue & green crane & black shoulder band...**$225-$250**

Teapot, cov., Oriental Shape, Intarsio decoration, Wileman & Co., patt. No. 3081, short production period, 1899........**$1,200-$1,500**

Vase, footed swelled cylindrical body tapering to a tiny flared neck, Pastello Ware, decorated with a country landscape with a cottage with smoke rising from the chimney, modern **$450**

Luncheon set (trio), cup & saucer & dessert plate, Queen Anne Shape, Archway of Roses patt., ca. 1928, 3 pcs.... **$150-$200**

Bowl-vase, 7" h., Art Deco style, wide low rounded lower body below sharply tapering cylindrical sides, Blocks patt., decorated in shades of blue **$750**

Luncheon set (trio), cup & saucer & dessert plate; Vogue shape, Blocks patt., #11785, 3 pcs............. **$250-$300**

Spatterware

SPATTERWARE TAKES ITS name from the "spattered" decoration, in various colors, used to trim pieces hand painted with rustic center designs of flowers, birds, houses, etc. Popular in the early 19th century, most was imported from England.

Related wares, called "stick spatter," had freehand designs applied with pieces of cut sponge attached to sticks, hence the name. Examples date from the 19th and early 20th century and were produced in England, Europe and America.

Some early spatter-decorated wares were marked by the manufacturers, but not many. Twentieth century reproductions are also sometimes marked, including those produced by Boleslaw Cybis.

Plate, 19th century, Thistle pattern, strong yellow border, numerous repairs to rim, 8-1/4" dia. **$420**

Bowl, 19th century, original blue and yellow tulip decoration, extremely rare, no imperfections or paint loss, 13-1/2" dia..........**$330**

Rainbow spatterware octagon platter, 19th century, green and red, no imperfections or loss, 14" x 17-3/4".. **$900**

Rainbow spatterware coffeepot in blue and red, repairs to lid and tip of spout, 9" h.. **$300**

Red spatterware with peafowl decoration, two small cups and saucer, American, 19th century, saucer 4-1/2" dia., larger cup 3-3/4" h **$180**

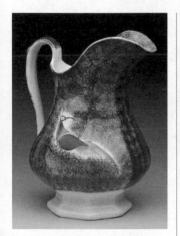

Large water pitcher, 19th century, strong blue spatter, original red, orange, and green peafowl decoration, colors on peafowl are unusual, pitcher has no imperfections, 10" h. .. **$570**

Pair of red spatterware peafowl plates, with large peafowls surrounded by strong red spatter decoration, larger plate 9-1/2" dia. **$360**

Rare cup and saucer, 19th century, double brown acorn decoration, original red spatterware decoration, both pieces with no loss or repairs, largest 6" dia. **$960**

Large milk pitcher, 19th century, fort or castle pattern, strong blue decoration, 8-1/2" h...**$270**

Group of spatterware, yellow spatterware sugar bowl with thistle pattern (missing cover), rainbow milk pitcher, blue and purple glazed octagonal plate, American, 19th century, plate 10" x 7-1/4", sugar bowl 5-1/2" h **$480**

Spongeware

SPONGEWARE: THE NAME says it all. A sponge dipped in colored pigment is daubed onto a piece of earthenware pottery of a contrasting color, creating an overall mottled, "sponged" pattern. A clear glaze is applied, and the piece fired. The final product, with its seemingly random, somewhat smudged coloration, conveys an overall impression of handmade folk art.

Most spongeware, however, was factory-made from the mid-1800s well into the 1930s. Any folk art appeal was secondary; the result of design simplicity intended to facilitate maximum production at minimum cost. Although mass-manufacturing produced most spongeware, it did in fact originate in the work of independent potters. Glasgow, Scotland, circa 1835, is recognized as the birthplace of spongeware. The goal: the production of utilitarian everyday pottery with appeal to the budget-conscious.

Batter pitcher, no cover, dark blue sponging, printed on front "1 1/2 Qt." **$625**

Sponged surface decorations were a means of adding visual interest both easily and inexpensively.

Since early spongeware was quickly made, usually by amateur artisans, the base pottery was often insubstantial and the sponging perfunctory. However, due to its general usefulness, and especially because of its low cost, spongeware quickly found an audience. Production spread across Great Britain and Europe, finally reaching the United States. Eventually, quality improved, as even frugal buyers demanded more for their money.

The terms "spongeware" and "spatterware" are often used interchangeably. Spatterware took its name from the initial means of application: A pipe was used to blow colored pigment onto a piece of pottery, creating a spattered coloration. Since the process was tedious, sponging soon became the preferred means of color application, although the "spatterware" designation remained in use. Specific patterns were achieved by means of sponge printing (aka "stick spatter"): A small piece of sponge was cut in the pattern shape desired, attached to a stick, and then dipped in color. The stick served as a more precise means of application, giving the decorator more control, creating designs with greater border definition. Applied colors varied, with blue (on white) proving most popular. Other colors included red, black, green, pink, yellow, brown, tan, and purple.

Because of the overlap in style, there really is no "right or wrong" in classifying a particular object as "spongeware" or "spatterware"; often the manufacturer's advertising designation is the one used. Spatterware, however, has become more closely identified with pottery in which the mottled color pattern (whether spattered or sponged) surrounds

Batter pitcher, no cover, dark blue sponging, printed on front "1 Qt."..................... **$625**

Butter crock, covered, dark blue sponging around oval reserved printed "BUTTER," 6" dia., 5" h.......**$80-$150**

a central image, either stamped or painted freehand. Spongeware usually has no central image; the entire visual consists of the applied "splotching." Any break in that pattern comes in the form of contrasting bands, either in a solid color matching the mottling, or in a portion of the base earthenware kept free of applied color. Some spongeware pieces also carry stampings indicating the name of an advertiser, or the use intent of a specific object ("Butter," "Coffee," "1 Qt.").

Much of what is classified as spatterware has a certain delicacy of purpose: tea sets, cups and saucers, sugar bowls, and the like. Spongeware is more down-to-earth, both in intended usage and sturdiness. Among the many examples of no-nonsense spongeware: crocks, washbowl and pitcher sets, jugs, jars, canisters, soap dishes, shaving mugs, spittoons, umbrella stands, washboards, and even chamber pots. These are pottery pieces that mean business; their shapes, stylings, and simple decoration are devoid of fussiness.

Spongeware was usually a secondary operation for the many companies that produced it, and was marketed as bargain-priced service ware; it's seldom marked. Today, spongeware is an ideal collectible for those whose taste in 19th century pottery veers away from the overly detailed and ornate. Spongeware's major appeal is due in large part to the minimalism it represents.

Pitcher, slightly tapering cylindrical body with rim spout and C-form applied handle, overall dark blue sponging, a few tight hairlines, 8-3/4" h. **$175**

Pitcher, embossed Pine Cone pattern, cylindrical with D-form handle, heavy overall dark blue sponging, Burley-Winter Pottery Co., 9-1/2" h. **$800**

Pitcher, slender ovoid body with pinched rim spout and pointed arched handle, overall dark blue patterned sponging, 8-1/4" h. **$250**

Vegetable dish, shallow rectangular shape with rounded corners, overall dark blue sponging, wear, minor clay separation at rim, 9-3/4" l. **$120**

Canister, covered, footed cylindrical shape with domed cover with knob finial, dark blue large sponging around zigzag oval reserved printed in fancy script, "Coffee," 6" h. **$1,000**

Canister, open, advertising-type, heavy dark blue sponging around reserve printed in dark blue fancy lettering, "Old Honesty Coffee," 6" h. **$1,000**

Pitcher, Hallboy-type, blue sponged bands around rim and base, wide dark blue body band flanked by pinstripe bands, angular handle, 6" h. **$250**

Butter crock, no cover, blue sponging, printed on front in black, "Butter," 6" dia., 5" h.......**$115**

Water filter, wide cylindrical body with stepped domed cover, heavy dark blue sponging with two thin bands near top, rectangular white panel printed "No. 7," large shield-form mark on lower front reading "Improved Natural Stone Germ Proof Filter – Fulper Pottery Co., Flemington, N.J. Est. 1895," crack at rim and chip on cover, 12-1/2" h. **$230**

Umbrella stand, cylindrical, decorated with narrow blue sponged bands around rim and base, each flanked by two wide blue bands, two wide blue sponged bands around middle flanked by two dark blue bands, 21" h. **$2,000**

Sumida Gawa Pottery

SUMIDA GAWA WARES were made in Japan for Western export from the late 19th century through 1941. The pottery pieces, the popular forms of which include teapots, bowls, vases, jugs and tankards, are often heavy, brightly glazed and covered with figures in relief. Inscribed in kanji, more than 70 different marks are known, but not all pieces are marked. Pieces marked "Nippon" date to 1890-1921; pieces marked "Foreign" were made for export to England.

Jardiniere with figures pulling cart along path on orange ground, circa 1900, mark of Ryosai, 9" x 12". **$375**

Cylindrical form vase with figures and vines in relief on orange ground, circa 1900-1910, mark of Ryosai, 13-7/8" **$313**

Urn-shaped vase with applied decorations of Japanese ceramics on black ground, circa 1900, Ryosai mark, 18-1/4".................. **$3,000**

Bulbous vase with bird on flowering vine in relief on deep red glossy ground, early 20th century, unidentified mark, 11-1/4". **$250**

Three pots with figures in relief on red ground, early 20th century, chocolate pot with figural head, teapot with figures in relief and covered pot with pouring spout, all marked, tallest 9". **$1,125**

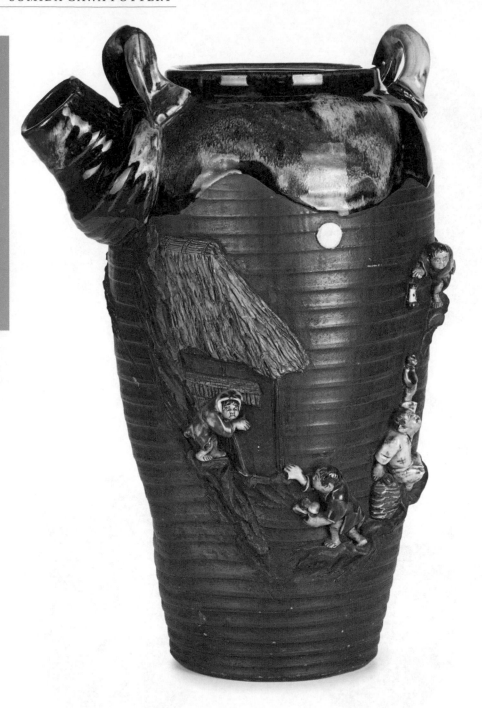

Lidded vessel, with handles and pouring spout with figures and thatched hut in relief on red ground, circa 1900, Ryosai mark, 18"...$750

Elephant-form candle-holder with child reading book, early 20th century, illegible mark, 7-1/8" x 7-1/4" x 4-1/2"... **$875**

Covered house-shaped tea box with female figure at top on black ground, early 20th century, unidentified, mark 6". **$250**

Figure of Girogin, god of longevity, with scroll in hand, circa 1900, unmarked, 9"........ **$313**

Pitcher with two figures on rock formations in mountain landscape, circa 1900, mark of Ryosai, 12-3/8". ... **$250**

Gourd vase with figures and creatures in celebratory poses on matte dark red ground, circa 1900, unidentified mark, 9" x 12". **$1,625**

Diorama bowl, with seven figures on ledge in relief on brown ground, early 20th century, unsigned, 5-1/4"..**$600-$800**

Pair of vases with woman and child in relief on brown and red ground, early 20th century, illegibly marked, 8-1/4". **$438**

Urn-form vase with pot of flowers with mother-of-pearl petals surrounded by porcelain vases on black ground, early 20th century, mark of Ryosai, 12". **$406**

Vase with bamboo stem and crane, early 20th century, Hara mark, 7-1/2" **$375**

Van Briggle Pottery

ARTUS VAN BRIGGLE, who formerly worked for Rookwood Pottery in Colorado Springs, Colorado, at the turn of the 20th century, established the Van Briggle Pottery. He died in 1904, but his widow and others carried on the pottery line. From 1900 until 1920, the pieces were dated. It remains in production today, specializing in art pottery.

Mug with embossed image of attacking eagle in light green mat glaze, 1905, incised marks include AA, company name, number 3 in circle, and date, impressed is shape number 355 B, excellent original condition, 4-3/4" h. **$325**

Early vase with stylized flowers, matte purple and green glazes, 1903, signed AA/1903/III/219, 6-1/2" x 4". **$2,125**

Bowl with arrow root design, mulberry mat glaze, 1920, marked on bottom with Van Briggle logo, name "Van Briggle" and "20" for date, excellent original condition, 4-7/8" x 9-1/2"...**$275**

Vase with poppy pods, thick matte green glaze, 1906, marked AA VAN BRIGGLE/illegible numbers/1906/X, 3-1/2" x 5-1/2". $813

Humidor encircled by red tulips against green ground with red accents at top and lined in red,
1902, marked with Van Briggle logo, name, 1902 date, Roman numeral III for clay type and
number 90, probably a process number; small glaze nick to tip of one leaf, open glaze bubble,
6-1/4" h..$3,700

Early vase with tulips, chartreuse and indigo glaze, 1903, signed AA/VAN BRIGGLE/1903/141/III, 8" x 3". **$5,625**

Early vase with daffodils, matte green glaze, 1903, signed AA/VAN BRIG-GLE/1903, 8-1/4" x 3"...................... **$1,875**

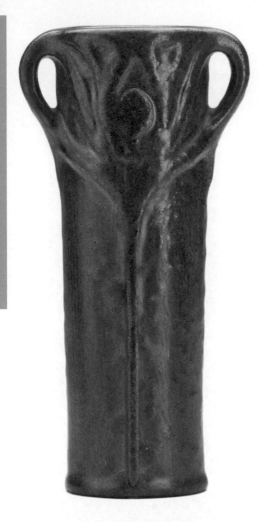

Two-handled vase with peacock feathers, sheer mottled indigo glaze on brown ground, 1906, signed AA/VAN BRIGGLE/COLO SPRINGS/1906, 6-1/2" x 3-1/4". **$1,500**

Vase with dark mat black-green glaze, 1916, marked in blue slip with Van Briggle logo and 1916 date, glaze skip at rim and base, 6-3/4" h. **$150**

Early bulbous vase with poppy pods, mauve glaze, 1905,
incised AA/VAN BRIGGLE/1905/V/21, 3-3/4" x 4"..........**$625**

Vase with trefoil, green glaze, 1907, marked AA VAN
BRIGGLE COLO. SPGS. 1907, 60?, 8-3/4" x 7-1/2". **$1,750**

Butterfly vase with two embossed swallowtails in rose over green mat glaze, AA and Van Briggle name visible, restoration to small rim chip, 3-3/4" h. **$200**

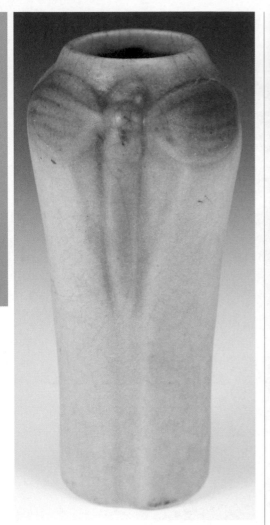

Art Nouveau pottery vase, dragonfly, Kathryn Hall, circa 1910, 7-1/4" h. x 3-1/4" dia.. **$275**

Lorelei vase, Art Nouveau woman grasping top of vase, her hair flowing forward and long gown flowing around side of vase, green shading to blue glaze, signed on underside with Van Briggle logo, "Van Briggle Colo Spgs" and artist initials "HVM," very good to excellent condition, 11" h. **$403**

Rare copper-clad vessel with chameleon handles, 1907, signed AA/11/15/Van Briggle/Colo. Springs/702.S.W., 5" x 8". **$2,250**

Large squat vessel with arrowroot leaves, matte green glaze, 1906, signed AA/VAN BRIGGLE/3/1906/439, 5-1/2" x 11-1/2". **$3,125**

Small vessel with anemone, light green and blue glaze, 1906, incised AA VAN BRIGGLE/323/1906/4, 3-1/2" x 4-3/4". **$500**

Early vessel with flowers and buds, lilac and green glaze, 1905, incised AA VAN BRIGGLE/354/VY/1905, 4-1/2" x 7". $625

Wedgwood

WEDGWOOD

THE NAME "WEDGWOOD" has, over the years, become nearly synonymous with "Jasperware," a specific pottery line produced by this British firm. But while Jasperware may be Wedgwood's most enduring contribution to the world of pottery, it is by no means the only one.

Wedgwood was founded in 1759 by Josiah Wedgwood in Burslem, England. The earliest Wedgwood efforts were focused on utilitarian earthenware. Ornamental pottery made its debut in 1770, with the opening of new production facilities in Etruria. Jasperware became the company's first artware success.

Wedgwood's Jasperware has been so often imitated that a brief description immediately conjures up its basics: solid-color, unglazed stoneware, the decoration consisting of white, bas-relief "classic" figures encircling the object. The most common Jasperware color is blue, although other shades have included black, white, yellow, green, and even lilac. Most pieces are single-color, but some of the most striking examples of Jasperware use three or more alternating colors.

Once established, the Jasperware format remained quite consistent. The reason was simple: It filled a niche for the sort of elegant yet relatively inexpensive décor

Emile Lessore decorated Queen's Ware double urn, England, circa 1865, raised rectangular shaped plinth set with two attached urns, each with two covers, all enamel decorated in typical palette, plinth with hand-painted cartouches in landscapes, artist signed and impressed mark, 8 3/4" high............. **$2,760**

pieces that buyers craved. The Jasperware appeal is particularly understandable during the Victorian era, as adventurers unearthed the wonders of ancient Greece and Rome. Jasperware's images of toga-clad warriors and water-bearing maidens effectively romanticized a theme occupying the public interest, presenting civilizations of the past at their most civilized.

As noted, Jasperware was just one of the Wedgwood successes. Among the others:

• Creamware. Of a lighter weight than traditional china, this Wedgwood line proved less expensive both to produce and transport. Creamware was so acclaimed that Queen

Charlotte of England eventually permitted it to be marketed as "Queen's Ware."

• Moonlight Lustre. Produced from 1805-1815, the "moonlight" decorative effect was achieved by varied colors, (pink, gray, brown, and sometimes yellow), intermingled and "splashed" across the ware.

• Varied lustrewares. In the early 20th century, Wedgwood produced an in-demand line of pottery in assorted lustre finishes, their names and multicolored hues once again stressing the romantic: Butterfly,

Emile Lessore decorated Queen's Ware dish, England, circa 1865, oval shape with scalloped rim, polychrome enamel decorated with man serenading woman in landscape setting, titled on reverse The Duet, artist signed and impressed mark, 9 3/8" long $240

Dragon, and Fairyland. Within each series, designs held true to the theme: Fairyland, for example, featured such pattern images as Woodland Elves, Fairy in a Cage, and Toad and Dwarf. The overall, dreamlike effect was often enhanced by the use of mottled colors and hypnotically repeating borders. Decades later, similarities to the Fairyland decorative technique could be found in the psychedelic stylings of the 1960s.

During its long history, Wedgwood also experimented, to alternating effect, with other processes and treatments. These included fine porcelain, bone china, stone china, majolica, and Pearlware.

Fortunately for collectors, most Wedgwood pieces carry the marking "Wedgwood." In 1891, the additional identifier "England" was added (later pieces are marked "Made In England"). A limited line of artware, produced from 1769 to 1780, carries the marking "Wedgwood & Bentley"; during that time Josiah Wedgwood was in partnership with Thomas Bentley.

Pottery marked "Wedgwood & Co." and "Wedgewood" (note the additional "e") was the work of competitors, hoping to capitalize on Josiah Wedgwood's fame. They have no relation to the Wedgwood firm; the only advantage of owning one of these pieces would be for its curiosity value.

Wedgwood has certainly set the record for endurance: Jasperware has remained in continuous production since first being introduced in the 1700s. Collectors remain drawn to this line, thanks to its eye-catching juxtaposition of vivid base colors with the stark-white relief images. And, while many are first exposed to the Wedgwood legacy through Jasperware, a significant number delight in exploring the numerous other directions in pottery the company has taken during its 250-year history.

Rosso Antico wine cooler, England, mid-19th century, barrel shape with handles of mask heads below leaf and berry headdress, molded body with fruiting grapevines, impressed mark, 9 3/4" high **$246**

Ivory Vellum potpourri and cover, England, late 19th century, globular shaped Queen's Ware body with pierced cover, gilded upturned loop handles, gold and enamel flowers and foliage, insert disc lid, impressed mark, 9 3/4" high **$369**

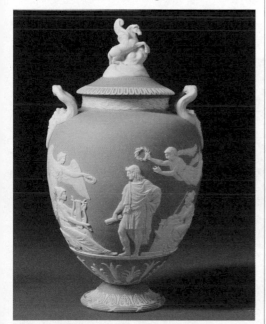

Light blue jasper dip apotheosis of Virgil vase and cover, England, mid-19th century, applied white relief with snake handles terminating at Medusa masks, classical figures in relief surrounding body within foliate borders, Pegasus finial, impressed mark, 17 3/4" high.......... **$12,000**

Yellow jasper dip biscuit barrel, England, circa 1930, cylindrical shape with applied black classical muses below fruiting grapevine festoons terminating at lion masks and rings, running grapevine at footrim, silver-plated rim, handle, and cover, impressed mark, 5 1/2" high **$600**

Crimson jasper dip Portland vase, England, circa 1920, applied classical figures in white relief, impressed mark, 6 1/8" high **$2,400**

Wedgwood-mounted cut-steel and fruitwood patch box, England, circa 1800, circular box trimmed in tortoiseshell with multifaceted steel beadwork surrounding central octagonal dark blue medallion with applied white classical figure in relief, 2 5/8" overall diameter............................**$240**

Majolica jardiniere on pedestal base, England, circa 1893, allover marigold-colored ground with molded body decorated in panels of floral urns, impressed marks, jardiniere 17" high, pedestal base, 24 1/4" high **$1,200**

Dark blue jasper dip Portland vase, England, 19th century, applied undraped classical figures in white relief, man wearing Phrygian cap under base, impressed mark, 10" high..**$2,160**

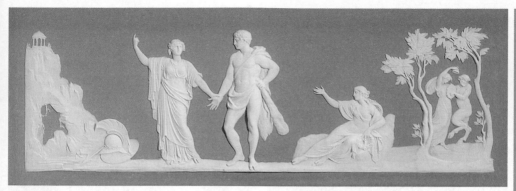

Light blue jasper plaque, long narrow rectangular shape, applied white relief scene of Judgment of Hercules, impressed mark, 19th century, mounted in ebonized wood frame, some surface wear, 5 3/4" x 16" **$1,763**

Crimson jasper teapot, covered, squatty bulbous body with short angled spout and C-form handle, domed cover with button finial, applied white classical figures, circa 1920, restoration to figure and rim chips on cover, 5 1/4" high ....**$400-$600**

Crimson jasper dip box and cover, England, circa 1920, scalloped rim with white applied classical figural group centering florets, box with classical figure groups, impressed mark, 3 3/4" long.................. **$720**

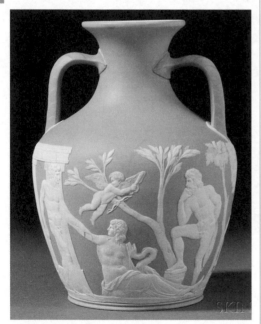

Light green jasper dip Portland vase, England, 19th century, applied undraped classical figures in white relief, man wearing Phrygian cap under base, impressed mark, 10 1/2" high **$720**

Three-color jasper dip barber bottle and cover, England, circa 1866, lilac ground with green medallions and applied white Bacchus heads to shoulders, classical figures and fruiting grapevine festoons in relief, impressed mark, 10 1/4" high...... **$431**

Pair of three-color jasper vases, England, mid-19th century, solid white ground with applied lilac and green classical motifs and white classical figural groups, impressed marks, 5 1/4" high **$492**

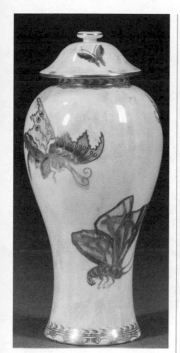

Butterfly Lustre vase and cover, England, circa 1920, shape 2046, pattern Z4832 with gilded and polychrome enameled butterflies to mother-of-pearl ground, printed mark, 10 7/8" high........................**$1,320**

Pair of slip-decorated white terra-cotta stoneware vases, England, late 18th century, each with white cut to brown with flower heads in relief to border, impressed marks, 6 3/4" high **$720**

Charles Bellows solid black jasper Portland vase, England, 1913, polished surface with applied classical undraped figures in white relief, man wearing Phrygian cap below base, inscribed Executed for Charles Bellows at Etruria 1913 No. 2, impressed mark, 10" high........................**$8,400**

Fairyland Lustre leapfrogging elves fruit bowl, England, circa 1920, pattern Z5360 with flame sky, interior with Woodland Bridge Variation I and Mermaid center, signed MJ and printed mark, 11 1/4" diameter **$18,000**

Butterfly Lustre vase, England, circa 1920, shape 2414, pattern Z4832 with gilded and polychrome enameled butterflies to mother-of-pearl ground, printed mark, 9 1/2" high **$1,560**

Pair of Dragon Lustre vases, England, circa 1920, pattern Z4829, mottled blue ground with gilded and polychrome enamel decorated dragons coiling body, printed marks, 12 3/8" high **$1,320**

Fairyland Lustre Picnic by a River plaque, England, circa 1920, rectangular shape with blue sky and purple bat, printed mark, set in an ebonized wood frame, by sight 4 1/4 x 9 3/4" **$7,200**

Fairyland Lustre Melba center bowl, England, circa 1920, pattern Z5462, exterior with Woodland Elves IV–Big Eyes to dark blue sky, interior with Jumping Faun to pale orange sky, printed mark, 8" diameter. **$7,200**

Fairyland Lustre vase, slightly tapering cylindrical body with flaring round foot and angled shoulder to short trumpet neck, decorated in Goblin pattern No. Z5367, brown goblins with red-spotted wings standing and kneeling on green grass alongside dark blue water with butterflies and fairies flying above, gold Wedgwood Portland vase mark, few glaze hairline cracks, small flake under foot, 8 1/2" high...................... **$6,500**

Fairyland lustre octagonal bowl decorated on exterior with gold castles against light blue sky, interior decorated with gnomes, toadstools and fairies, signed on underside with Portland vase mark "WEDGWOOD ENGLAND Z-5125," very good to excellent condition with minor wear to gilding in bottom of bowl, 4-3/4" dia..**$2,875**

Fairyland lustre plaque decorated with Picnic By a River design showing orange and green elves against lavender background with green river, green Roc bird and flame lustre sky, signed on reverse with gold Portland vase mark, "Wedgwood Made in England," black lacquered frame, very good to excellent condition, plaque 4-1/2" x 10", 7" x 12-3/4" overall......... **$5,000-$7,000**

Fairyland lustre geisha bowl, octagonal, decorated on exterior with Geisha or Angels pattern, interior decorated with running figures, signed with Portland vase mark "MADE IN ENGLAND Z-4968," very good to excellent condition.. **$5,000-$7,000**

Fairyland lustre chalice bowl, decorated on exterior with Twyford Garlands pattern against flame background, interior decorated with variation of Fairy Gondola against flame background, signed on underside with Portland vase mark "WEDGWOOD MADE IN ENGLAND Z-5360," very good to excellent condition with minor scratches to interior bottom of bowl, 10-3/4" dia........ **$10,350**

Fairyland Lustre lily tray, England, circa 1920, pattern Z4968 with Jumping Faun interior to daylit sky, exterior with mottled green ground and gilded birds, printed mark, 9" diameter **$9,600**

Fairyland Lustre Willow pattern vase and cover, England, circa 1920, shape 2410, pattern Z5228 to blue sky, printed mark, 9 1/2" high ...**$9,000**

Fairyland lustre bowl decorated on exterior with Fairy with Large Hat pattern with dark blue water and flame sky, interior decorated with Woodland Bridge pattern in a variation with no elves present, signed on underside with Portland vase mark "WEDGWOOD MADE IN ENG-LAND Z-5360," very good to excellent condition, 6-1/2" dia **$5,750**

Fairyland Lustre pillar vase, England, circa 1920, shape 3451, blue to daylit sky with paneled sides, printed mark, 12" high **$12,000**

Bowl, Dragon Lustre, low flaring round foot below deep flaring bell-form bowl, exterior in mottled blue and green with enameled gold dragons and red highlights, interior bottom with Oriental medallion in blue, green, red, and gold, Portland vase mark on bottom, 9" dia., 5 1/2" h. **$210**

Fairyland lustre vase decorated with Pillar pattern against creamy background, signed on underside with Portland vase mark "WEDGWOOD MADE IN ENGLAND Z-4968," very good to excellent condition, 14" t. ...**$10,925**

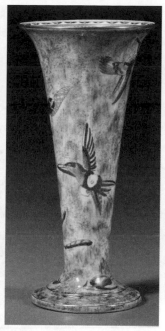

Hummingbird Lustre trumpet vase, England, circa 1920, mottled blue, pink, and green ground with gilded and polychrome decorated birds surrounding body, printed mark, 11" high. **$1,320**

Bowl, Butterfly Lustre, footed octagonal form, exterior in pale blue lustre with large blue and gold butterflies, interior in deep gold lustre, 6 1/2" w. **$463**

Fairyland lustre plate decorated with Roc Centre variation of Imps of a Bridge, scene depicts maroon imps walking across arched bridge with Roc bird flying above and other imps looking on, finished with blue and white floral rim, signed on underside with Portland vase mark "WEDGWOOD MADE IN ENGLAND," very good to excellent condition, 10-1/2" dia **$5,750**

Three Jasperware pieces including two pitchers with England only markings, 20th century, undamaged, large pitcher with firing separation at base of tree below spout, 3" to 8-3/4" h....... **$184**

Fairyland lustre melba center bowl, decorated on exterior with Garden of Paradise pattern against pink sky, interior decorated with Jumping Fawn pattern, signed on underside with Portland vase mark "MADE IN ENGLAND Z-4968," very good to excellent condition, 8" dia.....**$5,000-$8,000**

Fairyland lustre plate decorated with Firbolgs IV pattern showing purple Firbolgs in various stages of falling out of a tree, finished with border rim of blue and white flowers and gilded leaves against black border, signed on underside with Portland vase mark "WEDGWOOD MADE IN ENGLAND W-557," very good to excellent condition, 10-1/2" dia. **$5,750**

Fairyland lustre plate with center decoration of Thumbelina floating on a leaf, holding a stick with an insect on top, finished with Twyford border, signed on underside with Portland vase mark "WEDGWOOD MADE IN ENGLAND," no "Z" number, very good to excellent condition, 10-1/2" dia. **$7,188**

Fairyland lustre Nizami plate decorated with center medallion depicting Persian gentleman cutting down a tree, center medallion and gilded trim set against a moonlight blue background with mother of pearl lustre, signed on underside with Portland vase mark "WEDGWOOD MADE IN ENGLAND Z-5494," very good to excellent condition, 3-3/4" dia. **$1,553**

Teapot, covered, footed squatty bulbous body in creamy white with short angled spout, upright squared handle and tapering domed cover with knob finial, applied light blue grapevine band around shoulder and cover, marked "Wedgwood Embossed Queens Ware of Etruria & Barlaston," Josiah Wedgwood & Sons, England, circa 1940, 8 3/4" l., 5" h. **$70**

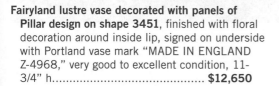

Fairyland lustre vase decorated with panels of Pillar design on shape 3451, finished with floral decoration around inside lip, signed on underside with Portland vase mark "MADE IN ENGLAND Z-4968," very good to excellent condition, 11-3/4" h.. **$12,650**

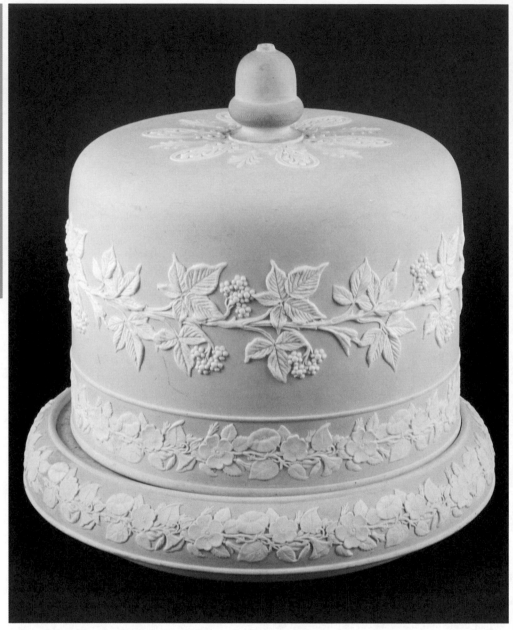

Chase dish in lilac jasperware, 10-1/2" h. x 10"dia. **$175**

Weller

WELLER POTTERY WAS made from 1872 to 1945 at a pottery established originally by Samuel A. Weller at Fultonham, Ohio and moved in 1882 to Zanesville, Ohio.

Mr. Weller's famous pottery slugged it out with several other important Zanesville potteries for decades. Cross-town rivals such as Roseville, Owens, La Moro, and McCoy were all serious fish in a fairly small and well-stocked lake. While Mr. Weller occasionally landed some solid body punches with many of his better art lines, the prevailing thought was that his later production ware just wasn't up to snuff.

Samuel Weller was a notorious copier and, it is said, a bit of a scallywag. He paid designers such as William Long to bring their famous discoveries to Zanesville. He then attempted to steal their secrets, and, when successful, renamed them and made them his own.

After World War I, when the cost of materials became less expensive than the cost of labor, many companies, including the famous Rookwood Pottery, increased their output of less expensive production ware. Weller Pottery followed along in the trend of production ware by introducing scores of interesting and unique lines, the likes of which have never been created anywhere else, before or since.

In addition to a number of noteworthy production lines, Weller continued in the creation of hand-painted ware long after Roseville abandoned them. Some of the more interesting Hudson pieces, for example, are post-World War I pieces. Even later lines, such as Bonito, were hand painted and often signed by important artists such as Hester Pillsbury. The closer you look at Weller's output after 1920, the more obvious the fact that it was the only Zanesville company still producing both quality art ware and quality production ware.

For more information on Weller pottery, see *Warman's Weller Pottery Identification and Price Guide* by Denise Rago and David Rago.

Brighton butterfly with flesh tone body and wings in gray, white, and black, unmarked, excellent original condition, without pin, 2 1/4" x 3 1/2".....................**$110**

Coppertone Gardenware Pan with Rabbit figure, impressed on bottom with Weller Pottery script logo, excellent original condition, 13 5/8" high **$3,000**

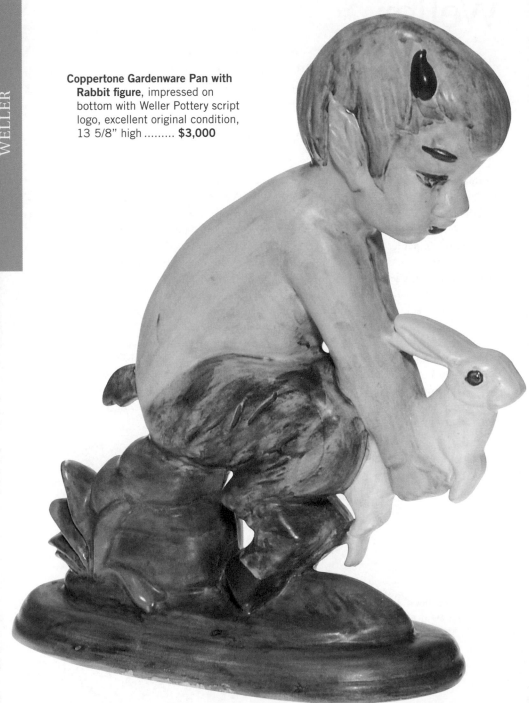

Eocean vase displaying flock of mallard ducks landing at eventide, water reeds below them, duck on back, executed by Albert Haubrich, lavender blue and pink evening sky, inscribed Eocean Weller, impressed X476 and painted cipher of artist on side, fine overall crazing, excellent condition, 13" high..................... **$2,300**

Clewell copper-clad corn vase on Weller L'Art Nouveau blank, Canton, Ohio, stamped L'ART NOUVEAU WELLER, 10" x 4"... **$1,625**

Rare Coppertone "Two Fish" vase, marked with Weller half-kiln ink stamp and marked with 2 and H in black slip, small chip to dorsal fin of smaller fish, good mold and color, 8".................. **$1,300**

Eocean vase decorated with pair of life-size white lilies, bud and foliage painted and signed by artisan Lillie Mitchell, incised X404 on bottom, excellent condition, 16 1/4" high **$1,900**

Coppertone bud vase with fluted rim and frog clinging to side, marked on base with number 12 in slip, good mold and color, 9" **$500**

Fru Russet "Lizard" vase in raspberry-colored glaze with lizard in mottled blue, incised Weller on bottom, excellent condition, 4 1/2" ... **$2,300**

Unusual Coppertone bowl with latticework rim, marked with full-kiln Weller Ware ink stamp logo and signed F.E.W. on bottom, excellent original condition, 3 1/4" high x 11 1/4" diameter .. **$190**

Cretone vase decorated in Art Deco style by Hester Pillsbury with leaping deer, flowers, leaves, and designs in white slip, applied via pastry bag, on satin black ground, impressed with Weller Pottery "script" mark and monogrammed by artist on side, fine crazing visible on interior and bottom, glaze inclusion at rim, 7" high......................................$500

Rare tall Cameo vase with birds and ferns, Fultonham, Ohio, stamped Weller 2P, 13 1/2" x 7" **$1,500**

Large Eocean vase with red poppies front and back, painted by Charles Chilcote, inscribed Eocean Weller on bottom, light crazing, minor surface scratches, 11 3/4" high...**$550**

Rare Etruscan jardinière by decorator Fredrick Hurten Rhead, terra cotta vessel with ebony glazed backdrop enclosing design of classical warriors within wreath of hearts encircling rim and base, signed beneath base in black slip "Etruscan" and "Rhead" with incised number 100 /2, 6 7/8" high............................ **$1,800**

WELLER

Jewell footed dresser box with cover, embossed face of maiden, fish around base portion, cosmetic repair to nose of maiden, very good condition, 4 1/2" high x 5 1/2" diameter **$400**

Flemish hanging shade with garlands embossed in surface, impressed Weller inside, brass hanging hooks attached, electrical fixture inside with opaque globe in center of shade, wiring not operative, excellent original condition with minor rubs, 17 1/2" diameter $550

Gardenware squirrel in natural mat colors, marked on base with Weller half-kiln ink stamp, fine overall crazing, professional restoration to ears, two toes on right foot, and small area on right paw, tiny chips to toes on left foot, 11 5/8" x 11 1/2" **$500**

Hen with six chicks, impressed Weller incised logo, fine crazing, professional restoration to comb and some small chips at base, 7 3/4" high x 7 3/4" long $850

Gardenware rooster, naturalistic mat tones, incised Weller logo, fine crazing, professional restoration to comb, some small chips at base, 12 7/8" high x 13" long..........................**$1,000**

Brighton butterfly, blue and white with accents in pink, green and black, unmarked, fine overall crazing, 2-1/4" x 3" h. **$140**

Forest jardinière displaying meadow of mature trees in summer, impressed Weller on bottom, glazed over line at rim, 10 1/2" high, 12 1/4" diameter **$400**

Hudson vase with white and yellow hollyhock decoration by Hester Pillsbury, impressed Weller in large block letters on bottom, signed by artist on side, paper label reads "From the White Pillars Museum," glaze bubbles near base, 11 5/8" high **$600**

Hudson vase decorated by Sara Reid McLaughlin with Dutch scene of several windmills, sailboats, and pink-roofed houses, signed by artist in black slip within scene and incised Weller Pottery and 15 on bottom, small glaze flake at base and fine overall crazing, 11 1/8" high.. **$1,700**

WELLER

Hudson twin-handled vase decorated with robin perched among blooms on tree branch, artist's initials, LBM, are at base of piece in black slip, bottom marked with Weller Pottery half-kiln stamp and possibly the letter "A" in green slip, light overall crazing, 7 3/4" high **$2,200**

Hudson vase displaying pair of black-throated warblers perched on juniper branch, Weller impression, faint line visible from inside, ivory backdrop, 9 3/8" high **$1,500**

LaSa signed gourd vase, with tropical view of palm trees and large lake with mountains in distance against evening sky, 9 1/4" high **$500**

LaSa vase encircled by scene of river flowing past shore with trees and clouds above, unmarked, few tiny scratches, good color, surface in excellent shape, 11 1/4" high **$550**

Tall LaSa scenic vase, with pine trees, clouds, mountains and red sky, signed Weller LaSa on side near base, excellent condition with minor abrasions, 16" high.................. **$1,000**

Tall LaSa vase with tropical scene of palm trees, mountains and red sky, unmarked, 1/8" glaze chip at base and minor abrasions, 16" high **$650**

LaSa footed vase with summertime trees in front of lake with hills on other side, large clouds, Weller LaSa scratched in above foot, minor surface scratches, excellent condition, 9 1/8" high $500

Tall LaSa vase with pine tree decoration and red and gold sky, unmarked, accompanied by 3" x 5" card on which is written: "The enclosed piece of pottery is given you with the compliments of THE LIMA ROTARY CLUB. This piece has been selected from the La Sl [sic] line, our latest creation. This line, which is strictly hand made, we consider the finest that we have ever produced. By reason of its artistic qualities, we hope that it will be used as a decorative piece of pottery, and not for fresh or cut flowers. Manufactured by The S.A. Weller Co., Pottery Zanesville, Ohio"; several scratches on lower third of body, 11 3/8" high $450

Louwelsa vase decorated with roses,
sterling silver overlay, impressed on base
Louwelsa Weller X 11, no artist mark or
marks on silver, overall crazing, 7 3/4"
high...$550

**Large Louwelsa vase with red tulips done
by Albert Haubrich**, impressed Louwelsa
Weller circular logo, incised F, impressed
number 11 and number 46, overall crazing, glaze nick off base, 16 1/2" high $900

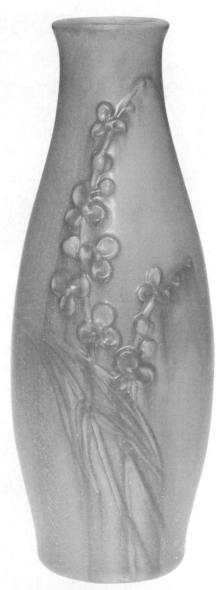

Sicard candlestick in green and gold with shamrock designs, signed Weller and Sicard on opposite sides near base, excellent condition, 7 1/2" high **$450**

Matt Ware vase with molded design of arrowroot plant, mat green glaze, impressed Weller in small block letters, no crazing, stilt pull to foot ring, 15 7/8" high **$550**

Matt Ware vase decorated with three mushrooms in heavy slip, impressed Weller in small block letters on bottom, some crazing to slip-decorated portion, bruise at base, 6 5/8" high........**$550**

**Scenic vase showing Japanese lanterns
hanging from tree after sunset**, unmarked, fine crazing and minor glaze
drips, 9" high $1,100

**Roma jardinière and pedestal displaying
pink flowers and arched leafy stems**,
unmarked, excellent condition, combined
height 32" $475

Rosemont vase, each side with bluebird and branches with pink flowers, one side also has yellow butterfly, impressed Weller in block letters, minor crazing and scratches, 7 5/8" high **$150**

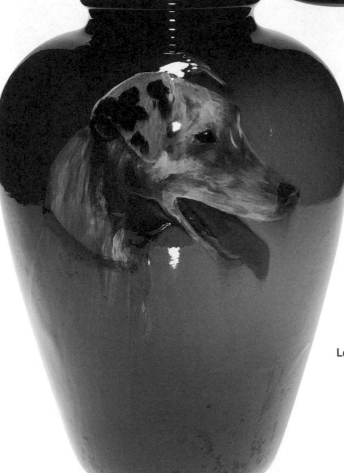

Louwelsa vase displaying portrait of Dalmatian, impressed circular Weller Louwelsa symbol and X 485, no artist mark visible, overall crazing, scratches, and small burst glaze bubbles, 10 3/4" high..........................**$450**

Selma covered jar with repeating pattern of bluebirds in apple tree, impressed with WELLER on bottom, restoration to small chip on lid and fine overall crazing, 7 7/8" high.. **$650**

Tall Aurelian vase decorated by Frank Ferrell, grape decor, incised Aurelian Weller K and impressed 518 10 on base and signed "Ferrell" in slip on side near base, exterior oversprayed, which indicates restoration of some sort, 20" h. **$325**

Sicard vase with cuttings of daisy flower heads and foliage strewn about circumference, metallic textured border surrounds base, Weller Sicard signature, excellent condition, 7 1/4" high............. **$600**

Sicard vase decorated and glazed with metallic luster glaze in magenta, green, and blue, incised on base 451 X and signed on side Sicardo Weller, overall crazing, loss of height at rim, base has been ground resulting in some small grinding chips, hole through bottom to facilitate turning vessel into lamp, 16" high **$500**

Sicard vase with stylized floral decoration and fine coloration, marked Weller Sicard on side near base and incised 10 on bottom, tiny bubbles in glaze, 4 3/4" high **$500**

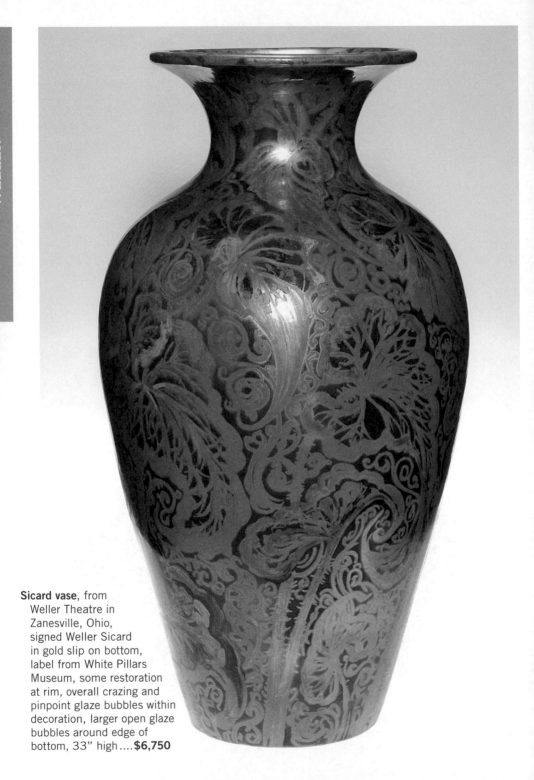

Sicard vase, from Weller Theatre in Zanesville, Ohio, signed Weller Sicard in gold slip on bottom, label from White Pillars Museum, some restoration at rim, overall crazing and pinpoint glaze bubbles within decoration, larger open glaze bubbles around edge of bottom, 33" high **$6,750**

Woodcraft wall pocket with two bluebirds, one in nest, one on branch, with red flowers and leaves, impressed Weller in block letters on rear, fine crazing with restoration to beak of bird on branch, minor firing separation to vine, 14 3/4" x 12" **$700**

Sicard vase decorated with green and gold dandelion and leaves against purple background, signed Weller on side of piece, excellent condition with minor abrasions, 7 3/8" high..... **$425**

Sicard vase with daisies, 1903-1917, signed Weller Sicard, 29M, 5 3/4" x 7 1/4".............. **$1,500**

Louwelsa vase with long stem flowers in green glaze, shape number 555, marked Louwelsa/Weller/555 on underside, 8-1/2" h. $360

Sicard vase decorated with ivy leaves in blue, purple, green, and gold, signed Weller and Sicard on opposite sides near base, 1/4" grinding chip at base, 7 1/4" high $450

Sicard vase with mistletoe decoration in green, purple, and gold, signed Weller Sicard on side near bottom, minor grinding chips at base and faint crazing, 7 1/4" high **$475**

Sicard pear-form vase decorated with English ivy over aqua, smooth surface with purplish blue coloration and green glazing, signed Weller Sicard on side, excellent condition, 4 1/2".................... **$425**

Pottery vase made for 1904 World's Fair in St. Louis, two slip decorated Jerusalem flowers and word Jerusalem, also in slip, no other markings, 2-1/2" h........... **$225**

Sicard lobed vase decorated with nasturtiums in green and purple, signed Weller Sicard on body with impressed Weller on bottom and number 37, minor abrasions and fine overall crazing, 5 3/8" high x 7" wide **$850**

Sicard star-shaped covered box scattered with four-leaf clover designs and lid arrayed with stars, unmarked, overspray to cover and box indicating repair, 2 1/2" high, 4 5/8" **$275**

WELLER

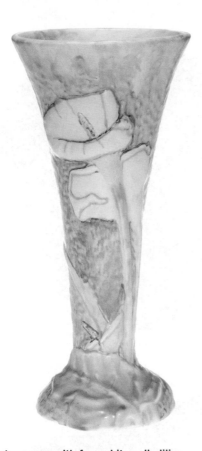

Silvertone vase with four white calla lilies and green foliage against backdrop of lilac and blue with pale yellow, stamped Weller Ware with number 3 beneath, minor crazing, excellent condition, 11 3/4" high **$225**

Rare etched mat scenic tankard showing swans in wooded pond, work of Albert Wilson, swans and water are incised, trees in background are painted, typical Weller numbers on bottom, signed A. Wilson on side in white slip, uncrazed with small glaze chip on spout and pinhead nick at base, 16 5/8" high **$600**

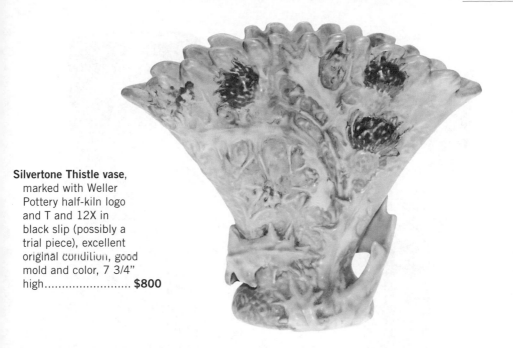

Silvertone Thistle vase, marked with Weller Pottery half-kiln logo and T and 12X in black slip (possibly a trial piece), excellent original condition, good mold and color, 7 3/4" high......................... **$800**

Three Hobart art pottery pieces, turquoise glaze, putti with grapes flower frog, girl with duck flower frog, and kneeling nude female two-part flower frog/bowl, first two marked, circa 1925, boy undamaged, girl marked second with glaze pops to head, nude with restoration to nose, each with some normal crazing, 4-1/4" to 7" h. **$126**

Voile jardinière and pedestal present-ing orchards bearing fruit, jardinière hand-marked 16 under glaze, excellent condition, combined height 32" **$500**

White and Decorated vase featuring exotic bird perched on branch with flowering rose of Sharon blooms, impressed Weller in block letters on base, excellent original condition with fine light crazing, 13 1/8" high.. **$1,200**

Eocean tankard displaying trio of red peonies in full bloom on long arched stems, impressed 580 below base, 12" h............. **$200**

WELLER

Three art pottery vases, including two pieces of Baldin, one signed, first half 20th century, undamaged except for minute flake to one leaf of largest example, 6" to 7-1/4" h. **$287**

Vase by May Timberlake, 20th century, initialed M.T., with cat decoration, 7" high..............**$972**

Large white pop-eyed dog, marked with incised Weller Pottery logo,
excellent original condition, 9 3/4" **$3,000**

Aurelian jug decorated with cherries, incised Aurelian Weller on base, roughness at spout, broad
crazing, 6" h. $80

Brighton kingfisher flower frog, bright colors, impressed Weller in block letters, excellent original condition, 9" h. **$300**

Chase vase depicting white horse, rider and three hounds with a tree to side, in thickly applied white slip on dark blue ground, Weller Pottery incised mark and a W, excellent original condition, 11-3/4" h... **$150**

Dickensware "The Turk" humidor, incised "Dickens Weller," a few minor nicks to top and base, 7-1/2" h..**$200**

Dickensware "The Irishman" humidor, incised "Dickens Weller," several chips to edge of top, label affixed to bottom and certificate within that indicates this came from White Pillars Museum, 6-1/2" h. **$150**

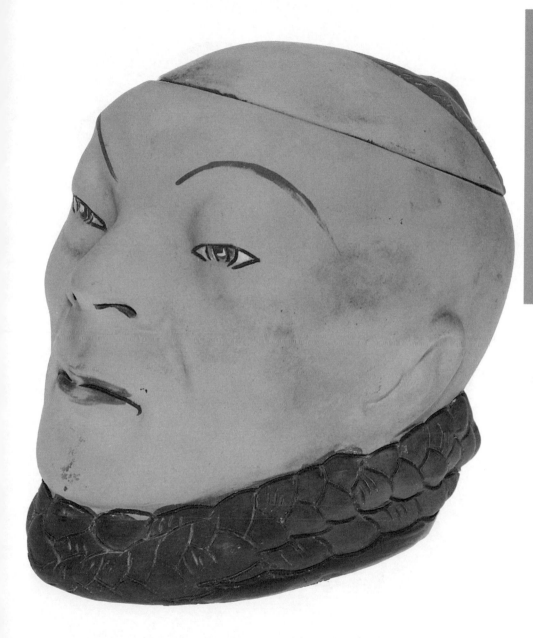

Dickensware "Chinaman" humidor, underside of lid incised "Dickens Weller," bottom bears a sticker identifying piece as being from White Pillars Museum, deteriorating restoration to top, small chip to inner rim of base, 6-1/4" h. **$120**

Second line Dickensware jug, front with vignette of Dombey and son seated at a table with crystal flacon and glass on top, on rear of flat vessel is name "Dombey and Son" in white slip, base incised 504 Dickens Weller, excellent original condition, 7-1/4" h. **$300**

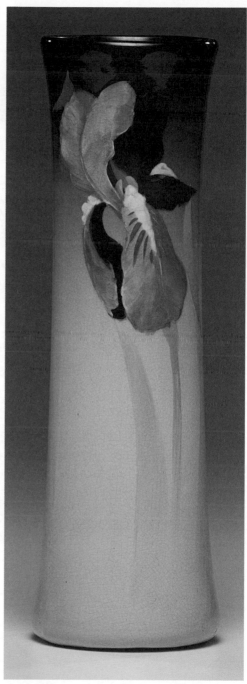

First Line Dickensware oil lamp decorated by Laura Cline with leaves and berries, impressed 385 on bottom and initialed by artist on side amid leaves, excellent original condition, original Bradley and Hubbard copper oil font, 5-1/4" x 8-1/2". A letter, dated 1975, from early dealers Gladys and Foster Hall, authors of Halls' Pricing Formulas, identifies this as a rare piece of Roseville Blue Ware. **$425**

Eocean iris vase of cylindrical form with flaring neck, marked Weller/ Eocean / 305 on bottom, 12-3/4" h. **$330**

Dedonatis vase encircled with Italianesque freehand floral design by Frank Dedonatis, impressed with "Weller Script" mark and marked "255 BPU," artist's monogram in blue slip,
very fine crazing, excellent original condition, 8-3/4" h. **$375**

Glendale vase with small bird seated in tree looking over nest containing four eggs, bears name McLaughlin in raised letters on back near base, restoration at rim, 10-1/8" h... $275

Flemish vase with magnolia decoration encircling vase, unmarked, excellent original condition. 14" h. $275

Two Hobart/Lavonia art pottery pieces, lilac to turquoise glaze, semi-nude female two-compart-ment vase and wall pocket, latter with ink-stamp mark, circa 1925, vase undamaged with light crazing around base, pocket with minor flake to side rim and moderate crazing, 10-1/2" and 8-1/2" h. $184

Two art pottery articles, comprising Knifewood vase with canaries and small Woodrose jar-dinière, each marked under base, first half 20th century, undamaged, 5" h. $230

Tall LaSa vase with pine tree decoration, some painted, some incised, allowing white clay body to show through, incised Weller LaSa near base, some wear, mostly at base, 13-3/8" h. **$200**

Hudson white and decorated vase with flower and berry decoration, impressed Weller in block letters with label from White Pillars Museum, overall fine crazing, 10-5/8" h. Warranty card from White Pillars Museum accompanies vase. **$190**

Unusual Hunter whiskey jug with two fish and lots of hand incising in design, incised "Hunter" on bottom along with paper label that reads "From White Pillars Museum," professional restoration to handle and spout, 5-5/8" h..$180

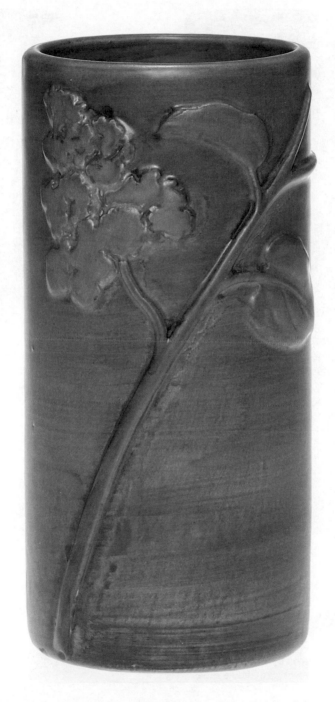

Kenova vase with relief decoration of flowering branch, flowers hand colored, impressed with 8
on bottom, excellent original condition, 8-3/4" h..$350

Sicard candlestick with swirls of green, gold, and purple, signed Weller and Sicard on opposite sides of base, excellent condition, 6 1/2" **$500**

LaSa vase showing trees by side of river, signed Weller LaSa near base, wear at rim and near base, several small scratches, 11-1/4" h. **$325**

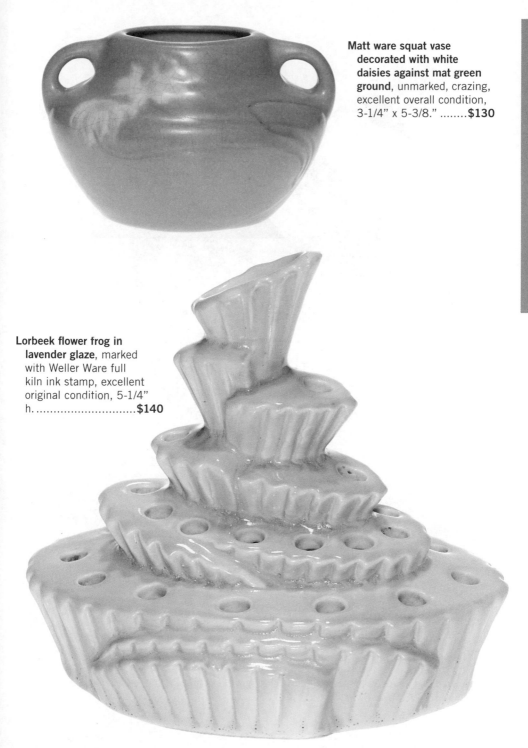

Matt ware squat vase decorated with white daisies against mat green ground, unmarked, crazing, excellent overall condition, 3-1/4" x 5-3/8." **$130**

Lorbeek flower frog in lavender glaze, marked with Weller Ware full kiln ink stamp, excellent original condition, 5-1/4" h. **$140**

WELLER

Small pop-eyed dog figure, impressed with Weller script mark, fine crazing, excellent original condition, 4-1/8" h. $250

Matt glaze 6-1/4 inch humidor encircled with molded band of animals, unmarked, some chips
to lid..$80

Muskota bowl with trio of white geese clustered at one end, marked with Weller Pottery ink stamp, crazing and chip to end of one reed, 6-5/8" x 10" h. **$250**

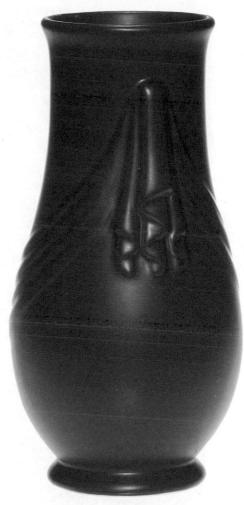

Ragenda vase, suggestive of draped fabric, early 1930s, dark maroon mat glaze, unmarked, in excellent original condition, 9-3/4" h. **$200**

Sicard vase covered with flower and leaf design, signed Sicard Weller on side and incised 94 on base, tight line on side, 8-7/8" h... **$350**

Rhead Faience vase of Geisha wearing formal garment kneeling beneath a canopy of trees,
squeeze bag and hand painting techniques, monogram "VMH," unidentified artist appears
on side, hand incised "Rhead, X, 504" beneath, crazed, a few surface scratches, otherwise
excellent condition, 6-7/8" h. $400

Rosemont vase with lilac tinted cockatoo swinging on hoop front and back, connected by bows and rose bouquets set against ebony backdrop, Weller in block letters is impressed beneath, 8-1/2" h. $300

Miniature Sicard pear-shape vase encompassed with leaves of dandelion, signed "Weller Sicard" on side, glaze nick at rim, minor surface scratches, 3-1/8" h. $325

Rosemont planter, each side picturing a bluebird and branches with pink flowers, impressed Weller in block letters, excellent original condition, 6-5/8" h. $200

Tutone vase with four loop handles in signature maroon mat with green accents color scheme, unmarked, excellent original condition, 12-7/8" h...$190

Glossary of Selected Ceramics Terms

Abino Ware: A line produced by the Buffalo Pottery of Buffalo, New York. Introduced in 1911, this limited line featured mainly sailing ship scenes with a windmill on shore.

Agate Ware: An earthenware pottery featuring a mixture of natural colored clays giving a marbled effect. Popular in England in the 18th century.

Albany slip: A dark brown slip glaze used to line the interiors of most salt-glazed stoneware pottery. Named for a fine clay found near Albany, New York.

Albino line: A version of Griffen, Smith and Hill's Shell & Seaweed majolica pattern with an off-white overall color sometimes trimmed with gold or with pink or blue feathering.

Albion Ware: A line of majolica developed by Edwin Bennett in the 1890s. It featured colored liquid clays over a green clay body decorated with various scenes. Popular for jardinieres and pedestals.

Bas relief: Literally "low relief," referring to lightly molded decorations on ceramic pieces.

Bisquit: Unglazed porcelain left undecorated or sometimes trimmed with pastel colors. Also known as bisque.

Bocage: A background of flowering trees or vines often used as a backdrop for figural groups, which were meant to be viewed from the front only.

Bone china: A porcelain body developed in England using the white ashes of bone. It has been the standard English porcelain ware since the early 19th century.

Coleslaw: A type of decoration used on ceramic figurines to imitate hair or fur. It is finely crumbled clay applied to the unfired piece and resembling coleslaw cabbage.

Crackled glaze: A glaze with an intentional network of fine lines produced by uneven contracting of the glaze after firing. First popular on Chinese wares.

Crazing: The fine network of cracks in a glaze produced by uneven contracting of the glaze after firing or later reheating of a piece during usage. An unintentional defect usually found on eathernwares.

Creamware: A light-colored fine earthenware developed in England in the late 18th century and used by numerous potters into the 19th century. Josiah Wedgwood marketed his version as Queensware.

Crystalline glaze: A glaze containing fine crystals resulting from the presence of mineral salts in the mixture. It was a popular glaze on American art pottery of the late 19th century and early 20th century.

Eared handles: Handles applied to ceramic pieces such as crocks. They are crescent or ear-shaped, hence the name.

Earthenware: A class of fine-grained porous pottery fired at relatively low temperature and then glazed. It produces a light and easily molded ware that was widely used by the potteries of Staffordshire, England in the late 18th and early 19th century.

Faience: A form of fine earthenware featuring a tin glaze and originally inspired by Chinese porcelain. It includes early Dutch Delft ware and similar wares made in France, Germany and other areas of Europe.

Fairyland Lustre: A special line of decorated wares developed by Susannah "Daisy" Makeig-Jones for the Josiah Wedgwood firm early in the 20th century. It featured fantastic or dreamlike scenes with fairies and elves in various colors and with a mother-of-pearl lustre glaze. Closely related to Dragon Lustre featuring designs with dragons.

Flambé glaze: A special type of glaze featuring splashed or streaked deep reds and purple, often dripping over another base color. Popular with some American art pottery makers but also used on porcelain wares.

Flint Enamel glaze: A version of the well-known brown mottled Rockingham pottery glaze. It was developed by Lyman Fenton & Co. of Bennington, Vermont and patented in 1849. It featured streaks and flecks of green, orange, yellow and blue mixed with the mottled brown glaze.

Glaze: The general term for vitreous (glass-like) coating fired onto pottery and porcelain to produce an impervious surface and protect underglaze decoration.

Hard-paste: Refers to true porcelain, a fine, white clay body developed by the Chinese and containing kaolin and petuntse or china stone. It is fired at a high temperature and glazed with powdered feldspar to produce a smooth, shiny glaze.

Lead glaze: A shiny glaze most often used on cheap redware pottery and produced using a dry powdered or liquid lead formula. Since it would be toxic, it was generally used on the exterior of utilitarian wares only

Lithophane: A panel of thin porcelain delicately molded with low-relief pattern or scenes that show up clearly when held to light. It was developed in Europe in the 19th century and was used for decorative panels or lamp shades and was later used in the bottom of some German and Japanese steins, mugs or cups.

Majolica: A type of tin-glazed earthenware pottery developed in Italy and named for the island of Majorca. It was revived in Europe and America in the late 19th century and usually featured brightly colored shiny glazes

Married: A close match or a duplicate of the original missing section or piece, such as a lid.

Mission Ware: A decorative line of pottery developed by the Niloak Pottery of Benton, Arkansas. It featured variously colored clays swirled together and was used to produce such decorative pieces as vases and candlesticks.

Moriage: Japanese term for the slip-trailed relief decorations used on various forms of porcelain and pottery. Flowers, beading and dragon decoration are typical examples.

Pâte-sur-pâte: French for "paste on paste," this refers to a decorative technique where layers of porcelain slip in white are layered on a darker background. Used on artware produced by firms like Minton, Ltd. of England.

Pearlware: A version of white colored creamware developed in England and widely used for inexpensive eathenwares in the late 18th and early 19th century. It has a pearly glaze, hence the name.

Pillow vase: a form of vase designed to resemble a flattened round or oblong pillow. Generally an upright form with flattened sides. A similar form is the Moon vase or flask, meant to resemble a full moon.

Porcelain: The general category of translucent, vitrified ceramics first developed by the Chinese and later widely produced in Europe and America. Hard-paste is true porcelain, while soft-paste is an artificial version developed to imitate hard-paste using other ingredients.

Pottery: The very general category of ceramics produced from various types of clay. It includes redware, yellowware, stoneware and various earthenwares. It is generally fired at a much lower temperature than porcelain.

PUG: An abbreviation for "printed under glaze," referring to colored decorations on pottery. Most often it is used in reference to decorations found on Mettlach pottery steins.

Relief-molding: A decorative technique, sometimes erroneously referred to as "blown-out," whereby designs are raised in bold relief against a background. The reverse side of such decoration is hollowed-out, giving the impression the design was produced by blowing from the inside. Often used in reference to certain Nippon porcelain wares.

Rocaille: A French term meaning "rockwork." It generally refers to a decoration used for the bases of ceramic figurines.

Salt-glazed stoneware: A version of stoneware pottery where common rock salt is thrown in the kiln during firing and produces hard, shiny glaze like a thin coating of glass. A lightly pitted orange peel surface is sometimes the result of this technique.

Sanded: A type of finish usually on pottery wares. Unfired pieces are sprinkled or rolled in fine sand, which, when fired, gives the piece a sandy, rough surface texture.

Sang-de-boeuf: Literally French for "ox blood," it refers to a deep red glaze produced with copper oxide. It was first produced by the Chinese and imitated by European and American potters in the late 19th and early 20th century.

Sgrafitto: An Italian-inspired term for decorative designs scratched or cut through a layer of slip before firing. Generally used on earthenware forms and especially with the Pennsylvania-German potters of America.

Slip: The liquid form of clay, often used to decorate earthenware pieces in a process known as slip-trailing or slip-quilling.

Soft-paste: A term used to describe a certain type of porcelain body developed in Europe and England from the 16th to late 18th centuries. It was used to imitate true hard-paste porcelain developed by the Chinese but was produced using a white clay mixed with a grit or flux of bone ash or talc and fired at fairly low temperatures. The pieces are translucent, like hard-paste porcelain, but are not as durable. It should not be used when referring to earthenwares such as creamware or pearlware.

Sprigging: A term used to describe the ornamenting of ceramic pieces with applied relief decoration, such as blossoms, leaves or even figures.

Standard glaze: The most common form of glazing used on Rookwood Pottery pieces. It is a clear, shiny glaze usually on pieces decorated with florals or portraits against a dark shaded backhground.

Stoneware: A class of hard, high-fired pottery usually made from dense grey clay and most often decorated with a salt glaze. American 19th century stoneware was often decorated with slip-quilled or hand-brushed cobalt blue decorations.

Tapestry ware: A form of late 19th century porcelain where the piece is impressed with an overall linen cloth texture before firing. The Royal Bayreuth firm is especially known for their fine "Rose Tapestry" line wherein the finely textured ground is decorated with colored roses.

Tin glaze: A form of pottery glaze made opaque by the addition of tin oxide. It was used most notably on early Dutch Delft as well as other early faience and majolica wares.

Underglaze-blue: A cobalt blue produced with metallic oxides applied to an unfired clay body. Blue was one of the few colors that did not run or smear when fired at a high temperature. It was used by the Chinese on porcelain and later copied by firms such as Meissen.

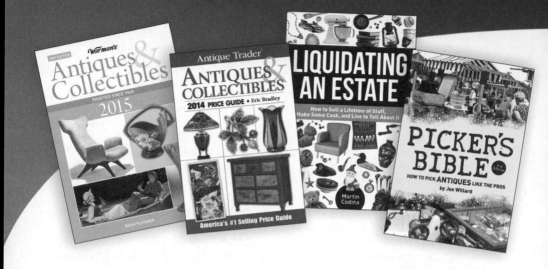